KENNIKAT PRESS SCHOLARLY REPRINTS

Dr. Ralph Adams Brown, Senior Editor

Series in

**AMERICAN HISTORY AND CULTURE
IN THE NINETEENTH CENTURY**

Under the General Editorial Supervision of
Dr. Martin L. Fausold
Professor of History, State University of New York

CAMPAIGNING IN CUBA

❥

BY

GEORGE KENNAN

KENNIKAT PRESS
Port Washington, N. Y./London

CAMPAIGNING IN CUBA

First published in 1899
Reissued in 1971 by Kennikat Press
Library of Congress Catalog Card No: 75-137918
ISBN 0-8046-1484-9

Manufactured by Taylor Publishing Company   Dallas, Texas

KENNIKAT SERIES ON AMERICAN HISTORY AND
CULTURE IN THE NINETEENTH CENTURY

CONTENTS

CAMPAIGNING IN CUBA

CAMPAIGNING IN CUBA

CHAPTER I

STARTING FOR THE FIELD

WAR broke out between the United States and Spain on April 21, 1898. A week or ten days later I was asked by the editors of the "Outlook" of New York to go to Cuba with Miss Clara Barton, on the Red Cross steamer *State of Texas*, and report the war and the work of the Red Cross for that periodical. After a hasty conference with the editorial and business staffs of the paper I was to represent, I accepted the proposition, and on May 5 left Washington for Key West, where the *State of Texas* was awaiting orders from the Navy Department. The army of invasion, under command of General Shafter, was then assembling at Tampa, and it was expected that a hostile movement to some point on the Cuban coast would be made before the end of the month.

I reached Tampa on the evening of Friday, May 6. The Pullman cars of the Florida express, at that time, ran through the city of Tampa and across the river into the spacious grounds of the beautiful Tampa Bay Hotel, which, after closing for the regular winter season, had been compelled to

reopen its doors—partly to accommodate the large number
of officers and war correspondents who had assembled there
with their wives and friends, and partly to serve as headquarters for the army of Cuban invasion.

It was a warm, clear Southern night when we arrived, and
the scene presented by the hotel and its environment, as we
stepped out of the train, was one of unexpected brilliancy
and beauty. A nearly full moon was just rising over the
trees on the eastern side of the hotel park, touching with
silver the drifts of white blossoms on dark masses of olean-
der-trees in the foreground, and flooding with soft yellow
light the domes, Moorish arches, and long façade of the whole
immense building. Two regimental bands were playing
waltzes and patriotic airs under a long row of incandescent
lights on the broad veranda; fine-looking, sunbrowned men,
in all the varied uniforms of army and navy, were gathered
in groups here and there, smoking, talking, or listening to
the music; the rotunda was crowded with officers, war correspondents, and gaily attired ladies, and the impression made
upon a newcomer, as he alighted from the train, was that
of a brilliant military ball at a fashionable seaside summer
resort. Of the serious and tragic side of war there was hardly
a suggestion.

On the morning after our arrival I took a carriage
and drove around the city and out to the camp, which was
situated about a mile and a half from the hotel on the other
side of the river. In the city itself I was unpleasantly disappointed. The showy architecture, beautiful grounds, semi-
tropical foliage, and brilliant flowers of the Tampa Bay Hotel
raise expectations which the town across the river does not
fulfil. It is a huddled collection of generally insignificant
buildings standing in an arid desert of sand, and to me it
suggested the city of Semipalatinsk—a wretched, verdure-
less town in southern Siberia, colloquially known to Russian

army officers as "the Devil's Sand-box." Thriving and prosperous Tampa may be, but attractive or pleasing it certainly is not.

As soon as I got away, however, from the hotel and into the streets of the town, I saw at almost every step suggestions of the serious and practical side, if not the tragic side, of war. Long trains of four-mule wagons loaded with provisions, camp equipage, and lumber moved slowly through the soft, deep sand of the unpaved streets in the direction of the encampment; the sidewalks were thronged with picturesquely dressed Cuban volunteers from the town, sailors from the troop-ships, soldiers from the camp, and war correspondents from everywhere; mounted orderlies went tearing back and forth with despatches to or from the army headquarters in the Tampa Bay Hotel; Cuban and American flags were displayed in front of every restaurant, hotel, and Cuban cigar-shop, and floated from the roofs or windows of many private houses; and now and then I met, coming out of a drug-store, an army surgeon or hospital steward whose left arm bore the red cross of the Geneva Convention.

The army that was destined to begin the invasion of Cuba consisted, at that time, of ten or twelve thousand men, all regulars, and included an adequate force of cavalry and ten fine batteries of field-artillery. It was encamped in an extensive forest of large but scattered pine-trees, about a mile from the town, and seemed already to have made itself very much at home in its new environment.

The first thing that struck me in going through the camp was its businesslike aspect. It did not suggest a big picnic, nor an encampment of militia for annual summer drill. It was manifestly a camp of veterans; and although its dirty, weather-beaten tents were pitched here and there without any attempt at regularity of arrangement, and its camp equipage, cooking-utensils, and weapons were piled or stacked between the tents in a somewhat disorderly fashion, as if thrown about at random, I could see that the irregularity and disorder were only apparent, and were really the irregularity and disorder of knowledge and experience gained by long and varied service in the field. I did not need the inscriptions —"Fort Reno." and "Fort Sill"—on the army wagons to assure me that these were veteran troops from the Plains, to whom campaigning was not a new thing.

As we drove up to the camp, smoke was rising lazily into the warm summer air from a dozen fires in different parts of the grounds; company cooks were putting the knives, forks, and dishes that they had just washed into improvised cupboards made by nailing boxes and tomato-crates against the trees; officers in fatigue-uniform were sitting in camp-chairs, here and there, reading the latest New York papers; and thousands of soldiers, both inside and outside the sentry-lines, were standing in groups discussing the naval fight off Manila, lounging and smoking on the ground in the shade of the army wagons, playing hand-ball to pass away the time, or swarming around a big board shanty, just outside the lines, which called itself "NOAH'S ARK" and announced in big letters its readiness to dispense cooling drinks to all comers at a reasonable price.

The troops in all branches of the army at Tampa impressed me very favorably. The soldiers were generally stalwart, sunburnt, resolute-looking men, twenty-five to thirty-five years of age, who seemed to be in perfect physical condition, and who looked as if they had already seen hard service and were ready and anxious for more. In field-artillery the force was particularly strong, and our officers in Tampa based their confident expectation of victory largely upon the anticipated work of the ten batteries of fine, modern field-guns which General Shafter then intended to take with him. Owing to lack of transportation facilities, however, or for some other reason to me unknown, six of these batteries were left in Tampa when the army sailed for Santiago, and the need of them was severely felt, a few weeks later, at Caney and San Juan.

Upon my return from the camp I called upon General Shafter, presented my letter of introduction from the President, and said I wished to consult him briefly with regard to the future work of the American National Red Cross. He received me cordially, said that our organization would soon have a great and important work to do in Cuba in caring for the destitute and starving reconcentrados, and that he would gladly afford us all possible facilities ·and protection. The Red Cross corps of the army medical department, he said, would be fully competent to take care of all the sick and wounded soldiers in the field; but there would be ample room for our supplementary work in relieving the distress of the starving Cuban peasants, who would undoubtedly seek refuge within our lines as soon as we should establish ourselves on the island. He deprecated and disapproved of any attempt on the part of the Red Cross to land supplies for the reconcentrados under a flag of truce in advance of the army of invasion and without its protection. "The Spanish authorities," he said, "under stress of starvation, would simply seize your stores and use them for the maintenance of their own army. The best thing for you to do is to go in with us and under our protection, and relieve the distress of the reconcentrados as fast as we uncover it." I said that I thought this was Miss Barton's intention, and that we had fourteen hundred tons of food-stuffs and medical supplies on the steamer *State of Texas* at Key West, and were ready to move at an hour's notice. With an understanding that Miss Barton should be notified as soon as the army of invasion embarked, I bade the general good-by and returned to the hotel.

In an interview that I had on the following day with
Colonel Babcock, General Shafter's adjutant-general, I was
informed, confidentially, that the army was destined for
"eastern Cuba." Small parties, Colonel Babcock said,
would be landed at various points on the coast east and west
of Havana, for the purpose of communicating with the insurgents and supplying them with arms and ammunition;
but the main attack would be made at the eastern end of
the island. He did not specifically mention Santiago by
name, because Cervera's fleet, at that time, had not taken
refuge there; but inasmuch as Santiago was the most important place in eastern Cuba, and had a deep and sheltered
harbor, I inferred that it would be made the objective point
of the contemplated attack. The Secretary of War, in his
reply to the questions of the Investigating Commission, says
that the movement against Santiago, as then planned, was
to be a mere "reconnaissance in force, to ascertain the
strength of the enemy in different locations in eastern
Cuba"; but Colonel Babcock certainly gave me to understand that the attack was to be a serious one, and that it
would be made with the whole strength of General Shafter's
command. The matter is of no particular importance now,
except in so far as the information given me by Colonel
Babcock indicates the views and intentions of the War Department two weeks before Admiral Cervera's fleet took
refuge in Santiago harbor.

I left Port Tampa for Key West on the Plant-line
steamer *Mascotte* at half-past ten o'clock Saturday evening,
May 7. The long, narrow, and rather sinuous channel out
of Tampa Bay was marked by a line of buoys and skeleton
wooden frames resting on driven spiles; but there were no
lights for the guidance of the mariner, except one at the
outer entrance, ten or twelve miles from the port; and if
the *Mascotte* had not been provided with a powerful search-

light of her own she would hardly have been able to find her
way to sea, as the night was cloudy and the buoys were invisible.   With the long, slender shaft of her search-light,
however, she probed the darkness ahead, as with a radiant
exploring finger, and picked up the buoys, one after another, with unfailing certainty and precision.   Every two
or three minutes a floating iron balloon, or a skeleton frame
covered with sleeping aquatic birds, would flash into the
field of vision ahead, like one of Professor Pepper's patent
ghosts, stand out for a moment in brilliant white relief
against a background of impenetrable darkness, and then
vanish with the swiftness of summer lightning, as the electric beam left it to search for another buoy farther away.

When I awoke the next morning we were out on the blue,
tumbling, foam-crested water of the Gulf, forty or fifty miles
from the Florida coast.   All day Sunday we steamed slowly
southward, seeing no vessels except a Jamaica "fruiter,"
whose captain shouted to us, as he crossed our bow, that
he had been blown off his course in a recent gale, and would
like to know his position and distance.   We should have
reached Key West at half-past two Sunday afternoon; but
an accident which disabled one of the *Mascotte's* boilers
greatly reduced her normal speed, so that when I went to
my state-room at eleven o'clock Sunday evening we were
still twenty or thirty miles from our destination.

Three hours later I was awakened by shouted orders, the
tramping of feet, and the rattling of heavy chain-cable on
the forward deck, and, dressing myself hastily, I went out
to ascertain our situation.   The moon was hidden behind
a dense bank of clouds, the breeze had fallen to a nearly
perfect calm, and the steamer was rolling and pitching
gently on a sea that appeared to have the color and con-
sistency of greenish-gray oil.   Two hundred yards away, on
the port bow, floated a white pyramidal frame in the fierce

glare of the ship's search-light, and from it, at irregular intervals, came the warning toll of a heavy bell. It was the bell-buoy at the entrance to Key West harbor, and far away on the southeastern horizon appeared a faintly luminous nebula which marked the position of Key West city. Under the war regulations then in force, no vessels other than those belonging to the United States navy were permitted to enter or leave the port of Key West between late evening twilight and early dawn, and we were, therefore, forced to anchor off the bell-buoy until 5 A. M. Just as day was breaking we got our anchor on board and steamed in toward the town. The comparatively shallow water of the bay, in the first gray light of dawn, had the peculiar opaque, bluish-green color of a stream fed by an Alpine glacier; but as the light increased it assumed a brilliant but delicate translucent green of purer quality, contrasting finely with the scarlet flush in the east which heralded the rising, but still hidden, sun. On our right, as we entered the wide, spacious harbor, were two or three flat-topped, table-like islands, or "keys," which, in general outline and appearance, suggested dark mesas of foliage floating in a tropical ocean of pale chrysolite-green. Directly ahead was the city of Key West—a long, low, curving silhouette of roofs, spires, masts, lighthouses, cocoanut-palms, and Australian pines, delicately outlined in black against the scarlet arch of the dawn, "like a ragged line of Arabic etched on the blade of a Turkish simitar." At the extreme western end of this long, ragged silhouette rose the massive walls of Fort Taylor, with its double tier of antiquated embrasures; and on the left of it, as the distance lessened and the light increased, I could distinguish the cream-colored front of the Marine Hospital, the slender white shaft of the lighthouse, the red pyramidal roof of the Government Building, and the pale-yellow walls and cupola

of the Key West Hotel—all interspersed with graceful leaning palms, or thrown into effective relief against dark
masses of feathery Australian pine.

Along the water-front, for a distance of half a mile, extended an almost unbroken line of steamers, barks, schooners, and brigantines, discharging or receiving cargo, while
out on the pale-green, translucent surface of the harbor
were scattered a dozen or more war-ships of the North
Atlantic Squadron, ranging in size from the huge, double-
turreted monitor *Puritan* to the diminutive but dangerous-
looking torpedo-boat *Dupont*. All were in their war-paint
of dirty leaden gray, which, although it might add to their
effectiveness, certainly did not seem to me to improve their
appearance as component parts of an otherwise beautiful
marine picture. Beyond the war-ships and nearer to the
eastern end of the island lay the captured Spanish prizes,
including the big black liners *Pedro* and *Miguel Jover*, the
snow-white *Argonauta*, the brigantine *Frascito*, and a dozen
or more fishing-schooners intercepted by the blockading
fleet while on their way back to Havana from the Yucatan
banks.

But none of these war-ships or prizes had, for me, the interest that attached to a large black two-masted steamer
of eighteen hundred tons, which was lying at anchor off
the government wharf, flying from her mainmast-head a
white flag emblazoned with the red Greek cross of the
Geneva Convention. It was the steamship *State of Texas*,
of the Mallory line, chartered by the American National
Red Cross to carry to Cuba supplies for the starving reconcentrados, and to serve as headquarters for its president,
Miss Clara Barton, and her staff of trained surgeons, nurses,
and field-officers.

CHAPTER II

UNDER THE RED CROSS

WHEN Miss Barton joined the *State of Texas* at Key West on April 29 there seemed to be no immediate prospect of an invasion of Cuba by the United States army, and, consequently, no prospect of an opportunity to relieve the distress of the starving Cuban people. Knowing that such distress must necessarily have been greatly intensified by the blockade, and anxious to do something to mitigate it,—or, at least, to show the readiness of the Red Cross to undertake its mitigation,—Miss Barton wrote and sent to Admiral Sampson, commander of the naval forces on the North Atlantic Station, the following letter:

S. S. "STATE OF TEXAS," May 2, 1898.

Admiral W. T. Sampson, U. S. N., Commanding Fleet before Havana.

ADMIRAL: But for the introduction kindly proffered by our mutual acquaintance Captain Harrington, I should scarcely presume to address you. He will have made known to you the subject which I desire to bring to your gracious consideration.

Papers forwarded by direction of our government will have shown the charge intrusted to me, viz., to get food to the starving people of Cuba. I have with me a cargo of fourteen hundred tons, under the flag of the Red Cross, the one international emblem of neutrality and humanity known to civilization. Spain knows and regards it.

Fourteen months ago the entire Spanish government at Madrid cabled me permission to take and distribute food to the suffering people in Cuba. This official permission was broadly published. If read by our people, no response was made and no action taken until two months ago, when, under the humane and gracious call of our honored President, I did go and distribute food, unmolested anywhere on the island, until arrangements were made by our government for all American citizens to leave Cuba. Persons must now be dying there by hundreds, if not thousands, daily, for want of the food we are shutting out. Will not the world hold us accountable? Will history write us blameless? Will it not be said of us that we completed the scheme of extermination commenced by Weyler?

Fortunately, I know the Spanish authorities in Cuba, Captain-General Blanco and his assistants. We parted with perfect friendliness. They do not regard me as an American merely, but as the national representative of an international treaty to which they themselves are signatory and under which they act. I believe they would receive and confer with me if such a thing were made possible.

I should like to ask Spanish permission and protection to land and distribute food now on the *State of Texas*. Could I be permitted to ask to see them under flag of truce? If we make the effort and are refused, the blame rests with them; if we fail to make it, it rests with us. I hold it good statesmanship at least to divide the responsibility. I am told that some days must elapse before our troops can be in position to reach and feed these starving people. Our food and our forces are here, ready to commence at once.

With assurances of highest regard,

I am, Admiral, very respectfully yours,

[Signed] CLARA BARTON.

At the time when the above letter was written, the American National Red Cross was acting under the advice and direction of the State and Navy departments, the War Department having no force in the field.

Admiral Sampson replied as follows:

U. S. Flagship "New York," First-Rate,
Key West, Florida, May 2, 1898.

Miss Clara Barton, President American National Red Cross:

1. I have received through the senior naval officer present a copy of a letter from the State Department to the Secretary of the Navy; a copy of a letter from the Secretary of the Navy to the commander-in-chief of the naval force on this station; and also a copy of a letter from the Secretary of the Navy to the commandant of the naval station at Key West.

2. From these communications it appears that the destination of the steamship *State of Texas*, loaded with supplies for the starving reconcentrados in Cuba, is left, in a measure, to my judgment.

3. At present I am acting under instructions from the Navy Department to blockade the coast of Cuba for the purpose of preventing, among other things, any food-supply from reaching the Spanish forces in Cuba. Under these circumstances it seems to me unwise to let a ship-load of such supplies be sent to the reconcentrados, for, in my opinion, they would be distributed to the Spanish army. Until some point be occupied in Cuba by our forces, from which such distribution can be made to those for whom the supplies are intended, I am unwilling that they should be landed on Cuban soil.

Yours very respectfully,
[Signed]   W. T. Sampson,
Rear-Admiral U. S. N.,
Commander-in-Chief U. S. Naval Force, North Atlantic Station.

After this exchange of letters Miss Barton had a conference with Admiral Sampson, in the course of which the latter explained more fully his reasons for declining to allow the *State of Texas* to enter any Cuban port until such port had been occupied by American troops.

On May 3 Miss Barton sent the following telegram to Stephen E. Barton, chairman of the Central Cuban Relief Committee in New York:

KEY WEST, May 3, 1898.

Stephen E. Barton, Chairman, etc.:

Herewith I transmit copies of letters passed between Admiral Sampson and myself. I think it important that you should present immediately this correspondence personally to the government, as it will place before them the exact situation here. The utmost cordiality exists between Admiral Sampson and myself. The admiral feels it his duty, as chief of the blockading squadron, to keep food out of Cuba, but recognizes that, from my standpoint, my duty is to try to get food into Cuba. If I insist, Admiral Sampson will try to open communication under a flag of truce; but his letter expresses his opinion regarding the best method. Advices from the government would enable us to reach a decision. Unless there is objection at Washington, you are at liberty to publish this correspondence if you wish.

[Signed]   CLARA BARTON.

On May 6 the chairman of the Central Cuban Relief Committee replied as follows:

WASHINGTON, D. C., May 6, 1898.

Clara Barton, Key West, Florida:

Submitted your message to President and cabinet, and it was read with moistened eyes. Considered serious and pathetic. Admiral Sampson's views regarded as wisest at present. Hope to land you soon. President, Long, and Moore send highest regards.

[Signed]   BARTON.

Under these circumstances, of course, there was nothing for the Red Cross steamer to do but wait patiently in Key West until the army of invasion should leave Tampa for the Cuban coast.

Meanwhile, however, Miss Barton had discovered a field of beneficent activity for the Red Cross nearer home. In Tampa, on her way south, she learned that in that city, and at various other points on the coast of southern Florida, there were large numbers of destitute Cuban refugees and escaped reconcentrados, who were in urgent need of help.

A local committee in Tampa, composed of representatives from the various churches, had been doing everything in its power to relieve the distress of these unfortunate people, but the burden was getting to be beyond its strength, and it asked the Red Cross for assistance. The desired aid was promptly given, and the committee was supplied with provisions enough to support the Cuban refugees in Tampa until the middle of June.

Upon her arrival at Key West Miss Barton found a similar, but even worse, state of affairs, inasmuch as the number of destitute refugees and reconcentrados there exceeded fifteen hundred. A local Cuban relief society had established a soup-kitchen in which they were feeding about three hundred, and Mr. G. W. Hyatt, chairman of the Key West Red Cross Committee, was trying to take care of the rest; but both organizations were nearly at the end of their resources, and the local committee had nothing left in the shape of food-stuffs except corn-meal. Miss Barton at once telegraphed the Central Red Cross Committee in New York to forward thirty tons of assorted stores by first steamer, and pending the arrival of these stores she fed the Key West refugees from the *State of Texas* and from such local sources of food-supply as were available.

But Cuban refugees and reconcentrados were not the only hungry and destitute victims of the war to be found in Key West. On May 9 Miss Barton received the following letter from the United States marshal for the southern district of Florida:

DEPARTMENT OF JUSTICE, OFFICE OF U. S. MARSHAL,
SOUTHERN DISTRICT OF FLORIDA,
KEY WEST, FLORIDA, May 9, 1898.
Miss Clara Barton, President American National Red Cross.

DEAR MISS BARTON: On board the captured vessels we find quite a number of aliens among the crews, mostly Cubans, and some

American citizens, and their detention here and inability to get away for want of funds has exhausted their supply of food, and some of them will soon be entirely out. As there is no appropriation available from which food could be purchased, would you kindly provide for them until I can get definite instructions from the department at Washington?

Very respectfully yours,
[Signed]   JOHN F. HORR,
U. S. Marshal.

Appended to the above letter was a list of fifteen Spanish vessels whose crews were believed by the marshal to be in need of food.

In less than three hours after the receipt of this communication two large ships' boats, loaded with provisions for the sailors on the Spanish prizes, left the *State of Texas* in tow of the steam-launch of the troop-ship *Panther*. Before dark that night, Mr. Cobb and Dr. Egan, of Miss Barton's staff, who were in charge of the relief-boats, had visited every captured Spanish vessel in the harbor. Two or three of them, including the great liners *Miguel Jover* and *Argonauta*, had provisions enough, and were not in need of relief, but most of the others—particularly the fishing-smacks—were in even worse straits than the marshal supposed. The large transatlantic steamer *Pedro*, of Bilbao, had no flour, bread, coffee, tea, sugar, beans, rice, vegetables, or lard for cooking, and her crew had lived for fifteen days exclusively upon fish. The schooner *Severito* had wholly exhausted her supplies, and had on board nothing to eat of any kind. Of the others, some had no matches or oil for lights, some were nearly out of water, and all were reduced to an unrelieved fish diet, of which the men were beginning to sicken. The Red Cross relief-boats made a complete and accurate list of the Spanish prizes in the harbor,—twenty-two in all,—with the numerical strength of every crew, the amount of provisions, if any, on every vessel, and the quantity and kind of food that each would require.

Finding that one of the prizes had a cargo of plantains and bananas, and that most of the fishing-smacks were provided with salt-water tanks in which they had thousands of pounds of living fish, Miss Barton and her staff determined to purchase from them such quantities of these perishable commodities as they were willing to sell at a low nominal price, and use such food to increase and diversify the rations furnished to the fifteen hundred Cuban refugees and reconcentrados on shore. This would give the latter a change of diet, and at the same time lessen the amount of more expensive food-stuffs to be taken from the cargo of the Red Cross steamer or brought from New York. With the approval of the United States marshal, this plan was immediately carried into effect, and it worked admirably. The captains of the Spanish prizes were glad to give to the Red Cross perishable commodities for which they had no accessible market, and ten thousand pounds of fish and large quantities of plantains and bananas were soon obtained for distribution among the Cuban refugees and reconcentrados in Key West. I refer to this incident of the relief-work, not because it has, intrinsically, any particular importance, but because it shows that the means adopted by the Red Cross to relieve distress in Key West were intelligent and businesslike.

On the day after our arrival Mr. Cobb, of Miss Barton's staff, called at the hotel to tell us that the Red Cross relief-boats were about to make another visit to the Spanish prizes in the harbor, and to ask us if we would like to go with them and see the work.

In half an hour Miss Barton and her staff, Mrs. Kennan and I, started in the steam-launch of the monitor *Puritan* to make the round of the captured Spanish ships, towing behind us two large boats loaded with assorted stores for the destitute crews. The first vessel we visited was a small black brigantine from Barcelona, named *Frascito*, which had been captured eight miles off Havana by the United States ·cruiser *Montgomery*. The swarthy, scantily clad Spanish sailors crowded to the bulwarks with beaming faces as we approached, and the hurried, almost frenzied eagerness with which they threw us a line, hung a ladder over the side, and helped us on board, showed that although we were incidentally Americans, and therefore enemies, we were primarily Red Cross people, and consequently friends to be greeted and welcomed with every possible manifestation of respect, gratitude, and affection.

The interior of the little brigantine presented an appearance of slovenly but picturesque dirt, confusion, and disorder, as if the crew, overwhelmed by the misfortune that had come upon them, had abandoned the routine of daily duty and given themselves up to apathy and despair. The main-deck, between the low after-cabin and the high forecastle, had not been washed down, apparently, in a week; piles of dirty dishes and cooking-utensils of strange, unfamiliar shapes lay here and there around the little galley forward; coils of running rigging were kicking about underfoot instead of hanging on the belaying-pins; a pig-pen, which had apparently gone adrift in a gale, blocked up the gangway to the forecastle on the port side between the high bulwark and a big boat which had been lashed in V-shaped supports amidships; and a large part of the space between the cabin and the forecastle on the starboard side was a chaos of chain-cable, lumber, spare spars, pots, pans, earthen water-jars, and chicken-coops.

The captain of the little vessel was a round-faced, boyish-looking man, of an English rather than a Spanish type, with clear gray honest eyes and a winning expression of friendli-

2

ness and rustic bonhomie, like that of an amiable, intelligent
young peasant. He greeted us cordially, but with a slight
trace of shy awkwardness, and invited us into the small,
dark cabin, where we drank one another's health in a bottle
of sweet, strong liqueur, and he told us the rather pathetic
story of his misfortune. The brigantine *Frascito* ("Little
Flask"), he said, belonged in part to him and in part to a
company in Barcelona. The cargo, consisting chiefly of
South American jerked beef, was owned by his father and
himself, and ship and cargo represented all that he and his
family had in the world. He left Montevideo for Havana
about the middle of March, and had no intimation whatever
that Spain and the United States were at war, until a round
shot was fired across his bow by the cruiser *Montgomery,*
about eight miles off Morro Castle. The officers of the
cruiser treated him very kindly—"I could n't have done it
better," he said, with simple sincerity, "if I had done it myself; but it was very hard to lose everything just because I
did n't know. Of course I should n't have tried to get into
Havana if I had known there was war; but I left Montevideo
in March, and had no thought of such a thing." We tried
to cheer him up by telling him that the prize-court would
hardly condemn and confiscate his vessel under such circumstances, but he was still sad and troubled. He thanked
us with simple, unaffected earnestness for the provisions we
had put on board his ship, and said that the unexpected kindness of the Red Cross to him and his crew had cheered and
encouraged them all. He seemed anxious to do something
to show us his gratitude and appreciation, and when a
member of our party manifested interest in a large cage of
red-crested tropical birds which hung beside the cabin
door, he promptly took it down and presented it "to the
señorita for the Red Cross steamer, with the compliments
and thanks of the *Frascito*."

After putting on board the little brigantine such supplies, in the shape of bread, beans, rice, canned meats, etc., as the crew required, we bade the captain and mate good-by, and left them apparently somewhat cheered up by our visit.

From the *Frascito* we went successively to the *Oriente*, the *España*, the *Santiago Apostol*, the *Poder de Dios*, and fifteen or sixteen other vessels of the prize-fleet, ascertaining their wants, furnishing them with such food-supplies as they needed, and listening to the stories of their captains.

Among the sailors on the fishing-smacks were many unfamiliar and wild-looking Cuban and Spanish types—men with hard, dark faces, lighted up by fierce, brilliant black eyes, who looked as if they would have been in their proper sphere fighting under a black flag, on the Spanish Main, in the good old days of the bucaneers. But hard and fierce as many of them looked, they were not wholly insensible to kindness. On the schooner *Power of God*, where there seemed to be more wild, cruel, piratical types than on any other vessel except, perhaps, *St. James the Apostle*, I noticed a sailor with a stern, hard, almost black face and fierce, dark eyes, who—had such a thing been possible—might have stepped, just as he stood, out of the pages of "Amyas Leigh." He was regarding me with an expression in which, if there was no actual malevolence, there was at least not the slightest indication of friendliness or good will. Taking from my haversack a box of the cigarettes with which I had provided myself in anticipation of a tobacco famine among the Spanish sailors, I sprang over the bulwark, and, with as cordial a smile of comradeship as I could give him, I placed it in his hand. For an instant he stared at it as if stupefied with amazement. Then his hard, set face relaxed a little, and, throwing his head forward and raising his fierce black eyes to mine, he gave me a long look of surprise and intense, passionate gratitude, which seemed to say,

"I don't know your language, and I can't *tell* you how grateful I am, but I can *look* it" —and he did. He had evidently been out of tobacco many days, and in a moment he went below where he could light a match out of the wind, and presently reappeared, breathing smoke and exhaling it through his nostrils with infinite satisfaction and pleasure.

Nearly all the sailors on the fishing-smacks were barefooted, many were bareheaded, and all had been tanned a dark mahogany color by weeks of exposure to the rays of a tropical sun. Their dress consisted, generally, of a shirt and a pair of loose trousers of coarse gray cotton, like the dress worn in summer by Siberian convicts. Dr. Egan prescribed and furnished medicines for the sick wherever they were found, and on one vessel performed a rather difficult and delicate surgical operation for the relief of a man who was suffering from a badly swollen neck, with necrosis of the lower jawbone.

At half-past six o'clock we returned to the *State of Texas*, having attended to all the sick that were found, relieved all the distress that was brought to our attention, and furnished food enough for a week's consumption to the crews of nineteen vessels.

Two days later, at the suggestion of Miss Barton, Mr. Cobb purchased a quantity of smoking- and chewing-tobacco for the Spanish sailors, and we made another double round of the prize-ships, in the steam-launch of the New York "Sun," which was courteously placed at the disposal of the Red Cross for the whole afternoon. On our outward trip we left on every vessel tobacco and matches enough to last the crew for a week, and Mr. Cobb notified all the captains that if they or their crews wished to write open letters to their relatives and friends in Cuba or Spain, the Red Cross would collect them, submit them to the United States prize-court for approval, and undertake to forward them.

The tobacco and the offer to forward letters seemed to excite more enthusiastic gratitude in the hearts of the Spanish prisoners than even the distribution of food. On one schooner my attention was attracted to a ragged sailor who was saying something very earnestly in Spanish, and pointing, in a rather dramatic manner, to the sky. "What is he saying?" I inquired of Mr. Cobb. "He says," replied the latter, with a smile, "that if they were prisoners up in heaven, they could n't be better treated than they have been here."

I was touched and gratified to see the interest and sympathy excited by the work of the Red Cross in all who came in contact with it, from the commodore of the fleet to the poorest fisherman. The captains of the monitor *Puritan* and the auxiliary cruiser *Panther* offered us the use of their swift steam-launches in the work of distributing food; the representative of the New York "Sun" followed their example; the marines on the *Panther* doffed their caps to our boats as we passed, and even a poor Key West fisherman pulled over to us in his skiff, as we lay alongside a Spanish vessel, and gave us two large, lobster-like crawfish, merely to show us, in the only way he could, his affectionate sympathy and good will. Mr. Cobb offered him some of the tobacco that we were distributing among the Spanish sailors, but he refused to take it, saying : "I did n't bring the fish to you to beg tobacco, or for money, but just because I wanted to help a little. I hoped to get more, but these were all I could catch."

One touch of kindness makes all the world kin. Even the engineer of the New York "Sun's" naphtha-launch gave his cherished pipe to a sailor on a Spanish vessel who had none, and when one of his mates remonstrated with him, saying, "You 're not going to give him your own brier-wood pipe!" he replied, with a shamefaced smile : "Yes, poor devil! he can't get one away out here.   I can buy another ashore."

Late in the afternoon we made a second round of all the Spanish ships to collect their letters, and then returned to the *State of Texas*.   Mr. Cobb that same evening submitted the open letters to the United States prize-court for approval, and I made an arrangement with Mr. E. F. Knight, war correspondent of the London "Times," who was just starting for Havana, to take the Cuban letters with him and mail them there.   The letters for Spain were sent to the National Red Cross of Portugal.

CHAPTER III

ON THE EDGE OF WAR

UNTIL the illuminating search-light of war was turned upon the island of Key West, it was, to the people of the North generally, little more than a name attached to a small, arid coral reef lying on the verge of the Gulf Stream off the southern extremity of Florida. Few people knew anything definitely about it, and to nine readers out of ten its name suggested nothing more interesting or attractive than Cuban filibusters, sponges, and cigars. In less than a month, however, after the outbreak of hostilities, it had become the headquarters, as well as the chief coaling-station, of two powerful fleets; the news-distributing center for the whole Cuban coast; the supply-depot to which perhaps a hundred vessels resorted for water, food, and ammunition; the home station of all the newspaper despatch-boats cruising in West Indian waters; the temporary headquarters of more than a hundred newspaper correspondents and reporters, and the most advanced outpost of the United States on the edge of war. In view of the importance which the place had at that time, as well as the importance which it must continue to have, as our naval base in Cuban waters, a description of it may not be wholly without interest.

The island on which the city of Key West stands forms one of the links in a long, curving chain of shoals, reefs, and keys extending in a southwesterly direction about a hundred miles from the extreme end of the peninsula of Florida. It is approximately six miles long, has an average width of one mile, and resembles a little in shape a huge comma, with the city of Key West for its head and a diminishing curve of low, swampy chaparral and mangrove-bushes for a tail. The shallow bay of pale-green water between the head and the tail on the concave side of the comma is known as "the bight." It is the anchorage of the sponging-fleet, and is the eastern limit of settlement on that side of the island. Beyond it are sandy flats and shallow, salt-water lagoons, shut in by a dense growth of leather-leaved bushes and low, scrubby China-berry, sea-grape, and Jamaica-apple trees. The highest part of the Key is occupied by the city, and the highest part of the city is the low bluff on its western side, where the slender shaft of the lighthouse stands at a height of fifteen or eighteen feet above the level of tide-water. Owing to its geographical position in a semi-tropical sea, just north of the Gulf Stream and within the zone of the northeast trade-winds, Key West has a climate of remarkable mildness and equability. Twenty years' observations show that its lowest monthly mean of temperature is 70° F. in January, and its highest 84° in August—an annual range of only 14°. Between the years 1886 and 1896 the highest temperature recorded was 92°, and the lowest 40°— a range of only 52° between maximum and minimum in a period of ten years. New York and Chicago often have a greater variation of temperature than this in the course of ten days.

Equability, however, is not the only noteworthy characteristic of the Key West climate. It is also remarkable for its sunniness in winter and its breeziness at all seasons of the year. The average number of cloudy days there is only sixty-four per annum, and between October and April the sun often shines, day after day, in a cloudless sky, for weeks at a time. But even more constant and continuous than the sunshine are the cool breezes from the foam-crested waters of the Atlantic, which temper the heat of the almost perpetual summer. From the reports of the Weather Bureau it appears that the average number of calm days at Key West is only ten per annum. In 1895 only three days were calm, and in 1894 there were only twenty-seven hours, of day or night, in which there was not breeze enough to ripple, at least, the pale-green water of the harbor. For all practical purposes, therefore, the sea-breeze at Key West may be regarded as perennial and incessant. It varies in strength, of course, from day to day and from hour to hour; but in the two weeks that I spent there it was never strong enough to be unpleasant in the city, nor to necessitate the reefing of small sail-boats in the comparatively open and unsheltered bay.

The average annual rainfall on the island is about thirty-nine inches, and nearly the whole of this precipitation is confined to the so-called "rainy season," between May and November, when showers fall, now and then, at irregular intervals of from three to ten days. For their fresh water the inhabitants depend entirely upon this rainfall, which is carefully collected and saved in large roof-covered cisterns. There are a few wells on the island, but the water in them is generally brackish, or is so impregnated with lime and earthy salts as to be unfit either for drinking or for irrigation. To sum up briefly, the climate of Key West may be roughly described as mild and dry in winter, warm but showery in summer, and breezy and sunny at all seasons.

In this geographical and climatic environment there has grown up on the island an interesting but rather sleepy and unprogressive city of twenty-two thousand inhabitants. The most important of the elements that go to make up its

population are, first, whites from the United States, who
are chiefly engaged in shipping or commerce; second, Cubans
of mixed blood, employed, for the most part, in the cigar
factories; third, immigrants from the Bahamas, known as
"conchs," who devote themselves mainly to fishing, spong-
ing, and wrecking; and, fourth, negroes from America and
the West Indian Islands, who turn their hands to anything
they can find to do, from shoveling coal to diving into the
clear water of the bay after the pennies or nickels thrown
by Northern tourists from the deck of the *Mascotte* or the
Olivette.   Nothing in the shape of fruit, grain, or vegetables
is raised on the island for export, and the greater part of
the city's food-supply comes either from Florida or from the
islands of the West Indies.

The first thing that strikes a newcomer in Key West is
the distinctly and unmistakably foreign aspect of the city.
In spite of the English names on many of the sign-boards
over the shops, the American faces on the streets, and the
crowd of American officers and war correspondents smoking or talking on the spacious piazzas of the Key West
Hotel, one cannot get rid of the impression that he has left
the United States and has landed in some such town as San
Juan de Guatemala or Punta Arenas, on the Pacific coast of
Central America.   Everything that meets the eye seems
new, unfamiliar, and, in some subtle, indefinable way, un-
American.   The vivid but pale and delicate green of the
ocean water; the slender, fern-headed cocoanut-palms which
stand in clumps here and there along the streets; the feathery
Australian pines and dark-green Indian laurels which shade
the naval storehouse and the Marine Hospital; the masses of
tamarind, almond, sapodilla, wild-fig, banana, and cork-tree
foliage in the yards of the white, veranda-belted houses; the
Spanish and Cuban types on the piers and in front of the
hotels; the unfamiliar language which strikes the ear at

almost every step—all suggest a tropical environment and
Spanish, rather than American, influences and characteristics.

The two features of Key West scenery that appear, at
first glance, to be most salient, and that contribute most to
the impression of strangeness and remoteness made by the
island as a whole, are, unquestionably, the color of the water
and the character of the vegetation. The ocean in which
the little coral key is set has a vividness and a delicacy of
color that I have never seen equaled elsewhere, and that is
not even so much as suggested by the turbid, semi-opaque
water of the Atlantic off the coast of Massachusetts or
New Jersey. It is a clear, brilliant, translucent green, pale
rather than deep in tone, and ranging through all possible
gradations, from the color of a rain-wet lawn to the pure, delicate, ethereal green of an auroral streamer. Sometimes,
in heavy cloud-shadow, it is almost as dark as the green of
a Siberian alexandrite; but just beyond the shadow, in the
full sunshine, it brightens to the color of a greenish tur-
quoise. In the shallow bay known as "the bight," the yellowish brown of the marine vegetation on the bottom blends
with the pale green of the overlying water so as to repro-
duce on a large scale the tints of a Ural Mountain chrysolite,
while two miles away, over a bank of sand or a white coral
reef, the water has the almost opaque but vivid color of a pea-
green satin ribbon. Even in the gloom and obscurity of
midnight, the narrow slit cut through the darkness by the
sharp blade of the Fort Taylor search-light reveals a long
line of green, foam-flecked water. Owing to the very limited
extent of the island, the ocean may be seen at the end of
every street and from almost every point of view, and its
constantly changing but always unfamiliar color says to you
at every hour of the day: "You are no longer looking out
upon the dull, muddy green water of the Atlantic coast; you

are on a tropical, palm-fringed coral reef in the remote solitude of the great South Sea."

Next to the color of the ocean, in its power to suggest remoteness and unfamiliarity, is the character of the vegetation. The flora of Key West is wholly tropical, and in my first ramble through the city I did not discover a single plant, shrub, tree, or flower that I had ever seen in the North except the oleander. Even that had wholly changed its habits and appearance, and resembled the pot-grown plant of Northern households only as the gigantic sequoia of California resembles the stunted Lilliputian pine of the Siberian tundra. The Key West oleander is not a plant, nor a shrub; it is a tree. In the yard of a private house on Carolina Street I saw an oleander nearly thirty feet in height, whose branches shaded an area twenty feet or more in diameter, and whose mammoth clusters of rosy flowers might have been counted by the hundred. Such an oleander as this, even though its leaves and blossoms may be familiar, seems like a stranger and an exotic, and, instead of modifying the impression of remoteness and alienation made by the other features of the tropical environment, it deepens and intensifies it. Among the vines, plants, shrubs, and trees that I noticed and identified in the streets and private grounds of Key West were jasmine, bergamot, poinsettia, hibiscus, almond, banana, sapodilla, tamarind, Jamaica apple, mango, Spanish lime, cotton-tree, royal poinciana, "Geiger flower" (a local name), alligator-pear, tree-cactus, sand-box, corktree, banian-tree, sea-grape, cocoanut-palm, date-palm, Indian laurel, Australian pine, and wild fig. Most of these trees and shrubs do not grow even in southern Florida, and are to be found, within the limits of the United States, only in southern California and on the island of Key West.

A mere perusal of this long list of unfamiliar names will enable the reader to understand why the vegetation of the island reinforces the impression of strangeness and remoteness already made by the color of the sea.

Key West, after the outbreak of war, had two chief centers of interest and excitement: first, the harbor, between Fort Taylor and the government wharf, where lay all the monitors, cruisers, and gunboats of the North Atlantic Squadron that were not actually engaged in sea service; and, second, the Key West Hotel, which was the headquarters of the war correspondents, as well as of naval officers assigned to shore duty, and visitors on all sorts of business from the North.   I found it hard to decide which of these two centers would offer better opportunities and facilities for observation and the acquirement of knowledge.   If I stayed on board a vessel in the harbor, I should miss the life and activity of the city, the quick delivery of daily papers from the North, the news bulletins posted every few hours in the hotel, and all the stories of fight, peril, or adventure told on shady piazzas by officers and correspondents just back from the Cuban coast; while, on the other hand, if I established myself at the hotel, I could not see the bringing in of Spanish prizes from the Florida Strait, the arrival and departure of despatch-boats with news and orders, the play of the searchlights, the gun practice of the big war-ships, the signaling, the saluting, and the movements generally of the fleet.

After having spent a week at the hotel, I decided to go on board the Red Cross steamer *State of Texas*, which was lying off the government wharf, nearly opposite the customhouse, and within one hundred yards of the two big monitors *Puritan* and *Miantonomoh*.   I made the change just in time to see, from the best possible point of vantage, the great event of the week—the arrival of the two powerful fleets commanded respectively by Admiral Sampson and Commodore Schley.   Early Wednesday morning the graceful, black, schooner-rigged despatch-boat of the New York "Sun" came racing into the harbor under full head of steam, followed closely by the ocean-going tug of the Associated Press and two or three fast yachts in the service of New York papers, all blowing their whistles vigorously to attract attention from the shore. Something, evidently, had happened, and, looking seaward with a powerful glass, I had no difficulty in making out on the horizon, at a distance of eight or ten miles, the cruiser *Brooklyn*, the battle-ships *Texas* and *Massachusetts*, and two or three smaller cruisers and gunboats of the United States navy. The Flying Squadron from Hampton Roads had arrived.

The harbor at once became a scene of rapid movement and intense activity. Steam-launches darted out from the piers carrying war correspondents to their respective despatch-boats, and naval officers to the monitors and the huge four-masted colliers; a long line of party-colored flags was displayed from the signal-halyards of the *Miantonomoh;* two or three fast sea-going tugs carrying the naval commandant and other harbor officers started seaward at full speed, with long plumes of black smoke trailing to leeward from their lead-colored stacks; and the eight hundred marines on the auxiliary cruiser *Panther* swarmed on deck and crowded eagerly aft to gaze at the dim, distant outlines of the newly arrived vessels.

About the middle of the forenoon the swift, heavily armed gunboat *Scorpion* entered the harbor flying the commodore's pennant, and was received with a salute of eleven guns from the monitor *Miantonomoh*. The remainder of the day passed without any other unusual or noteworthy incident, but sometime in the night the fleet of Admiral Sampson joined the Flying Squadron in the offing, and Thursday morning the people of Key West saw, in their harbor and at sea off Fort Taylor, the largest and most powerful fleet of war-vessels that had ever assembled, perhaps, under the American flag.

All day Thursday the harbor was the center of incessant movement, activity, and excitement. The lighter vessels of the Flying Squadron, which had come in to coal, rejoined the heavier cruisers and battle-ships in the offing, and their places were taken by the big monitors *Amphitrite* and *Terror*, the cruisers *Detroit* and *Marblehead*, and the gunboats *Wilmington*, *Helena*, *Castine*, and *Machias*, which steamed in one after another from the fleet of Admiral Sampson. When all these vessels had anchored off Fort Taylor and the government wharf, there were in the harbor more than twenty ships of war, including three torpedo-boats and four monitors; six or eight armed yachts of the mosquito fleet; twelve or fifteen big transports, troop-ships, and colliers awaiting orders; twenty-two Spanish prizes of all sorts, from the big liner *Argonauta* to the little brigantine *Frascito;* and, finally, a fleet of newspaper tugs, launches, and despatch-boats almost equal, numerically, to the fleets of Commodore Schley and Admiral Sampson taken together. The marine picture presented by the harbor with all these monitors, cruisers, gunboats, yachts, transports, troop-ships, torpedo-boats, colliers, despatch-boats, and Spanish prizes lying at anchor, with flags and signals flying in the clear sunshine and on the translucent green water of the tropics, was a picture of more than ordinary interest and beauty, and one that Key West, perhaps, may never see again.

About two o'clock in the afternoon I was able, through the courtesy of Mr. Trumbull White in offering me the use of the Chicago "Record's" despatch-boat, to go off to the flagship *New York* and present my letter of introduction from the President to Admiral Sampson. I was received most cordially and hospitably, and, after conferring with him for half an hour with regard to the plans and work of the Red Cross, so far as they depended upon or related to the navy, I returned to the *State of Texas*. The fleet sailed

again at half-past ten o'clock that night for the coast of
Cuba.

After the departure of the blockading fleet and the Flying Squadron on May 19 and 20, the small army of war
correspondents at Key West had little to do except watch
for the arrival of vessels with news from the Cuban coast.
Most of them regarded this work—or rather absence of
work—as tedious and irksome in the extreme; but if they
had been living on board ship instead of at the hotel they
would have found a never-failing source of interest and entertainment in the constantly changing picture presented
by the harbor. Six or eight war-ships, ranging in size and
fighting power from monitors to torpedo-boats, were still
lying at anchor off the custom-house and the Marine Hospital; transports with stores and munitions of war were
discharging their cargoes at the piers; big four-masted
schooners, laden with coal for the blockading fleet, swung
back and forth with the ebbing and flowing tides as they
awaited orders from the naval commandant; graceful steam-
yachts, flying the flag of the Associated Press, were constantly coming in with news or going out in search of it;
swift naphtha-launches carrying naval officers in white uniforms darted hither and thither from one cruiser to another,
whistling shrill warnings to the slower boats pulled by sailors
from the transports; officers on the monitors were exchanging "wigwag" flag-signals with other officers on the gunboats or the troop-ships; and from every direction came
shouts, bugle-calls, the shrieks of steam-whistles, the peculiar jarring rattle of machine-guns at target practice, and
the measured beats of twenty or thirty ships' bells, striking,
at different distances, but almost synchronously, the half-
hours.

Interesting, however, as Key West harbor might seem
in the daytime, it was far more beautiful and impressive

at night. One clear, still evening late in May, when the
rosy flush of the short tropical twilight had faded, and the
Sand Key beacon began to glow faintly, like a setting planet,
on the darkening horizon in the west, I went up on the hur-
ricane-deck alone and looked about the harbor. The city,
the war-ships, and the massive square outlines of Fort Taylor had all vanished in the gathering darkness and gloom,
but in their places were rows, clusters, and constellations
innumerable of steadily burning lights. A long, slender
shaft of bluish radiance streamed out from the corner of
Fort Taylor, widening as it extended seaward, until it struck
and illuminated with a sort of ghostly phosphorescence the
whitish hull of a gunboat stealing noiselessly into the harbor
from the direction of the Cuban coast. The strange craft
hung out a perpendicular string of red and white lights,
which winked solemnly once or twice, changed color two or
three times, and then vanished. A second search-light from
the monitor *Miantonomoh* sent another slender electric ray
of inquiry in the direction of the intruder, as if still doubtful of its character; but when the straight blue sword of
the Fort Taylor search-light rose to the clouds and fell to
the water three times, as if striking a whole league of ocean
three successive and measured blows, the *Miantonomoh* understood that all was well, and her own search-light left the
gunboat and swept across the starry sky overhead like the
tail of a huge blue comet swinging at its perigee around a
darkened sun.

In a moment the monitor itself hung out a string of lights
which winked, changed color, vanished, reappeared, and again
vanished, leaving only a red light at the masthead. In a
moment an answering signal-rocket was thrown up by an invisible war-ship in the direction of Fort Taylor, and instantly
two powerful search-lights were focused upon a pale, whitish object, far out at sea, which looked in the bluish, ghostly
3

glare like the mainsail of the *Flying Dutchman*. Before I had time to form a conjecture as to the significance of these mysterious signals and apparitions, I was startled by a sudden flash and the thunder of a heavy gun from the darkness ahead; and away out at sea, in the strip of green water illuminated by the search-lights, a heavy projectile plunged into the ocean, near the sail of the *Flying Dutchman*, and sent a column of white spray thirty feet into the air. Then I understood what it all meant. The *Wilmington* was engaged in night gun practice. For half an hour or more the war-ship threw solid shot and explosive shells into that illuminated strip of green water, and the thunder of her cannon, which could be heard all over the island, suggested to the startled negro and Cuban population that the Spanish fleet had arrived and was bombarding the city. Then the *Miantonomoh* hung out another string of colored lanterns, the uproar ceased, and the pallid, ghostly canvas of the *Flying Dutchman* suddenly vanished as the search-lights left it and resumed their slow, sweeping exploration of the harbor, the channel, and the open sea.

CHAPTER IV

WAR CORRESPONDENTS AND DESPATCH-BOATS

FEW things impressed me more forcibly, in the course of my two weeks' stay at Key West, than the costly, far-sighted, and far-reaching preparations made by the great newspapers of the country to report the war. There were in the city of Tampa, at the time of my arrival, nearly one hundred war correspondents, who represented papers in all parts of the United States, from New England to the Pacific coast, and who were all expecting to go to Cuba with the army of invasion. Nearly every one of the leading metropolitan journals had in Tampa and Key West a staff of six or eight of its best men under the direction of a war-correspondent-in-chief, while the Associated Press was represented by a dozen or more reporters in Cuban waters, as well as by correspondents in Havana, Key West, Tampa, Kingston, St. Thomas, Port-au-Prince, and on the flagships of Admiral Sampson and Commodore Schley. Every invention and device of applied science was brought into requisition to facilitate the work of the reporters and to enable them to get their work quickly to their home offices. The New York "Herald," for example, paid fifty dollars an hour for a special leased wire between New York and Key West, and set up, in the latter place and in Tampa, newly invented, long-distance phototelegraph instruments, by means of which its artist in the field could transmit a finished picture to the home office every twenty minutes.

In their efforts to get full and accurate news of every event at the earliest possible moment, the war correspondents shrank from neither hardship nor danger. A week or two before my arrival in Key West, for example, Mr. Scovel, one of the most daring and enterprising of the war correspondents, landed from a despatch-boat on the coast of Cuba in the night, with the intention of making his way to the camp of General Gomez. As he had not had a previous understanding with the latter, no arrangements had been made to meet him, he could get no horses, and, with only two or three companions, he walked eighty miles through tropical forests and swamps, dodging Spanish sentinels and guerrillas, living wholly upon plantains and roots, and sleeping most of the time out of doors in a hammock slung between two trees. He finally succeeded in obtaining horses, reached the insurgent camp, had an interview with General Gomez, rode back to the coast at a point previously agreed upon, signaled to his despatch-boat, was taken on board, and returned safely to Key West after an absence of two weeks, in the course of which he had not once tasted bread nor slept in a bed.

Upon the record of such an achievement as this most men would have been satisfied, for a time, to rest; but Mr. Scovel, with untiring energy, went from Key West to the coast of Cuba and back three times in the next seven days. On the last of these expeditions he joined a landing force carrying arms and ammunition to the insurgents, participated in a hot skirmish with the Spanish troops, wrote an account of the adventure that same night while at sea in a small, tossing boat on his way back to Key West, and filed six thousand words in the Key West cable-station at two o'clock in the morning.

I speak of this particular case of journalistic enterprise, not because it is especially noteworthy or exceptional, but because it illustrates the endurance and the capacity for sustained toil in unfavorable circumstances, which are quite as characteristic of the modern war correspondent as are his courage and his alert readiness for any emergency or any opportunity.

Owing to the distance of the seat of war from the American coast and the absence of telegraphic communication between Cuba and the mainland, newspapers that made any serious attempt to get quick and exclusive information from the front had not only to send correspondents into the field, but to furnish them with means of moving rapidly from place to place and of forwarding their despatches promptly to an American telegraph office or a West Indian cable-station. Every prominent New York paper, therefore, had at least one despatch-boat for the use of its correspondents, several of them had two or three, and the Associated Press employed four. These boats were either powerful sea-going tugs like the *Hercules* and the *Premier*, or swift steam-yachts of the class represented by the *Wanda*, the *Kanapaha*, and the *Bucaneer*. Exactly how many of them there were in West Indian waters I have been unable to ascertain; but I should say not less than fifteen or twenty, with almost an equal number of naphtha- and steam-launches for harbor and smooth-water work. In these despatch-boats the war correspondents went back and forth between Key West and Cuba; watched the operations of the blockading fleet off Havana, Matanzas, or Cardenas; cruised along a coast-line nearly a thousand miles in extent, and, if necessary, went with Admiral Sampson's squadron to a point of attack as remote as Santiago de Cuba or San Juan de Porto

Rico.   Whenever anything of importance happened in any
part of this wide area, they were expected to be on the spot
to observe it, and then to get the earliest news of it to the
nearest cable-station—whether that station were Kingston,
Cape Haitien, St. Thomas, Port-au-Prince, or Key West.
All of the newspaper despatch-boats were small, many of
them had very limited coal-carrying capacity, and some were
nothing but sea-going tugs, with hardly any comforts or conveniences, and with no suitable accommodations for passengers.   The correspondents who used these boats were, therefore, compelled to live a rough-and-tumble life, sometimes
sleeping in their clothes on benches or on the floor in a small,
stuffy cabin, and always suffering the hardships and privations necessarily involved in a long cruise on a small vessel
in a tropical climate and on a turbulent sea.   The Florida
Strait between Key West and the north Cuban coast is as
uncomfortable a piece of water to cruise on as can be found
in the tropics.   It is the place where the swiftly running Gulf
Stream meets the fresh northeast trade-winds; and in the
conflict between these opposing terrestrial forces there is
raised a high and at the same time short, choppy, and irregular sea, on which small vessels toss, roll, and pitch about like
corks in a boiling caldron.   I was told by some of the correspondents who had cruised in these waters that often, for
days at a time, it was almost impossible to get any really
refreshing rest or sleep.   The large and heavy war-ships of
the blockading fleet rode this sea, of course, with comparatively little motion; but it is reported that even Captain
Sigsbee was threatened with seasickness while crossing the
strait between Havana and Key West in a small boat.

Discomfort, however, was perhaps the least of the war
correspondent's troubles.   He expected discomfort, and accepted it philosophically; but to it was added constant and
harassing anxiety.   As he could not predict or anticipate

the movements of the war-ships, and had no clue to the plans and intentions of their commanding officer, he was compelled to stay constantly with the fleet, night and day, in order to be on the scene of action when action should come. This part of his duty was not only difficult, but often extremely hazardous. As soon as night fell, every light on the war-ships was extinguished, and they cruised or drifted about until daybreak in silence and in darkness. Owing to their color, it was almost impossible to follow them, or even to see them at a distance of a mile, and the correspondent on the despatch-boat was liable either to lose them altogether if he kept too far away, or be fired upon if he came too near.

On my visit to the flagship *New York* I was accompanied by Mr. Chamberlain, one of the war correspondents of the Chicago "Record." Just before we went over the side of the ship on our return to the "Record's" despatch-boat, Mr. Chamberlain said to Admiral Sampson: "Can you give me any directions or instructions, admiral, with regard to approaching your fleet in hostile waters? I don't want to be in your way or to do anything that would imperil my own vessel or inconvenience yours."

"Where do you propose to go?" inquired the admiral.

"Anywhere," replied the war correspondent, "or rather everywhere, that you do."

The admiral smiled dryly and said: "I can't give you any definite instructions except, generally, to keep away from the fleet—especially at night. You may approach and hail us in the daytime if you have occasion to do so, but if you come within five miles of the fleet at night there is likely to be trouble."

This was all that Mr. Chamberlain could get from the admiral; but the officer of the deck, whose name I did not learn, had no hesitation in explaining fully to us the nature of the "trouble" that would ensue if, through design or inadvertence, a newspaper despatch-boat should get within five miles of the fleet at night. "We can't afford to take any chances," he said, "of torpedo-boats. If you show up at night in the neighborhood of this ship, we shall fire on you first and ask questions afterward."

"But how are we to know where you are?" inquired the correspondent.

"That's your business," replied the officer; "but if you approach us at night, you do it at your own peril."

When we had returned to the despatch-boat, Mr. Chamberlain said to me: "Of course that's all right from their point of view. I appreciate their situation, and if I were in their places I should doubtless act precisely as they do; but it's my business to watch that fleet, and I can't do it if I keep five miles away at night. I think I'll go within two miles and take the chances. Some of us will probably lose the numbers of our mess down here," he added coolly, "if this thing lasts, but I don't see how it can be helped."

The difficulty of keeping five miles away, or any specified distance away, from a blockading fleet of war-ships at night can be fully realized only by those who have experienced it. Except on Morro Castle at Havana there were no lights on the northern coast of Cuba; if it was cloudy and there happened to be no moon, the darkness was impenetrable; the war-ships did not allow even so much as the glimmer of a binnacle lamp to escape from their lead-colored, almost invisible hulls, as they cruised noiselessly back and forth; and the correspondent on the despatch-boat not only did not know where they were, but had no means whatever of ascertaining where he himself was. Meanwhile, at any moment, there might come out of the impenetrable darkness ahead the thunder of a six-pounder gun, followed by the blinding glare of a search-light. Unquestionably the correspondents were to be believed when they said privately to one another that it was nervous, harassing work.

But the list of difficulties and embarrassments which confronted the correspondent in his quest of news is not yet at an end. If he escaped the danger of being sunk or disabled by a shell or a solid projectile at night, and succeeded in following a fleet like that of Admiral Sampson, he had to take into serious consideration the question of coal. Fuel is quite as essential to a despatch-boat as to a battle-ship. The commander of the battle-ship, however, had a great advantage over the correspondent on the despatch-boat, for the reason that he always knew exactly where he was going and where he could recoal; while the unfortunate newspaper man was ignorant of his own destination, was compelled to follow the fleet blindly, and did not know whether his limited supply of coal would last to the end of the cruise or not. When Mr. Chamberlain sailed from Key West at night with the fleet of Admiral Sampson, he believed that the latter was bound for Santiago, on the southeastern coast of Cuba. The *Hercules* could not possibly carry coal enough for a voyage there and back; in fact, she would reach that port with only one day's supply of fuel in her bunkers. What should be done then? The nearest available source of coal-supply would be Kingston, Jamaica, and whether he could get there from Santiago before his fuel should be wholly exhausted Mr. Chamberlain did not know. However, he was ready, like Ladislaw in "Middlemarch," to "place himself in an attitude of receptivity toward all sublime chances," and away he went. Nothing can be more exasperating to a war correspondent than to have a fight take place while he is absent from the scene of action looking for coal; but many newspaper men in Cuban waters had that unpleasant and humiliating experience.

The life of the war correspondent who landed, or at-

tempted to land, on the island of Cuba, in the early weeks
of the war, was not so wearing and harassing, perhaps, as
the life of the men on the despatch-boats, but it was quite
as full of risk. After the 1st of May the patrol of the
Cuban coast by the Spanish troops between Havana and Cardenas became so careful and thorough that a safe landing
could hardly be made there even at night. Jones and Thrall
were both captured before they could open communications
with the insurgents; and the English correspondents, Whig-
ham and Robinson, who followed their example, met the
same fate. Even Mr. Knight, the war correspondent of the
London "Times," who landed from a small boat in the harbor of Havana with the express permission of the government at Madrid and under a guaranty of protection, was
seized and thrown into Cabanas fortress.

If a war correspondent succeeded in making a safe landing and in joining the insurgents, he had still to suffer
many hardships and run many risks. Mr. Archibald, the
correspondent of a San Francisco paper, was wounded on
the Cuban coast early in May, in a fight resulting from an
attempt to land arms and ammunition for the insurgents;
and a correspondent of the Chicago "Record" was killed
after he had actually succeeded in reaching General Gomez's
camp. He was sitting on his horse, at the summit of a little
hill, with Gomez and the latter's chief of staff, watching a
skirmish which was taking place at a distance of a quarter
of a mile or more, between a detachment of insurgents and
a column of Spanish troops. One of the few sharp-shooters
in the enemy's army got the range of the little group on
the hill, and almost the first ball which he sent in that direction struck the "Record" correspondent in the forehead between and just above the eyes. As he reeled in the saddle
Gomez's chief of staff sprang to catch him and break his
fall. The next Mauser bullet from the hidden marksman

pierced the pommel of the saddle that the staff-officer had just vacated; and the third shot killed Gomez's horse. The general and his aide then hastily escaped from the dangerous position, carrying the "Record" correspondent with them; but he was dead. In the first two months of the war the corps of field correspondents, in proportion to its numerical strength, lost almost as many men from death and casualty as did the army and navy of the United States. The letters and telegrams which they wrote on their knees, in the saddle, and on the rocking, swaying cabin tables of despatch-boats while hurrying to West Indian cable-stations were not always models of English composition, nor were they always precisely accurate; but if the patrons of their respective papers had been placed in the field and compelled to write under similar conditions, they would be surprised, perhaps, not at the occasional imperfection of the correspondents' work, but at the fact that in so unfavorable and discouraging an environment good work could be done at all.

CHAPTER V

OFF FOR SANTIAGO

THE most important event in the early history of the war, and the event that controlled the movements of the Red Cross steamer *State of Texas*, as well as the movements of General Shafter's army, was the arrival of the Spanish fleet of cruisers and torpedo-boats at Santiago de Cuba on May 19. There had been skirmishes and bombardments before that time, at Matanzas, Cardenas, and various other points on the Cuban coast; but none of them had any strategic importance, or any particular bearing upon the course or the conduct of the war. It was the appearance of Admiral Cervera at Santiago which determined the field of action, and, to some extent, the plan of campaign. The invasion of eastern Cuba had already been under consideration, and when the Spanish fleet took refuge in Santiago harbor the President and his counselors decided, definitely and finally, to begin operations at that end of the island, and to leave the western provinces unmolested until fall. The regular army, it was thought, would be strong enough, with the aid and coöperation of Admiral Sampson's fleet, to reduce the defenses of Santiago, and the volunteers might be left in camp at Chickamauga, Tampa, and Jacksonville, to get in training for an attack upon Havana at the end of the rainy season.

The preparations for the invasion of Cuba seemed, at that

time, to be nearly, if not quite, complete. The whole regular army, consisting of seven regiments of cavalry, twenty-two regiments of infantry, and fourteen batteries of artillery, had been mobilized and transported to the Gulf coast; the quartermaster's department had, under charter, twenty-seven steamers, with a carrying capacity of about twenty thousand men; immense quantities of food and munitions of war had been bought and sent to Tampa, and there seemed to be no good reason why General Shafter's command should not embark for Cuba, if necessary, at twenty-four hours' notice.

On May 26, just a week after the appearance of Admiral Cervera and his fleet at Santiago, the President held a consultation at the Executive Mansion with the Secretary of War, the Secretary of the Navy, and the members of the Board of Strategy, and decided to begin the invasion of Cuba at once. Orders were presumably sent to General Shafter to prepare for an immediate movement, and Secretary Long telegraphed Admiral Sampson as follows:

WASHINGTON, May 27, 1898.

Sampson, Care Naval Base, Key West:

If Spanish division is proved to be at Santiago, it is the intention of the department to make a descent immediately upon that port with ten thousand United States troops, landing about eight nautical miles east of the port. You will be expected to convoy transports. . . .   [Signed]   LONG.

Three days later General Shafter was directed, in the following order, to embark his command and proceed at once to Santiago:

WAR DEPARTMENT, WASHINGTON, May 30, 1898.

Major-General William R. Shafter, Tampa, Florida:

With the approval of the Secretary of War you are directed to take your command on transports, proceed under convoy of the navy to the vicinity of Santiago de Cuba, land your force at such place east or west of that point as your judgment may dictate, under the protection of the navy, and move it on to the high ground and bluffs overlooking the harbor, or into the interior, as shall best enable you to capture or destroy the garrison there and cover the navy as it sends its men in small boats to remove torpedoes, or, with the aid of the navy, capture or destroy the Spanish fleet now reported to be in Santiago harbor.

You will use the utmost energy to accomplish this enterprise, and the government relies upon your good judgment as to the most judicious use of your command, but desires to impress upon you the importance of accomplishing this object with the least possible delay. . . .   [Signed]   H. C. CORBIN,
Adjutant-General.

In view of the fact that General Shafter had been nearly a month at Tampa, and of the further fact that his command was composed wholly, or almost wholly, of regular troops, who were completely equipped for service when they left their stations, he should have been able, it seems to me, to comply with this order at once; but, apparently, he was not ready. Day after day passed without any noticeable change in the situation, and on June 7 the army at Tampa was apparently no nearer an advance than it had been when Cervera's fleet entered Santiago harbor on May 19.

Admiral Sampson, who was anxious to strike a decisive blow before the enemy should have time to concentrate and intrench, then telegraphed Secretary Long as follows:

MOLE, HAITI, June 7, 1898.

Secretary of Navy, Washington:

Bombarded forts at Santiago 7:30 A. M. to 10 A. M. to-day, June 6. Have silenced works quickly without injury of any kind, though stationary within two thousand yards. If ten thousand men were here [1] city and fleet would be ours within forty-eight hours. Every consideration demands immediate army movement. If delayed city will be defended more strongly by guns taken from fleet.

[Signed]   SAMPSON.

[1] Referring to the ten thousand men spoken of in the secretary's telegram of May 27.

When this despatch reached Washington, the Secretary of War sent General Shafter two peremptory telegrams, as follows:

WAR DEPARTMENT, June 7.

Major-General Shafter, Port Tampa, Florida:
You will sail immediately, as you are needed at destination at once. Answer.   [Signed]   R. A. ALGER,
Secretary of War.

EXECUTIVE MANSION, WASHINGTON,
June 7, 1898, 8:50 P. M.

Major-General Shafter, Port Tampa, Florida:
Since telegraphing you an hour since, the President directs you to sail at once with what force you have ready.
[Signed]   R. A. ALGER,
Secretary of War.

Upon receipt of these "rush" orders, General Shafter hastily embarked his army, amid great confusion and disorder, and telegraphed the Secretary of War that he would be ready to sail, with about seventeen thousand officers and men, on the morning of June 8. Before the expedition could get away, however, Commodore Remey cabled the Secretary of the Navy from Key West that two Spanish war-ships—an armored cruiser and a torpedo-boat destroyer —had been seen in Nicholas Channel, off the northern coast of Cuba, on the night of June 7, by Lieutenant W. H. H. Southerland of the United States gunboat *Eagle*. Fearing that these Spanish vessels would intercept the fleet of transports and perhaps destroy some of them, Secretary Alger telegraphed General Shafter not to leave Tampa Bay until he should receive further orders.

Scouting-vessels of the navy, which were promptly sent to Nicholas Channel in search of the enemy, failed to locate or discover the two war-ships reported by the commander of the *Eagle*, and on June 14 General Shafter's army, after having been held a week on board the transports in Tampa Bay, sailed for Santiago by way of Cape Maysi and the Windward Passage. The Spanish fleet under command of Admiral Cervera had then been in Santiago harbor almost four weeks.

It is hard to say exactly where the responsibility should lie for the long delay in the embarkation and despatch of General Shafter's expedition. When I passed through Tampa on my way south in June, the two railroad companies there were blaming each other, as well as the quartermaster's department, for the existing blockade of unloaded cars, while army officers declared that the railroad companies were unable to handle promptly and satisfactorily the large quantity of supplies brought there for the expedition. Naval authorities said that they had to wait for the army, while army officers maintained that they were all ready to start, but were stopped and delayed by reports of Spanish war-ships brought in by scouting-vessels of the navy.

That there was unnecessary delay, as well as great confusion and disorder, there seems to be no doubt. As one competent army officer said to me, in terse but slangy English, "The fact of the matter is, they simply got all balled up, and although they worked hard, they worked without any definite, well-understood plan of operations."

The principal trouble seemed to be in the commissary and quartermaster's departments. Many of the officers in these departments were young and inexperienced; army supplies from the North came down in immense quantities on two lines of railway and without proper invoices or bills of lading; it was often utterly impossible to ascertain in which, out of a hundred cars, certain articles of equipment or subsistence were to be found; and there was a lack everywhere of cool, trained, experienced supervision and direction. It was the

business of some one somewhere to see that every car-load of
supplies shipped to Tampa was accompanied by an invoice
or bill of lading, so that the chief commissary at the point of
destination might know the exact nature, quantity, and car-
location of supplies brought by every train.   Then, if he
wanted twenty-five thousand rations of hard bread or fifty
thousand pounds of rice before the cars had been unloaded,
he would know exactly where and in what cars to look for it.
As it was, he could not tell, often, what car contained it
without making or ordering personal examination, and it was
almost impossible to know how much of any given commodity
he had on hand in trains that had not yet been unloaded or
inspected.   As the result of this he had to telegraph to
Jacksonville at the last moment before the departure of the
expedition for three or four hundred cases of baked beans
and forty or fifty thousand pounds of rice to be bought there
in open market and to be sent him in "rush shipment."   It
is more than probable that there were beans and rice enough
to meet all his wants in unloaded trains at Tampa, but he
had no clue to their car-location and could not find them.
Such a state of things, of course, is wholly unnecessary,
and it should not occur a second time.   To take another
example:

When our army embarked at Port Tampa it was the business of some officer somewhere to know the exact capacity of
every transport and the numerical strength of every regiment.   Then it was some one's business to prearrange the
distribution of troops by assigning one or more designated
regiments to one or more designated steamers and giving
necessary orders to the colonels.   As it was, however, according to the testimony of every witness, a train-load of troops
would come to the docks at Port Tampa, apparently without
orders or assignment to any particular steamer, and while
they were waiting to learn what they should do, and while

4

their train was still blocking the way, another train-load of soldiers would arrive in a similar state of ignorance and add to the disorder and confusion. As a natural consequence, men got on wrong steamers and had to be unloaded, and often, after transports had moved out into the bay, parts of companies and regiments had to be transferred in small boats from one vessel to another. These are examples of what seems to have been bad management. In another class of cases the trouble was apparently due to mistaken judgment. To the latter class belongs the loading and treatment of horses and mules. It would have been much better and safer, I think, to load these animals on vessels especially prepared for and exclusively devoted to them than to put them into stifling and unventilated holds of steamers that also carried troops. If, however, this was impracticable, it was manifestly best to load the animals last, so as to expose them for as short a time as possible to such murderous conditions. The mules, however, were loaded first, and held in the holds of the transports while troops were embarking. They began to die from heat and suffocation, and then they were unloaded and reshipped after the troops were on board. This caused unnecessary delay, as well as the loss of many valuable animals. Eighteen perished, I am told, on one transport while the troops were embarking.

These cases of disorder and bad judgment are only a few out of many which were the subject of common talk among officers and civilians in Tampa. I could specify many others, but criticism is at best unpleasant duty, and the only justification for it is the hope that, if mistakes and disorders are pointed out and frankly recognized, they may be guarded against in future.

The army of invasion, when it finally left Tampa Bay for the Cuban coast, consisted of 803 officers and 14,935 enlisted men.[1] With its animals and equipment it filled thirty-five transports. It comprised (in addition to regular infantry) four batteries of light field-artillery, two batteries of heavy siege-guns, a battalion of engineers, a detachment of the Signal Corps, twelve squadrons of dismounted cavalry, and one squadron of cavalry with horses. All of the troops were regulars with the exception of three regiments, namely, the First Cavalry (Rough Riders, dismounted), the Seventy-first New York, and the Second Massachusetts. The command was well supplied with food and ammunition, but its facilities for land transportation were inadequate; its equipment, in the shape of clothing and tentage, was not adapted to' a tropical climate in the rainy season; it carried no reserve medical stores, and it had no small boats suitable for use in disembarkation or in landing supplies on an unsheltered coast. Some of these deficiencies in equipment were due, apparently, to lack of prevision, others to lack of experience in tropical campaigning, and the rest to lack of water transportation from Tampa to the Cuban coast; but all were as unnecessary as they afterward proved to be unfortunate.

When the army of invasion sailed, the Red Cross steamer *State of Texas*, laden with fourteen hundred tons of food and medical supplies, lay at anchor in Tampa Bay, awaiting the return of Miss Barton and a part of her staff from Washington. As soon as they arrived, the steamer proceeded to Key West, and on the morning of Monday, June 20, after a brief consultation with Commodore Remey, we sailed from that port for Santiago de Cuba. In the group assembled on the pier to bid us good-by were United States Marshal Horr;

---

[1] Report of General Miles ("Army and Navy Register," November 12, p. 311). General Shafter reported to the Secretary of War, September 13, that he sailed from Tampa with 815 officers and 16,072 men. General Miles is probably right.

Mr. Hyatt, chairman of the local Red Cross committee; Mr. White, correspondent of the Chicago "Record," whose wife was going with us as a Red Cross worker; and Mrs. Porter, wife of the President's secretary, who had come with Miss Barton from Washington to Key West in order to show her interest in and sympathy with the work in which the Red Cross is engaged.   About ten o'clock the steamer's lines were cast off, the gang-plank was drawn ashore, the screw began to churn the green water into boiling foam astern, and, amid shouted good-bys and the waving of handkerchiefs from the pier, we moved slowly out into the stream, dipped our ensign to the *Lancaster*, Commodore Remey's flagship, and proceeded down the bay in the direction of Sand Key light.

CHAPTER VI

THE CUBAN COAST

THE course usually taken by steamers from Key West to Santiago lies along the northern coast of Cuba, through the Nicholas and Old Bahama channels, to Cape Maysi, and thence around the eastern end of the island by the Windward Passage. Inasmuch, however, as we were going without a convoy, and Commodore Remey had advised us to keep out of sight of land, in order to avoid possible interception by a Spanish gunboat from some unblockaded port on the coast, we decided to go around the western end of the island, doubling Cape San Antonio, and then proceeding eastward past the Isle of Pines to Cape Cruz and Santiago. Tuesday afternoon we saw the high mountains in the province of Pinar del Rio looming up faintly through the haze at a distance of twenty-five or thirty miles, and late that same evening we passed the flash-light at the extremity of Cape San Antonio and turned eastward toward Cape Cruz and Santiago. After rounding the western end of the island we had a succession of thunder-storms and rain-squalls, with a strong easterly breeze and a heavy head sea; but Thursday night the weather moderated, and at half-past six o'clock Friday morning we sighted Cape Cruz rising out of the dark water ahead in a long, transverse stretch of flat table-land, backed by mountains and terminating on the sea in a high, steep bluff.

The coast of Cuba between Cape Cruz and Santiago is formed by a striking and beautiful range of mountains, known to the Spaniards as the "Sierra Maestra," or "Master Range," which extends eastward and westward for more than a hundred miles and contains some of the highest peaks to be found on the island. As seen from the water its furrowed slopes and flanks are deceptively foreshortened, so that they appear to fall with extraordinary steepness and abruptness to the sea; its rocky, wave-worn base is whitened by a long line of snowy breakers; its deep, wild ravines are filled with soft blue summer haze; and down from the clouds which shroud its higher peaks tumble in white, tortuous streaks the foaming waters of unnamed and almost unknown mountain torrents. As one sails, at a distance of two or three miles, along this wild, beautiful coast, the picture presented by the fringe of feathery palms over the white line of surf, the steep slopes of the foot-hills, shaggy with dark-green tropical vegetation, and the higher peaks broken in places by cliffs or rocky escarpments and rising into the region of summer clouds, is one hardly to be surpassed, I think, in the tropics. The average height of this range is three or four thousand feet; but in many places it is much greater than this, and the summit of the peak of Turquino, about midway between Cape Cruz and Santiago, is eighty-four hundred feet above the level of the sea.

Our captain thought that we should be off the entrance to Santiago harbor about three o'clock Saturday morning, and at half-past three I was on the bridge. There was not a sign, as yet, of dawn, and although I could make out faintly the loom of high land to the northward, it was so dark on the water that nothing could be distinguished at a distance of five hundred yards, and in the absence of all lights on the coast it was almost impossible to determine our exact position. Somewhere ahead of us,—or perhaps around us,—in the impenetrable gloom, were twelve or fifteen ships of war; but they were cruising about in silence and darkness, and the first evidence that we should probably have of their proximity would be the glare of a search-light and the thunder of a gun. About four o'clock the lookout forward shouted to the captain, "Vessel on the port bow, sir," and a large, dark object stole silently out toward us from under the shadow of the land. I took it, at first, for a gunboat; but it proved to be the transport *Santiago*, which had not yet disembarked her troops and was cruising aimlessly back and forth, as we were, waiting for daylight.

At a quarter past four the sky in the east began to grow lighter, and as the hidden sun climbed swiftly to the horizon the world about us began to assume form and color. Almost directly in front of us were two fine groups of high, forest-clad mountains, separated by an interval of perhaps ten or fifteen miles. In this gap and nearer the sea was a long stretch of lower, but still high, table-land, which extended from one group of mountains to the other and seemed to form the outer rampart of the coast. About the middle of this rocky, flat-topped rampart there was a deep, narrow notch, on the eastern side of which I could see with a glass a huge grayish-stone building, elevated a little above the level of the table-land on one side and extending down the steep declivity of the notch in a series of titanic steps on the other. I hardly needed to be informed that the notch was the entrance to the harbor of Santiago, and that the grayish-stone building was Morro Castle. Between us and the land, in a huge, bow-shaped curve, lay the war-ships of the blockading fleet, with Commodore Schley's flagship, the *Brooklyn*, at one end, Admiral Sampson's flagship, the *New York*, at the other, and the battle-ships *Texas, Indiana,*

Iowa, Massachusetts, and half a dozen gunboats and cruisers lying at intervals between. The convex side of the crescent was nearest to Morro Castle, and in this part of the curve were the battle-ships *Texas, Indiana,* and *Iowa,* with the small gunboat *Suwanee* thrown out as scout or skirmisher in the position that the head of the arrow would occupy if the line of the blockading vessels were a bent bow eight miles long.

We steamed directly in toward the entrance to the harbor, without being stopped or questioned, and took a position in front of Morro Castle, about one thousand yards south of the battle-ship *Indiana.* From this point of view, with the aid of a good glass, we could make out quite distinctly the outlines of the castle, and were a little disappointed to see still floating over it the red-and-yellow banner of Spain. We had had no news for more than a week, and thought it possible that both the castle and the city were in the possession of General Shafter's army.

The entrance to the Bay of Santiago appears, from a distance of three or four miles, to be a narrow cleft or notch in the high, flat-topped rampart which forms the coast-line. On account of an eastward curve in the channel just beyond Morro Castle, one cannot look through the notch into the upper harbor. At a distance of a quarter of a mile from the entrance, the line of vision strikes against a steep hill, which forms one side of the curving, fiord-like passage leading to the city. Owing to the great depth of water off the entrance to the bay, it is impossible for vessels to anchor there, and the ships of the blockading fleet simply drifted back and forth with the winds and tides, getting under way occasionally, when it became necessary to change position.

After breakfast I went off in a boat to the flagship *New York,* called upon Admiral Sampson, and obtained from him a brief account of all that had happened off that coast since the 1st of May.

Admiral Cervera, with a fleet of seven Spanish war-ships, left the Cape Verde Islands for West Indian waters on the 29th of April. On the 13th of May he was reported at the French port of St. Pierre, Martinique, and from there he sailed to Curaçao, an island off the coast of Venezuela, nearly due south of Haiti. From Curaçao it was thought he would be likely to go either to Cienfuegos or Havana; and on the 19th of May Commodore Schley, with the Flying Squadron, was sent to watch the former port, while Admiral Sampson, who had just returned from Porto Rico, resumed the blockade of Havana. Cervera, however, did not go to either place. Leaving Curaçao on the 16th, he crossed the Caribbean Sea, and at daybreak on the morning of Thursday, May 19, he entered the harbor of Santiago de Cuba for the purpose of obtaining a fresh supply of coal. His fleet then consisted of the second-class battle-ship *Cristobal Colon*, the armored cruisers *Vizcaya*, *Almirante Oquendo*, and *Maria Teresa*, and the torpedo-boat destroyers *Furor* and *Pluton*. What he expected to do, after coaling his vessels, does not clearly appear; but certain of his Spanish friends in the United States have recently published what seems to be an authorized statement, in which they set forth his views as follows:

Admiral Cervera did not enter Santiago harbor with any intention of remaining there, or of seeking refuge from the pursuit of the American fleets. His object was merely to make some slight repairs to his vessels, obtain a fresh supply of coal, and then run out to sea. As a result of interference from Havana, however, he was prevented from carrying out his plans. No sooner had he reported his arrival in Santiago than " Captain-General Blanco communicated with Spain and asked the Minister of Marine to place Admiral Cervera and his fleet under his (Blanco's) orders. Blanco then ordered

Cervera to remain in Santiago and assist in the defense of the shore batteries. Admiral Cervera protested strongly against this, and appealed to Spain; but it is doubtful whether his appeal ever reached the government. He asked to be allowed to coal up and then leave Santiago, where he might be free to meet the American fleet, rather than to be bottled up in a blockaded harbor. He contended that he could not possibly be useful to Spain by remaining in Santiago harbor, with the certainty of American ships coming to keep him there, whereas, outside and free, his strong fleet could be of great value to the Spanish cause. The answer of General Blanco was that Admiral Cervera was now subject to his orders; that he, and not Admiral Cervera, was in command of affairs in Cuba, and that the admiral must obey his command. Cervera could then do nothing."

If this semi-official statement of Admiral Cervera's case is an accurate one, the Santiago campaign, which ended in the destruction of Cervera's fleet and the capture of the city, was the direct result of General Blanco's interference. The Spanish admiral had plenty of time to coal his vessels and make his escape before either of our fleets reached the mouth of the harbor, and if he had done so there might have been no Santiago campaign, and the whole course of the war might have been changed. But the opportunity soon passed.

On the 20th of May the news of Cervera's appearance at Santiago was reported to the Navy Department in Washington, and Secretary Long immediately cabled it to Admiral Sampson by way of Key West. On the following day, May 21, Sampson sent the *Marblehead* to the southern coast of Cuba with an order directing Commodore Schley to proceed at once to Santiago unless he had good reason to believe that the Spanish fleet was really in Cienfuegos.

When this order reached Schley, on the 23d of May, he felt sure that he had Cervera "bottled up" in Cienfuegos harbor, and he did not become aware of his error until the 25th. He then proceeded with his fleet to Santiago, but did not reach there until the 26th. Cervera had then had a whole week in which to coal his vessels and make his escape. That he fully intended to do this seems to be evident from the statement of Mr. Frederick W. Ramsden, British consul at Santiago, whose recently published diary contains the following entry, under date of May 23: "The Spanish fleet is taking in coal, water, and provisions in a hurry, and it is evident that it is preparing to go to sea, probably to-night or in the morning, as I hear the pilots have been ordered for this evening."

If Cervera had gone to sea on the evening of May 23, or the morning of the 24th, as was plainly his intention, he would have made his escape without the slightest difficulty, because Admiral Sampson was then cruising off Havana, while Schley was still blockading Cienfuegos. What would have been the course of the war in that event, it is impossible to say; but General Shafter would certainly have been held at Tampa until the Spanish fleet had been overtaken and destroyed, and then, very likely, the army of invasion would have landed at some point nearer to Havana. Admiral Cervera, however, for some reason not yet positively known, remained in Santiago a whole week, and at the expiration of that time it is doubtful whether he could have made his escape, even had he wished to do so, because Commodore Schley, with the Flying Squadron, was off the entrance to the harbor. Six days later, when Schley's squadron was reinforced by the powerful fleet of Admiral Sampson, Cervera's last chance of escape vanished, and there was nothing left for him to do but assist the forts and the garrison to defend the city to the last, or make a desperate

and almost hopeless attempt to break through the line of the
blockading fleet.

Late in May, while Admiral Sampson was still cruising off
Havana, he sent an order, by the captain of the *New Orleans*,
to Commodore Schley, directing the latter to "use the collier
Sterling to obstruct the [Santiago] channel at its narrowest
part leading into the harbor," so as to make the escape of
the Spanish fleet absolutely impossible.   "I believe," he said,
"that it would be perfectly practicable to steam this vessel
into position, drop all her anchors, allow her to swing across
the channel, and then sink her, either by opening the valves,
or whatever means may be best."

Commodore Schley, for some reason, did not obey this
order; but as soon as Admiral Sampson reached the mouth
of Santiago harbor, he proceeded to carry out the plan himself.   At three o'clock on the morning of June 3, Lieutenant R. P. Hobson, with a volunteer crew of seven men,
ran the steam-collier *Merrimac* into the mouth of the harbor,
under a heavy fire from the Spanish batteries, dropped her
anchors in mid-channel between Churruca Point and Smith
Cay, opened her sea connections, exploded a number of torpedoes hung along her sides at the water-line, and when she
sank, hung on to a raft attached by a rope to the sunken
vessel.   They were rescued from this position by the Spaniards and thrown into Morro Castle, but were treated with
the consideration and courtesy to which their gallantry entitled them.   On the afternoon of the same day, Admiral
Cervera, who with his own hand had dragged Hobson from
the water, sent his chief of staff out to the *New York*, under
a flag of truce, with a letter to Admiral Sampson, in which
he informed the latter that the lieutenant and his men were
safe, and referred in terms of admiration and respect to their
courage and devotion to duty.

Unfortunately,—or perhaps fortunately,—the object for

which Lieutenant Hobson and his men risked their lives
was not attained. The *Merrimac* failed to swing around so
as to lie transversely across the channel, but sank in such a
way as to place her hull parallel with the middle of it and
near its eastern edge. This left plenty of water and plenty
of room for vessels to pass on the western, or Smith Cay,
side. Egress, however, although still possible, was extremely
difficult and dangerous, on account of the strictness and
closeness of the blockade which was established when
Admiral Sampson arrived and took command of the combined fleets. The battle-ships and larger vessels, which
formed the outer line of the blockade, were disposed in a
semicircle around the mouth of the harbor, at a distance of
four or five miles, with the flagship *New York* at one end of
the line and the *Brooklyn* at the other. Inside of this semicircle, and much nearer the entrance, were stationed two
or three small cruisers or gunboats, whose duty it was to
watch the mouth of the harbor incessantly and give instant
warning of the appearance of any hostile vessel. At night,
when the danger from the Spanish torpedo-boats was greatest and when Cervera's fleet was most likely to escape, a
powerful and piercing search-light was held constantly on
the mouth of the narrow cañon between Morro and Socapa;
the battle-ships closed in so as to diminish the radius of their
semicircle by nearly one half; the cruisers and gunboats,
under cover of the blinding radiance of the search-light,
moved a mile nearer to the mouth of the harbor; and three
steam-launches patrolled the coast all night within pistol-
shot of the enemy's batteries. In the face of such a blockade it was virtually impossible for Cervera to escape, and
almost equally impossible for his torpedo-boats to come out
of the harbor unobserved, or to reach any of our larger
vessels even if they should venture out. Long before they
could get across the mile and a half or two miles of water

that separated the harbor entrance from the nearest battle-ship, they would be riddled with projectiles from perhaps a hundred rapid-fire guns. Torpedo-boats, however, did not play an important part on either side. Our own were prevented from entering the harbor by a strong log boom stretched across the channel just north of the Estrella battery, and those of the Spaniards never even attempted to make an aggressive movement in the period covered by the blockade. Admiral Cervera evidently thought that the chance of accomplishing anything by means of a torpedo-boat attack was too remote to justify the risk.

On the 6th of June Admiral Sampson bombarded the shore batteries and the mouth of the harbor for two hours and a half, destroying a number of houses on Smith Cay, setting fire to the Spanish cruiser *Reina Mercedes*, which was moored near the end of the Socapa promontory, and killing or wounding twenty-five or thirty officers and men on the cruiser, in the batteries, and in Morro Castle. The earth-work batteries east and west of the entrance did not prove to be very formidable and were quickly silenced; but the submarine mines in the narrow channel leading to the upper harbor, which prevented our fleet from forcing an entrance, could not be removed without the coöperation of a land force. All that Admiral Sampson could do, therefore, was to bombard the harbor fortifications now and then, so as to prevent further work on them; occupy the lower part of Guantanamo Bay, forty miles east of Santiago, as a coaling-station; and urge the government in Washington, by telegraph, to send the army forward as speedily as possible.

The fleet of transports which conveyed General Shafter's command to the southern coast of Cuba arrived off the entrance to Santiago harbor at midday on the 20th of June, after a tedious and uneventful voyage of five days from the Dry Tortugas around the eastern end of the island. General Shafter at once held a conference with Admiral Sampson and with the Cuban general Garcia, who had come to the coast to meet the fleet, and, after considering every possible line of attack, decided to land his force at two points, within supporting distance of each other, ten or fifteen miles east of the entrance to Santiago harbor, and then march toward the city through the interior. The points selected for debarkation were Siboney, a small village about ten miles east of Morro Castle, and Daiquiri,[1] another similar village five miles farther away, which, before the war, was the shipping-port of the Spanish-American Iron Company. From Daiquiri there was a rough wagon-road to Siboney, and the latter place was connected with Santiago by a narrow-gage railroad along the coast and up the Aguadores ravine, as well as by a trail or wagon-road over the foothills and through the marshy, jungle-skirted valleys of the interior.

When we reached the entrance to Santiago harbor in the Red Cross steamer *State of Texas* on the 25th of June, the Fifth Army-Corps—or most of it—had already landed, and was marching toward Santiago along the interior road by way of Guasimas and Sevilla. The landing had been made, Admiral Sampson told me, without the least opposition from the Spaniards, but there had been a fight, on the day before our arrival, between General Wheeler's advance and a body of troops supposed to be the rear-guard of the retiring enemy, at a place called Guasimas, three or four miles from Siboney, on the Santiago road. Details of the fight, he said, had not been received, but it was thought to be nothing more than an unimportant skirmish.

In reply to my question whether he had any orders for us, or any suggestions to make with regard to our movements,

[1] I spell this word as it is spelled by the officers of the Spanish-American Iron Company, who say that "Baiquiri" is erroneous.

he said that, as there seemed to be nothing for the Red Cross
to do in the vicinity of Santiago, he should advise us to go
to Guantanamo Bay, where Captain McCalla had opened
communications with the insurgents under General Perez,
and where we should probably find Cuban refugees suffering
for food.   Acting upon this suggestion, we got under way
promptly, steamed into the little cove of Siboney to take a
look at the place and to land Mr. Louis Kempner of the
Post-Office Department, whom we had brought from Key
West, and then proceeded eastward to Guantanamo Bay.

CHAPTER VII

THE FIGHT AT GUANTANAMO

AS the southeastern coast of Cuba is high and bold, with deep water extending close up to the line of surf, vessels going back and forth between Santiago and Guantanamo run very near to the land; and the ever-changing panorama of tropical forest and cloud-capped mountain which presents itself to the eye as the steamer glides swiftly past, within a mile of the rock-terraced bluffs and headlands, is a constant source of surprise and delight, even to the most experienced voyager. It is an extremely beautiful and varied coast. In the foreground, only a rifle-shot away across the blue undulating floor of the Caribbean, rises a long terraced mesa, fronting on the sea, with its rocky base in a white smother of foaming surf, and its level summit half hidden by a drooping fringe of dark-green chaparral and vines. Over the cyclopean wall of this mesa appear the rounded tops of higher and more distant foot-hills, densely clad in robes of perennial verdure, while beyond and above them all, at a distance of five or six miles, rise the aërial peaks of the splendid Sierra del Cobre, with a few summer clouds drifting across their higher slopes and casting soft violet shadows into the misty blue of their intervening valleys. Here and there the terraced mesa, which forms the coast-line, is cut into picturesque castle-like bluffs by a

series of wedge-shaped clefts, or notches, and through the
openings thus made in the rocky wall one may catch brief
glimpses of deep, wild ravines down which mountain torrents
from the higher peaks tumble to the sea under the dense
concealing shade of mango- and mimosa-trees, vines, flowering shrubs, and the feathery foliage of cocoanut and royal
palms.

Wild, beautiful, and picturesque, however, as the coast
appears to be, not a sign does it anywhere show of a bay, an
inlet, or a safe sheltered harbor.   For miles together the
surf breaks almost directly against the base of the terraced
rampart which forms the coast-line, and even where streams
have cut deep V-shaped notches in the rocky wall, the strips
of beach formed at their mouths are wholly unsheltered
and afford safe places of landing only when the sea is
smooth and the wind at rest.   Often, for days at a time,
they are lashed by a heavy and dangerous surf, which makes
landing upon them in small boats extremely difficult, if not
absolutely impracticable.

About thirty-five miles from Santiago harbor, as one sails
eastward, the wall-like mesa on the left sinks from a height
of two or three hundred feet to a height of only twenty or
thirty; the mountains of the Sierra del Cobre come to an
end or recede from the coast, leaving only a few insignificant
hills; and through a blue, tremulous heat-haze one looks far
inland over the broad, shallow valley of the Guantanamo
River.

We entered the beautiful Bay of Guantanamo about half-
past five o'clock on Saturday afternoon, and found it full
of war-ships and transports.   The white hospital steamer
Solace lay at anchor over toward the western side of the
harbor, and between her and the eastern shore were the
Dolphin, the *Eagle*, the *Resolute*, the *Marblehead*, and three or
four large black colliers from Key West.   As we rounded

the long, low point on the western side of the entrance and
steamed slowly into the spacious bay, a small steam-launch
came puffing out to meet us, and, as soon as she was within
hailing distance, an officer in the white uniform of the navy
rose in the stern-sheets, put his hands to his mouth, and
shouted: "Captain McCalla presents his compliments to the
captain of the *State of Texas*, and requests that you follow me
and anchor between the *Marblehead* and the Haitian cable-
steamer."

"All right," replied Captain Young, from the bridge.

"That sounds well," I said to one of the Red Cross men
who was standing near me. "It shows that things are not
allowed to go helter-skelter here."

We followed the little launch into the harbor and dropped
anchor in the place indicated, which was about one hundred
yards from shore on the eastern side of the channel, and
just opposite the intrenched camp of Colonel Huntington's
marines. I was impatient to land and see the place where
the American flag had first been raised on Cuban soil; but
darkness came on soon, and it did not seem worth while to
leave the ship that night.

After breakfast on the following morning, I took a small
boat and went off to the *Marblehead* to call upon Captain
McCalla, who was in command of the station. I had made
his acquaintance in Washington, when he was one of the
members of a board appointed to consider means of sending
relief to the Greely arctic expedition; but I had not seen him
in many years, and it is not surprising, perhaps, that I almost
failed to recognize him in his Cuban costume. The morning
was hot and oppressive, and I found him clad in what was,
in the strictest sense of the words, an undress uniform,
consisting of undershirt, canvas trousers, and an old pair of
slippers. Like the sensible man I knew him to be, he made
no apology for his dress, but welcomed me heartily and intro-

duced me to Captain Philip of the battle-ship *Texas,* who had
just come into the harbor after a fresh supply of coal. As
I entered, Captain McCalla was telling Captain Philip, with
great glee, the story of his experience off the Cuban coast
between Morro Castle and Aguadores, when his vessel, the
Marblehead, was suddenly attacked one night by the whole
blockading fleet.

"They saw a railroad-train," he said, "running along the
water's edge toward Siboney, and in the darkness mistook it
for a Spanish torpedo-boat. The train, of course, soon disappeared; but I happened to be cruising close inshore, just
there, as it passed, and they all turned their search-lights on
me and opened fire."

"All except the *Iowa,*" corrected Captain Philip, with a
smile.

"Yes, all except the Iowa," assented Captain McCalla,
laughing heartily, as if it were the funniest of jokes.
"Even the *Texas* did n't show me any mercy; but Bob
Evans knew the difference between a railroad-train and a
torpedo-boat, and did n't shoot. I told him, the last time I
saw him, that he was clearly entitled to take a crack at me.
Every other ship in the fleet had had the privilege, and it
was his turn. I 'm the only man in the navy," he said, with
renewed laughter, "who has ever sustained the fire of a
whole fleet of battle-ships and cruisers and got away alive."

After Captain Philip had made his call and taken his
leave, I explained to Captain McCalla the object of our coming to Guantanamo Bay, and asked whether there were any
Cuban refugees in the vicinity who needed food and could be
reached. He replied unhesitatingly that there were. He
was in almost daily communication, he said, with General
Perez, an insurgent leader who was then besieging Guantanamo city, and through that officer he thought he could
send food to a large number of people who had taken refuge

in the woods north of the bay and were in a destitute and
starving condition. He had already sent to them all the
food he himself could spare, but it was not half enough to
meet their wants. With characteristic promptness and
energy he called his stenographer and dictated a letter to
General Perez, in which he said that Miss Clara Barton,
president of the American National Red Cross, had just
reached Guantanamo Bay in the steamer *State of Texas*, with
fourteen hundred tons of food intended for Cuban reconcentrados, and asked whether he (Perez) could furnish
pack-animals and an escort for, say, five thousand rations, if
they could be landed on the western side of the lower bay.
This letter he sent to General Perez by a special courier
from the detachment of Cubans then serving with the
marines, and said that he should probably receive a reply in
the course of two or three days.   As nothing more could be
done at that time, I returned to the *State of Texas*, reported
progress to Miss Barton, and then went on shore to send a
telegram to Washington by the Haitian cable, which had
just been recovered and repaired, and to take a look at the
camp of the marines.

When, on May 26, Commodore Schley, with the Flying
Squadron, arrived off the entrance to Santiago harbor, and
began the blockade of that port, the great need of his
vessels was a safe and sheltered coaling-station.   The heavy
swell raised along the southern coast of Cuba by the prevailing easterly winds makes it often dangerous and always
difficult to lay a collier alongside a battle-ship in the open
sea and transfer coal from one to the other.   Understanding and appreciating this difficulty, Secretary Long telegraphed Admiral Sampson on May 28 to consider the
question whether it would not be possible to "seize Guantanamo and occupy it as a coaling-station."   Sampson
replied that he thought it might be done, and immediately

cabled Commodore Schley off Santiago as follows: "Send a ship to examine Guantanamo with a view to occupying it as a base, coaling one heavy ship at a time." The official correspondence thus far published does not show whether Commodore Schley received this order in time to act upon it before Sampson arrived or not; but as soon as the latter came he caused a reconnaissance of Guantanamo Bay to be made, decided that the lower part of it might be seized by a comparatively small land force if protected by the guns of a few war-ships, and immediately sent to Key West for the first battalion of marines, which was the only available landing force at his command. Meanwhile the auxiliary cruiser *Yankee* bombarded and burned a Spanish blockhouse situated on a hill near the entrance to the lower harbor of Guantanamo, and on June 8 Captain McCalla, in the *Marble-head*, seized and occupied—as far as he could do so without a landing force—all that part of the bay which lies between the entrance and the narrow strait leading to the fortified post of Caimanera.

The marines, under command of Lieutenant-Colonel Huntington, arrived on the steamer *Panther*, Friday, June 10, and proceeded at once to disembark. The place selected for a landing was a low, rounded, bush-covered hill on the right, or eastern, side of the bay, about a quarter of a mile from the entrance. On the summit of this hill the Spaniards had made a little clearing in the chaparral and erected a small square blockhouse; but inasmuch as this blockhouse had already been destroyed and its garrison driven to the woods by the fire of the *Yankee*, all that the marines had to do was to occupy the abandoned position and again fortify the hill. In some respects this hill, which was about one hundred and fifty feet in height, made a strong and easily defended position; but, unfortunately, it was covered nearly to the summit with a dense growth of bushes and scrub, and was commanded by a range of higher hills a little farther to the eastward. The enemy, therefore, could not only creep close up to the camp under cover of the dense chaparral, but could fire down upon it from the higher slopes of the wooded range which runs parallel with the bay on its eastern side.

The landing was made, without opposition, about two o'clock on the afternoon of Friday, June 10. Under cover of the guns of the war-ships, the marines disembarked on the strip of beach at the foot of the hill; burned all the houses and huts left by the Spaniards, so as to guard against the danger of infection with yellow fever; and then deployed up the hill, pitched their shelter-tents on its eastern slope, and spent all the afternoon and a large part of the next day in landing ammunition and stores, establishing outposts, and making arrangements for a permanent camp.

The Spaniards, who must have been watching these operations from the concealment of the bushes and from the slopes of the adjacent hills, gave no sign, at first, of their presence; but seeing that the marines were comparatively few in number, they finally plucked up courage, and about five o'clock Saturday afternoon began a desultory, skirmishing attack which lasted the greater part of that day and night, and, indeed, continued, with an occasional intermission, for three or four days and nights. Major Cochrane, who described the fight to me, said that he slept only an hour and a half in four days, and that many of his men became so exhausted that they fell asleep standing on their feet with their guns in their hands.

The strength of the marine battalion at that time was between five and six hundred men. They were armed with rifles of the Lee or Lee-Metford pattern, and had, in addition, two automatic Colt machine-guns and three rapid-fire Hotchkiss cannon of three-inch caliber. The greatest disadvantage under which they labored was that due to the tangled, almost impenetrable nature of the chaparral that surrounded the camp, and the facilities which it afforded the enemy for concealment and stealthy approach. The gunboats shelled the woods from time to time, drove the hidden Spaniards back, and silenced their fire; but as soon as night fell they would creep silently up through the bushes until they were so near to the camp that the pickets of the marines could smell the smoke of their cigarettes, and yet could neither see them nor hear them. Then the nocturnal skirmishing would begin again. There were six successive attacks from different directions on the night of the 11th, and a still greater number on the night of the 12th, with more or less desultory skirmishing during the day, so that for a period of forty-eight hours the gallant marines had no rest or sleep at all.

There was some danger, at first, that the enemy, reinforced from Caimanera or Guantanamo city, would assemble in force on the slopes of the eastern hills, creep up through the scrub until they were within a short distance of the camp, and then overwhelm the marines in a sudden rush-assault. They were known to have six thousand regulars at Guantanamo city, only about fifteen miles away, and it was quite within the bounds of possibility that they might detach a large part of this force for offensive operations on the eastern side of the lower bay. To provide for this contingency, and to strengthen his defensive position, Lieutenant-Colonel Huntington withdrew his men from the eastern slope of the hill, where they had first been stationed, and posted them on the crest and upper part of the western slope, where they would be nearer the fleet and better protected by its guns. At the same time our small force, in the intervals of fighting, dug a trench and erected a barricade around the crest of the hill on the land side, so as to enlarge the clearing, give more play to the automatic and rapid-fire guns, and make it more difficult for the enemy to approach unseen. When this had been done, there was little probability that a rush-assault would succeed. The best troops in the world, unless they were in overwhelming force, could hardly hope to cross a clearing that was swept by the fire of six hundred rifles, two machine-guns, and three Hotchkiss cannon hurling canister or shrapnel.

In the course of the first three days' engagement the marines were joined by eighty or a hundred Cuban insurgents; but opinions differ as to the value of the latter's coöperation. Some officers with whom I talked spoke favorably of them, while others said that they became wildly excited, fired recklessly and at random, and were of little use except as guides and scouts. Captain Elliott, who saw them under fire, reported that they were brave enough, but that their efficiency as fighting men was on a par with that of the enemy; while Captain McCalla called attention officially to their devotion to freedom, and said that one of them, who had been shot through the heart, died on the field, crying with his last breath: "Viva Cuba libre!"

At the end of the third day's fighting, all attacks of the Spaniards having been repulsed, Lieutenant-Colonel Huntington determined to take the offensive himself. About six miles southeast of the camp, at a place called Cuzco, there was a well from which the Spanish troops were said to obtain all their drinking-water, and a heliograph signal-station by means of which they maintained communication with Caimanera. On the morning of June 14 Captain Elliott, with two companies of marines and about fifty Cuban volunteers, was sent to attack this place, drive the Spaniards away, and destroy the well and signal-station. The expeditionary force engaged the enemy, five hundred strong, about eleven o'clock in the morning, and fought with them until three in the afternoon, driving them from their position and inflicting upon them a loss of sixty men killed and one hundred and fifty wounded.   Then, after capturing the heliograph outfit, burning the station, and filling up the well, the heroic little detachment returned, exhausted but triumphant, to its camp, with a loss of only two men killed, six wounded, and twenty or thirty overcome by heat.

On the fourth day of the long struggle for the possession of Guantanamo Bay, the Spaniards virtually gave up the contest and abandoned the field.   A few guerrillas still remained in the chaparral, firing occasionally at long range either into the camp or at the vessels of the fleet; but, finally, even this desultory, long-range target practice ceased, and the last of the enemy fled, either to the fort at Caimanera or to Guantanamo city, leaving the plucky marines in undisputed control of the whole eastern coast of the lower bay.   Our total loss in the series of engagements was only six men killed and twelve or fifteen wounded; but among the killed was the lamented Dr. Gibbs, acting assistant surgeon, United States navy, who was shot at one o'clock on the night of the 11th.

After the four days of fighting were over, Captain McCalla, with the *Marblehead*, the auxiliary cruiser *St. Louis*, and the battle-ship *Texas*, steamed up the bay to the little village of Caimanera, demolished the fort there with a few well-directed shots, and drove the garrison back into the woods.   In the course of this expedition the *Marblehead* and the *Texas* ran into a number of submarine contact mines, or fouled them with their screws; but, fortunately, none of them exploded.   The firing-pins had become so incrusted with barnacles and other marine growths during their long immersion that the force of the blow when the ships struck them did not drive them in far enough to explode the charges.   When we reached Guantanamo in the *State of*

Texas, Captain McCalla's boats and launches had thoroughly explored and dragged the lower bay, and had taken out safely no less than thirteen contact mines, each containing about one hundred pounds of guncotton.   The upper bay was still in the possession of the Spaniards; but its control was not a matter of any particular importance.   What Admiral Sampson wanted was a safe and sheltered coaling- and repairing-station for the vessels of his fleet, and this he obtained when his war-ships and marines, after four days of almost incessant fighting, drove the Spanish troops from the whole eastern coast of the lower bay.

CHAPTER VIII

THE LANDING AND ADVANCE OF THE ARMY

EARLY Sunday morning, at the little zinc-walled telegraph office under the camp of the marines at Guantanamo, I happened to meet two war correspondents—one of them, if I remember rightly, Mr. Howard of the New York "Journal"—who had just come from the front with a detailed account of the fight at Guasimas. This fight, they said, was not a mere insignificant skirmish, as Admiral Sampson supposed when I saw him on Saturday, but a serious battle, in which a part of General Wheeler's division was engaged, for several hours, with a force of Spanish regulars estimated at two or three thousand men. More than one hundred officers and men on our side had been killed or wounded, among them Captain Capron and Sergeant Hamilton Fish, both of whom were dead. The wounded, Mr. Howard said, had been brought back to Siboney and put into one of the abandoned Spanish houses on the beach, where, only the night before, he had seen them lying, in their blood-stained clothing, on the dirty floor, without blankets or pillows, and without anything that seemed to him like adequate attendance or care. At my request the two correspondents went on board the *State of Texas* and repeated their statement to Miss Barton, who, after consultation with the officers of her staff, decided to take the steamer back at once to Siboney. We could do nothing more at Guantanamo until General Perez should furnish transportation and an escort for the food that we intended to send to the refugees north of the bay, and, meanwhile, we might, perhaps, render some service to the wounded soldiers of General Wheeler's command whom Mr. Howard had seen lying, without blankets or pillows, on the floor. We had on board the *State of Texas*, at that time, one hundred or more cots, with plenty of bedding, and if the medical officers of the army could not get hospital supplies ashore, we thought that we could. At any rate, we would try. Calling again upon Captain McCalla, I explained to him the reasons for our sudden change of plan, and told him that, although we had decided to go to Siboney, we should try to get back in time to meet the pack-train and escort to be furnished by General Perez. I then returned to the *State of Texas*, and we sailed for Siboney at two o'clock.

In order to follow intelligently the course of the Santiago campaign, and to understand and appreciate the difficulties with which the medical department of the army had to contend, one must know something of the coast upon which that army landed and the nature of the environment by which it was surrounded. The southeastern coast of Cuba, between the entrance to Santiago harbor and the Bay of Guantanamo, is formed by three parallel ranges of hills and mountains which may be roughly characterized as follows: first, what I shall call the rampart—a high, flat-topped ridge, or narrow table, very steep on the sea side, and broken into long terraces by outcropping ledges of limestone; second, the foot-hills, which rise out of a wooded valley or valleys behind the rampart; and, third, the high mountains of the coast, or Sierra del Cobre, range, which lie back of the foot-hills, at a distance of five or six miles from the sea. This is not a strictly accurate topographical description of the coast, but it is roughly and generally true and will answer my purpose.

In the vicinity of Santiago the rampart, or mesa-like elevation which borders the sea, has a height of two or three
hundred feet, and stretches eastward and westward, like a
stone wall, for a distance of nearly twenty miles. At three
points it is cut down to the sea-level in narrow, V-shaped
clefts, or notches, which have a width at the bottom of from
seventy-five to two hundred yards, and which serve as out-
lets for three small streams. The first of these notches, as
one goes eastward from Morro Castle, is that formed by the
mouth of the Aguadores ravine, where the Juragua Railroad,
on its way from Siboney to Santiago, crosses the Aguadores
or Guamo River, and where the iron railroad-bridge and the
approach to the city are guarded by a wooden blockhouse
and an old stone fort. In the second notch, about six miles
from Aguadores and ten from Morro Castle, are the hamlet
and railroad-station of Siboney; and in the third, five miles
farther to the eastward, lies the somewhat larger and more
important mining village of Daiquiri, which, before the war,
was the shipping-port of the Spanish-American Iron Company. There is no harbor, shelter for vessels, or safe
anchorage at any of these places; but as the rampart, everywhere else, presents an almost insurmountable barrier, an
invading force must either disembark in these notches, or
go eastward to the Bay of Guantanamo and march forty
miles to Santiago through the foot-hills. General Shafter,
after inspecting the coast, decided to land in the notches
occupied by the villages of Daiquiri and Siboney. He could
then advance on Santiago either along the strip of beach
under the rampart, by way of Aguadores and Morro Castle,
or over a rough wagon-road running through the valleys and
across the foot-hills of the interior, three or four miles back
of the rampart.

The first difficulty which confronted him was that due to
the lack of landing facilities. Not anticipating, apparently,

that he might be forced to disembark on an unsheltered coast, he had neglected to provide himself with suitable surf-boats, and was wholly dependent upon the small boats of the transports and a single scow, or lighter, which he had brought with him from Tampa. Seeing that it would be impossible to land sixteen thousand men safely and expeditiously with such facilities, he applied for help to Admiral Sampson, and was furnished by the latter with fifty-two small boats and a number of steam-launches, all manned by officers and sailors from the fleet. Thus provided, he began the work of disembarkation on the morning of June 22 at Daiquiri, the vessels of the fleet, meanwhile, making feigned attacks at several other points along the coast, and shelling the notches and villages of both Siboney and Daiquiri, in order to drive the enemy back and cover the advance of the loaded boats.

Fortunately for General Shafter and for his troops, the Spaniards did not attempt to oppose the landing. If the sides of the notches and the foot-hills back of them had been fortified with earthworks and held by a daring enemy with a battery or two of light guns, it would have been extremely difficult, if not absolutely impossible, to get the troops ashore. Even without artillery, ten or fifteen hundred men armed with Mausers on the heights which command the notches and the approaches to them might have held off a landing force for days, if not weeks. The war-ships might have shelled them, or swept the heights with machine-guns, but it would have been easy for them to find shelter under the crest of the rampart on the land side, and I doubt whether a force so sheltered could have been dislodged or silenced by Admiral Sampson's whole fleet. In order to drive them out it would have been necessary to land in the surf under fire, and storm the heights by scaling the precipitous terraced front of the rampart on the sea side.

This might, perhaps, have been done, but it would have involved a great sacrifice of life. The Spanish officers in Cuba, however, were not skilful tacticians. Instead of anticipating General Shafter's movements and occupying, with an adequate force, the only two places in the vicinity of Santiago where he could possibly land, they overlooked or neglected the splendid defensive positions that nature herself had provided for them, and allowed the army of invasion to come ashore without firing a shot. It was great luck for us, but it was not war.

Before night on the 22d, General Lawton's division, consisting of about six thousand men with a Gatling-gun battery, had landed at Daiquiri, and on the morning of the 23d it marched westward along the wagon-road to Siboney. The Spanish garrison at the latter place retreated in the direction of Santiago as General Lawton appeared, and the village fell into our hands without a struggle. Disembarkation continued throughout the 23d and 24th, at both Daiquiri and Siboney, and before dark on the afternoon of the 24th nine tenths of the army of invasion had landed, with no other accident than the loss of two men drowned.

In the meantime, General Linares, the Spanish commander at Santiago, had marched out of the city, with a force of about three thousand men, to meet the invaders, and had occupied a strong defensive position on the crest of a wooded hill at Guasimas, three or four miles northwest of Siboney, where the two roads from the latter place—one up the valley of the stream and the other over the end of the mesa —come together. He did not know certainly which of these two roads the invading force would take, and therefore posted himself on the hill at their junction, where he could command both.

On the afternoon of the 23d, Cuban scouts reported the position of the enemy to General Wheeler, who was then in command of our advance, and, after a council of war, it was decided to attack simultaneously by both roads. Early on the morning of Friday, June 24, therefore, General Young, with the First and Tenth dismounted cavalry, marched out of Siboney on the main road to Santiago, and proceeded up the valley of the little stream which empties into the sea through the Siboney notch; while Colonel Wood, at the head of the Rough Riders, climbed the end of the rampart, on the western side of the notch, and advanced toward Guasimas by the mesa trail, which is considerably higher than the main road and lies half a mile to a mile farther west.

The two columns encountered the enemy at about the same time. The Rough Riders, under Colonel Wood, began the attack on the mesa trail, and a few moments later General Young's command, on the Siboney-Santiago road, opened fire with three Hotchkiss mountain guns and began the ascent of the hill from the valley. The whole country was so overgrown with trees, shrubs, and tropical vines that it was almost impossible to see an object fifty yards away, and as the Spaniards used smokeless powder, it was extremely difficult to ascertain their position, or even to know exactly where our own troops were. Colonel Wood deployed his regiment to the right and left of the trail, and endeavored, as he advanced, to extend his line so as to form a junction with General Young's command on the right, and at the same time outflank the enemy on the left; but the tropical undergrowth was so dense and luxuriant that neither of the attacking columns could see the other, and all that they could do, in the way of mutual support and coöperation, was to push ahead toward the junction of the two roads, firing, almost at random, into the bushes and vine-tangled thickets from which the Mauser bullets seemed to come. Colonel Roosevelt told me that once he caught a glimpse of the Spaniards, drawn up in line of battle; but

6

during the greater part of the engagement they were concealed in the chaparral, and could be seen only when they
broke from cover and fled, to escape the searching fire of our
steadily advancing line.   While Colonel Wood, on the left,
was driving the enemy out of the jungles intersected by the
mesa trail, General Young, with a part of the Tenth Cavalry
(colored) supported by four troops of the First, was engaged
in storming the hill up which ran the valley road; and at the
end of an hour and a half, after a stubborn defense, the
Spaniards were forced to abandon their chosen position and
retreat in the direction of Santiago, leaving the junction of
the two roads in our possession.   The battle of Guasimas—
the first fight of the Santiago campaign—had been won.

The number of men engaged in this affair, on our side,
was nine hundred and sixty-four, and our loss in killed and
wounded was sixty-six, including Captain Capron and
Hamilton Fish, both of whom died on the field.   The Spaniards, according to the statement of Mr. Ramsden, British
consul in Santiago, had a force of nearly three thousand men
and reported a loss of seven killed and fourteen wounded.
It seems probable, however, that their loss was much greater
than this.   General Linares would hardly have abandoned a
strong position and fallen back on the city after a loss of
only twenty-one men out of three thousand.

Two war correspondents, Mr. Richard Harding Davis and
Mr. Edward Marshall, took an active part in this engagement, and the latter was so severely wounded by a Mauser
bullet, which passed through his body near the spine, that
when he was carried from the field he was supposed to be
dying.   He rallied, however, after being taken to Siboney,
and has since partially recovered.

The effect of General Wheeler's victory at Guasimas was
to open up the Santiago road to a point within three or four
miles of the city; and when we returned in the *State of Texas*

from Guantanamo, the Rough Riders were in camp beyond
Sevilla, and a dozen other regiments were hurrying to the
front.

We reached Siboney after dark on Sunday evening, and
found the little cove and the neighboring roadstead filled
with transport steamers, whose twinkling anchor-lights—or
rather adrift lights, for there was no anchorage—swung
slowly back and forth in long curves as the vessels rolled and
wallowed in the trough of the sea. As soon as a boat could
be lowered, the medical officers of Miss Barton's staff went
on shore to investigate the state of affairs and to ascertain
whether the Red Cross could render any assistance to the
hospital corps of the army. They returned in the course of
an hour and reported that in two of the abandoned Spanish
houses on the beach they had found two hastily extemporized
and wholly unequipped hospitals, one of which was occupied
by the Cuban sick and wounded, and the other by our own.
No attempt had been made to clean or disinfect either of
the buildings, both were extremely dirty, and in both the
patients were lying, without blankets or pillows, on the
floor. The state of affairs, from a medical and sanitary point
of view, was precisely as the correspondents had described
it to us, except that some of the wounded of General
Wheeler's command had been taken on board the transports
Saratoga and *Olivette* during the day, so that the American
hospital was not so crowded as it had been when Mr.
Howard saw it the night before. The army surgeons and
attendants were doing, apparently, all that they could do to
make the sick and wounded comfortable; but the high surf,
the absence of landing facilities, the neglect or unwillingness of the quartermaster's department to furnish boats,
and the confusion and disorder which everywhere prevailed,
made it almost impossible to get hospital supplies ashore.
All that the surgeons could do, therefore, was to make the

best of the few medicines and appliances that they had
taken in their hands and pockets when they disembarked.
The things that seemed to be most needed were cots,
blankets, pillows, brooms, soap, scrubbing-brushes, and dis-
infectants. All of these things we had on board the *State
of Texas*, and the officers of Miss Barton's staff spent a large
part of the night in breaking out the cargo and getting the
required articles on deck.

Early the next morning, Dr. Lesser, with four or five
trained nurses, all women, and a boat-load of hospital supplies, landed at the little pier which had been hastily built
by the engineer corps, and walking along the beach through
the deep sand to the American hospital, offered their services to Dr. Winter, the surgeon in charge. To their
great surprise they were informed that the assistance of the
Red Cross—or at least their assistance—was not desired.
What Dr. Winter's reasons were for declining aid and supplies when both were so urgently needed I do not know.
Possibly he is one of the military surgeons, like Dr. Appel
of the *Olivette*, who think that women, even if they are
trained nurses, have no business with an army, and should
be snubbed, if not browbeaten, until they learn to keep
their place. I hope this suggestion does not do Dr. Winter
an injustice; but I can think of no other reason that would
lead him to decline the assistance of trained young women
who, although capable of rendering the highest kind of pro-
fessional service, were ready and willing to scrub floors, if
necessary, and who asked nothing more than to help him
make a clean, decent hospital out of an empty, dirty, abandoned Spanish house.

When told by Dr. Winter that they were not wanted, the
nurses went to the Cuban hospital, in a neighboring building, where their services were accepted not only with eagerness, but with grateful appreciation. Before night they had

swept, disinfected, and scrubbed out that hospital with soap and water, and had bathed the Cuban patients, fed them, and put them into clean, fresh cot-beds. Our own soldiers, at the same time, were lying, without blankets or pillows, on the floor, in a building which Dr. Winter and his assistants had neither cleaned nor attempted to clean.

Dr. Appel of the hospital steamer *Olivette*, in an official report to the surgeon-general of the army, published, in part, in the New York "Herald" of November 4, 1898, says:

"There was, at that time [the time when we arrived off Siboney], a number of surgeons on board the *State of Texas*, and four trained nurses; but, although we were working night and day, taking care of our sick and wounded, no assistance was given by them until some days afterward, when our own men were ready to drop from fatigue."

The idea conveyed by this ungenerous and misleading statement is that the surgeons and Red Cross nurses on the *State of Texas* neglected or evaded the very duty that they went to Cuba to perform, and remained, idle and useless, on their steamer, while Dr. Appel and his associates worked themselves into a state of complete physical exhaustion. So far as the statement contains this implication, it is wholly and absolutely false. The *State of Texas* arrived off Siboney at eight o'clock on the evening of Sunday, June 26. In less than an hour the Red Cross surgeons had offered their services to Major Havard, chief surgeon of the cavalry division, and as early as possible on the following morning Dr. Lesser and four or five Red Cross nurses reported at the American hospital, offered the surgeon in charge the cots, blankets, and hospital supplies which they had brought, or were ready to bring, on shore, and asked to be set to work. When, on account of some prejudice or misapprehension, Dr. Winter declined to let them help him in taking care of our own sick and wounded soldiers, what more could they do than devote themselves to the Cubans? Two days later, fortunately, Major Lagarde, chief surgeon at Siboney, over-ruled the judgment of his subordinate, accepted the services of the nurses, and set them at work in a branch of the military hospital, under the direction of Dr. Lesser. There they all worked, almost without rest or sleep, until Dr. Lesser, Mrs. Lesser, Mrs. White (a volunteer), and three of the Red Cross nurses were stricken with fever, and four of them were carried on flat-cars to the yellow-fever camp in the hills two miles north of the village. The surgeon of the *Olivette* would have shown a more generous and more manly spirit if, in his report to the surgeon-general, he had mentioned these facts, instead of adroitly insinuating that the Red Cross surgeons and nurses were loafing on board the *State of Texas* when they should have been at work in the hospitals.

But Dr. Appel further says, in the report from which I have quoted, that at the time when the *State of Texas* reached Siboney—two days after the fight at Guasimas—"there was no lack whatever of medical and surgical supplies."

If Major Lagarde, Dr. Munson, Dr. Donaldson, and other army surgeons who worked so heroically to bring order out of the chaos at Siboney, are to be believed, Dr. Appel's statement concerning hospital supplies is as false as his statement with regard to the Red Cross surgeons and nurses. In an official report to the surgeon-general, dated July 29 and published in the New York papers of August 9, Captain Edward L. Munson, assistant surgeon commanding the reserve ambulance company, says: "After the fight at Las Guasimas there were absolutely no dressings, hospital tentage, or supplies of any kind, on shore, within reach of the surgeons already landed." Dr. Munson was the adjutant of Colonel Pope, chief surgeon of the Fifth Army-Corps, and he probably knew a good deal more about the state of affairs at Siboney after the battle of Guasimas than Dr.

Appel did. Be that, however, as it may; I know from my own observation and experience that there *was* a lack of medical and hospital supplies at Siboney, not only when we arrived there, but for weeks afterward. Dr. Frank Donaldson, surgeon of the Rough Riders, in a letter from Siboney, published in the Philadelphia "Medical Journal" of July 23, says: "The condition of the wounded on shore here is beyond measure wretched, and excites the lively indignation of every one."

The neglect of our soldiers, both at Siboney and at the front, in the early days of the campaign, was discreditable to the army and to the country; and there is no reason why military surgeons should not frankly admit it, because it was not their fault, and they cannot justly be held accountable for it. The blame should rest, and eventually will rest, upon the officer or department that sent thirty-five loaded transports and sixteen thousand men to the Cuban coast without suitable landing facilities in the shape of surf-boats, steam-launches, and lighters.

In criticizing the condition of our hospitals, I cast no reflection upon the zeal, ability, and devotion to duty of such men as Colonel Pope, Major Lagarde, Major Wood, and the surgeons generally of the Fifth Army-Corps. They made the best of a bad situation for which they were not primarily responsible; and if the hospitals were in unsatisfactory condition, it was simply because the supplies furnished in abundance by the medical department were either left in Tampa for lack of water transportation, or held on board the transports because no adequate provision had been made by the commanding general or the quartermaster's department for landing them on a surf-beaten coast and transporting them to the places where they were needed.

CHAPTER IX

A WALK TO THE FRONT

WHEN I went on deck, the morning after our return to Siboney, I found that the *State of Texas* had drifted, during the night, half-way to the mouth of the Aguadores ravine, and was lying two or three miles off the coast, within plain sight of the blockading fleet. The sun was just rising over the foot-hills beyond Daiquiri, and on the higher slopes of the Cobre range it was already day; but the deep notch at Siboney was still in dark-blue shadow, and out of it a faint land-breeze was blowing a thin, hazy cloud of smoke from the recently kindled camp-fires of the troops on the beach. There was no wind where we lay, and the sea seemed to be perfectly smooth; but the languid rolling of the steamer, and a gleam of white surf here and there along the base of the rampart, showed that the swell raised by the fresh breeze of the previous afternoon had not wholly subsided. Fifteen or twenty transport-steamers were lying off the coast, some close in under the shadow of the cliffs, where the smoke from the soldiers' camp-fires drifted through their rigging; some five or six miles out in the open roadstead; and a few hull down beyond the sharply drawn line of the eastern horizon. Three miles away to the northwest the red-and-yellow flag of Spain was blowing out fitfully in the land-breeze over the walls of the stone fort at Aguadores, and four or five miles farther to the westward, at the end of the long, terraced rampart, I could make out, with a glass, the lighthouse, the tile-roofed barracks, and the gray battlements of the old castle at the entrance to Santiago harbor.

About seven o'clock the *State of Texas* got under way, steamed back to Siboney, and succeeded in finding an anchorage, in what looked like a very dangerous position, close to the rocks, on the eastern side of the cove. From this point of view the picture presented by the village and its environment was novel and interesting, if not particularly beautiful. On the right and left of the slightly curved strip of sand which formed the landing-place rose two steep bluffs to a height of perhaps two hundred and fifty feet. The summit of the one on the right, which was the steeper of the two, seemed, at first glance, to be inaccessible; but there must have been a hidden path up to it through the trees, bushes, and vines which clothed its almost precipitous face, because it was crowned with one of the small, square, unpainted log blockhouses which are a characteristic feature of almost every east-Cuban landscape. The western bluff, from which the trees had been cut away, sloped backward a little more than the other, and about half-way up it, in a network of yellow intersecting paths, stood another blockhouse, surrounded by a ditch and a circular "entanglement" of barbed-wire fencing. At the foot of this bluff, and extending westward under the precipitous declivity of the rampart, were two lines of unpainted, one-story wooden houses, which stood gable to gable at intervals of fifty or sixty feet, and looked, in their architectural uniformity, like buildings erected by a manufacturing company to shelter the families of its employees. The boundary of the village, at this end, was marked by still another small, square blockhouse, which was set, at a height of twenty feet, on a huge fragment of rock which had caved away and fallen from the cliff above.

Across the bottom of the ravine, between the two bluffs, extended a thickly planted strip of cocoanut-palms, whose gray trunks and drooping, feathery foliage served as a background for half a dozen leaf-thatched Cuban huts, an iron railway-bridge painted red, and a great encampment of white shelter-tents through which roamed thousands of blue-shirted soldiers, Cuban insurgents from the army of Garcia, and dirty, tattered refugees from all parts of the country, attracted to the beach by the landing of the army and the prospect of getting food. On the eastern side of the cove, near the ruins of an old stone fort, the engineer corps had built a rude pier, thirty or forty feet in length, and on either side of it scores of naked soldiers, with metallic identification tags hanging around their necks, were plunging with yells, whoops, and halloos into the foaming surf, or swimming silently, like so many seals, in the smoother water outside.

As the sun rose above the foot-hills and began to throw its scorching rays into the notch, the whooping and yelling ceased as the bathers came out of the water and put on their clothes; the soldiers of the Second Infantry struck and shouldered their shelter-tents, seized their rifles, and formed by companies in marching order; the Cubans of Garcia's command climbed the western bluff, in a long, ragged, disorderly line, on their way to the front by the mesa trail; small boats, laden with food and ammunition from the transports, appeared, one after another, and made their way slowly under oars to the little pier; and the serious work of the day began.

In order to ascertain what progress our forces were making in their march on Santiago, and to get an idea of the difficulties with which they were contending or would have to contend, I determined, about nine o'clock, to go to the front. It was impossible to get a horse or mule in Siboney, for love or money; but if our soldiers could march to the front under the heavy burden of shelter-tent, blanket roll, rifle, rations, and ammunition, I thought I could do it with no load at all, even if the sunshine were hot. Mr. Elwell, who had lived some years in Santiago and was thoroughly acquainted with the country, agreed to go with me in the capacity of guide and interpreter, and, just before we were ready to start, Dr. Lesser, who had returned to the ship after setting the nurses at work in the Cuban hospital, said that he would like to go.

"All right," I replied. "Get on your togs."

He went to his state-room, and in ten minutes returned dressed in a neat black morning suit, with long trousers, low shoes, a fresh white-linen shirt, and a high, stiffly starched, standing collar.

"Good heavens, doctor!" I exclaimed, as he made his appearance in this Fifth Avenue costume. "Where do you think you are going? To church?"

"No," replied the doctor, imperturbably; "to the front."

"In that dress?"

"Certainly; what's the matter with it?"

"Oh, nothing in particular. As a dress it is a very good dress, and reflects credit on your tailor; but for a tramp of ten or fifteen miles over a muddy trail and through a tropical jungle, would n't a neat, simple undershirt, with canvas trousers and a pair of waterproof leggings, be better? Your starched collar, in this heat, won't last ten minutes."

The doctor demurred, and protested that the clothes he was wearing were the oldest he had; but I finally persuaded him to take off his waistcoat and collar, tie a handkerchief around his neck, and put on a pair of my leggings; and in this slightly modified costume he went ashore with us for a march to the camp of the Rough Riders.

About fifteen hundred Cubans, of General Garcia's command, had been brought to Siboney the day before on one

of our transports; and although most of them had started
for the front, several hundred were still roaming through
the village, or standing here and there in groups on the
beach.   They did not, at first sight, impress me very favorably.   Fully four fifths of them were mulattoes or blacks;
the number of half-grown boys was very large; there was
hardly a suggestion of a uniform in the whole command;
most of the men were barefooted, and their coarse, drooping straw hats, cotton shirts, and loose, flapping cotton
trousers had been torn by thorny bushes and stained with
Cuban mud until they looked worse than the clothes that a
New England farmer hangs on a couple of crossed sticks in
his corn-field to scare away the crows.   If their rifles and
cartridge-belts had been taken away from them they would
have looked like a horde of dirty Cuban beggars and ragamuffins on the tramp.   I do not mean to say, or even to
suggest, that these ragamuffins were not brave men and
good soldiers.   They may have been both, in spite of their
disreputable appearance.   When, for months together, a
man has lived the life of an outlaw in the woods, scrambling
through tropical jungles, wading marshy rivers, and sleeping,
without tent or blankets, on the ground, he cannot be expected to look like a veteran of the regular army on dress-
parade in a garrison town.   Many of our own men, in the
later weeks of the Santiago campaign, were almost as ragged
and dirty as the poorest of the soldiers who came with General Garcia to Siboney.   The Cubans disappointed me, I
suppose, because I had pictured them to myself as a better
dressed and better disciplined body of men, and had not
made allowance enough for the hardships and privations of
an insurgent's life.

Turning our backs on the cove, the pier, the white tents
of the quartermasters, the tarpaulin-covered piles of provi-
sion-boxes, and the throng of soldiers, insurgents, and refu-

gees on the beach, we climbed a steep bank, crossed the railroad-track just west of the red-iron bridge, and joined a company of the Second Infantry on its way to the front.

The Santiago road, after leaving the village of Siboney, runs up a wide marshy valley, full of stagnant ponds and lagoons, and sparsely set with clumps of cocoanut and royal palm. Although this valley heads in the mountains of the Cobre range, and opens on the sea through the Siboney notch, its atmosphere seems hot and close, and is pervaded by a foul, rank odor of decaying vegetation, which is unpleasantly suggestive of malaria and Cuban fever, and makes one wish that one could carry air as one carries water, and breathe, as well as drink, out of a canteen. But one soon escapes from it. A mile or two from the village the road leaves the valley, turns to the left, and begins to ascend a series of densely wooded ridges, or foot-hills, which rise, one above another, to the crest of the watershed just beyond Sevilla. From the point where we left the valley to the summit of the divide, we never had an unobstructed outlook in any direction. Dense tropical forests, almost impenetrable to the eye, closed in upon the road, and when the sea-breeze was cut off and the sun stood vertically overhead, we lost all means of orientation and could hardly guess in what direction we were going. Now and then, at the bottom of a valley or on a sloping hillside, we passed a small, grassy opening, which would be called, in West Virginia, a glade or an interval; but during most of the time we plodded along in the fierce heat, between walls of dark-green foliage which rose out of an impenetrable jungle of vines, piñon-bushes, and Spanish bayonet. I saw no flowers except the clustered heads of a scarlet-and-orange blossom which I heard some one call the "Cuban rose," and I did not see a bird of any kind until we approached the battle-field of Guasimas, where scores of vultures were soaring and circling above the tree-tops, as if aware of the fact that in the leafy depths of the jungle below were still lying the unburied and undiscovered bodies of Spanish dead.

Nothing surprised me more, as I walked from Siboney to the front, than the feebleness of the resistance offered by the Spaniards to our advance. The road, after it enters the hills, abounds in strong defensive positions, and if General Chaffee or General Wood, with five thousand American regulars, had held it, as General Linares attempted to hold it at Guasimas, a Spanish army would not have fought its way through to Santiago in a month. There are at least half a dozen places, between the Siboney valley and the crest of the divide beyond Sevilla, where a few simple intrenchments in the shape of rifle-pits and barricades would have enabled even a small force, fighting as General Vara del Rey's command afterward fought at Caney, to detain our army for days, if not to check its advance altogether. The almost impenetrable nature of the undergrowth on either side would have made flanking movements extremely difficult, and a direct attack along the narrow road, in the face of such a fire as might have been delivered from intrenched positions in front and at the sides, would almost certainly have been disastrous to the advancing column. Even if the Spaniards had been driven from their first line of defense, they could have fallen back a mile or two to a second position, equally strong, and then to a third, and by thus fighting, falling back, and then fighting again, they might have inflicted great loss upon the attacking force long before it got within sight of Santiago.

I can think of only two reasons for their failure to adopt this method of defense. The first is that they did not know certainly whether General Shafter would make his main attack by way of Guasimas and Sevilla, or along the sea-coast by way of Aguadores; and they feared that if they sent the greater part of their small army to check an advance by the former route, the city, which would be left almost undefended, might be attacked suddenly by a column moving rapidly along the sea-coast and up the Aguadores ravine, or, possibly, by a force which should land at Cabanas and march around the bay. This reason, however, seems to me to have little force, because from the signal-station at Morro Castle they could watch and report all our movements along the coast, and a march of three or four hours would bring the army on the Siboney road back to the city, in ample time to meet an attacking column from either Aguadores or Cabanas.

The second reason is that, for lack of adequate means of transportation, they were unable to keep a large force supplied with food and ammunition at a distance from its base. I doubt whether this reason has any greater force than the other. I saw a large number of native horses and mules in Santiago after the surrender, and as the distance from the city to the strong positions on the Siboney road is only six or eight miles, it would not have required extraordinary transportation facilities to carry thither food and ammunition for three or four thousand men. But even half that number, if they fought as the San Luis brigade afterward fought at Caney, might have held General Shafter's advance in check for days, and made the capture of Santiago a much more serious and costly business than it was.

The truth probably is that General Linares was intimidated by the great show made by our fleet and transports—sixty steam-vessels in all; that he credited us with a much larger army than we really had; and that it seemed to him better to make the decisive fight at once on the commanding hills just east of Santiago than to lose perhaps one third of his small available force in the woods on the Siboney road, and then be driven back to the city at last with wearied and discouraged troops. But it was a mistaken calculation. If

he had delayed General Shafter's column, by obstinately resisting its advance through the woods on the Siboney road,
he would have given Colonel Escarrio time enough to reach
Santiago with the reinforcements from Manzanillo before
the decisive battle, and would also have given the climate
and the Cuban fever more time to sap the strength and de-
press the spirits of our badly equipped and improperly fed
troops. The final struggle on the hills east of the city
might then have had a very different termination.

The policy that General Linares should have adopted was
the Fabian policy of obstruction, harassment, and delay.
Every hour that he could detain General Shafter's advancing army on the Siboney road increased his own chances
of success and lessened those of his adversary; because the
army of defense, already acclimated, could stand exposure
to sun, rain, and miasma much better than the army of
invasion could. Besides that, a column of five thousand
regulars from Manzanillo was hurrying to his assistance, and
it was of the utmost importance that these reinforcements
should reach him before he should be forced into a decisive
battle. Instead of resisting General Shafter's advance,
however, with obstinate pertinacity on the Siboney road, he
abandoned his strong position at Guasimas, after a single
sharp but inconclusive engagement, and retreated almost to
Santiago without striking another blow. As I have already
said with regard to the unopposed landing at Daiquiri and
Siboney, it was great luck for General Shafter, but it was
not war.

We passed the battle-field of Guasimas about noon, without stopping to examine it, and pushed on toward Sevilla
with a straggling, disorderly column of soldiers belonging to
the Second and Twenty-first Infantry, who were following a
battery of light artillery to the front. The men seemed to
be suffering intensely from the heat, and every few hundred

yards we would find one of them lying unconscious in the
bushes by the roadside, where he had been carried by his
comrades after he had fainted and fallen under the fierce,
scorching rays of the tropical sun.   In one place, where the
road was narrow and sunken, we met a pack-train of mules
returning from the front.   Frightened at something, just
before they reached the artillery, they suddenly broke into
a wild stampede, and as they could not escape on either side,
owing to the height of the banks and the denseness of the
undergrowth, they jumped in among the guns and caissons
and floundered about until the whole battery was involved in
an almost inextricable tangle, which blocked the road for
more than an hour.   I tried to get around the jam of mules,
horses, and cannon by climbing the bank and forcing my way
through the jungle; but I was so torn by thorns and pricked
by the sharp spines of the Spanish bayonet that I soon gave
up the attempt, and, returning to the road, sat down, in the
shadiest place I could find, to rest, take a drink from my
canteen, and await developments.   If General Linares, when
he retreated, had left behind a squad or two of sharp-
shooters and bushwhackers to harass our advance at narrow
and difficult places in the road, what a chance they would
have had when the pack-mules jumped into that battery!
With the help given by a detachment of engineers, who were
working on the road a short distance ahead, the mules were
finally extricated, and the procession moved on.

Six or eight miles from Siboney we passed a solitary, and
of course empty, house, standing back a little from the road,
in a farm-like opening, or clearing.   This house, Mr. Elwell
informed me, was Sevilla.   I had supposed, before I left the
ship, that Guasimas and Sevilla were villages—as, indeed,
they are represented to be on all the Spanish maps of
the country.   But I soon learned not to put my trust in
Spanish maps.   Most of them have not been revised or cor-

rected in half a century, and they were full of errors in the
first place.   There is not a village, nor a hamlet, on this
whole road from Siboney to Santiago; and the only two
houses I saw had been abandoned for weeks, if not months.
The road runs, almost everywhere, through a tangled, tropical wilderness; and if there ever were any villages on it, they
have long since disappeared.

The Sevilla house seems to stand on or near the crest of
the highest ridge that the road crosses; and a short distance
beyond it, through an opening in the trees, we caught sight,
suddenly and unexpectedly, of the city of Santiago itself—
a long, ragged line of pink barracks, thatched houses, church
steeples, and wide-spreading trees, standing upon a low hill
on the other side of what looked like a green, slightly rolling
meadow, which was five or six hundred feet below the position
that we occupied, and perhaps three miles away.   This
meadow, as I subsequently ascertained, was itself made up
of hills, among them El Pozo and the high, bare ridge of San
Juan; but from our elevated point of view the hills and valleys seemed to blend into a gently rolling and slightly inclined
plain, which was diversified, here and there, by patches of
chaparral or clumps of royal palm, but which presented,
apparently, no obstacles at all to the advance of an attacking
force.   I could not discover anything that looked like a fort
or an extensive earthwork; but I counted sixteen Red Cross
flags flying over large buildings on the side of the city next
to us, and with the aid of a good field-glass I could just see,
in front of the long pink barrack, or hospital, two or three
faint brown lines which might possibly be embankments or
lines of rifle-pits.   The houses on the El Pozo and San Juan
heights ought to have been well within the limits of vision
from that point of view, but, as I did not notice them, I
presume they were hidden by the forest on one side or the
other of the opening through which we looked.

After studying the city for ten minutes, and wondering a little at its apparent defenselessness, we pushed on down the western slope of the ridge to the camp of the Rough Riders, which we found about half a mile from the Sevilla house, in an open glade, or field, on the right-hand side of the road. The long grass had been beaten down into such trails as a bear would make in wandering hither and thither among the dirty shelter-tents; and following one of these devious paths across the encampment, we found Lieutenant-Colonel Roosevelt standing with two or three other officers in front of a white-cotton rain-sheet, or tent-fly, stretched across a pole so as to protect from rain, or at least from vertical rain, a little pile of blankets and personal effects. There was a camp-chair under the tree, and near it, in the shade, had been slung a hammock; but, with these exceptions, Lieutenant-Colonel Roosevelt's quarters were no more comfortable than those of his men. He was dressed in the costume which he wore throughout the Santiago campaign—a coarse blue-flannel shirt, wide open at the throat; brown-canvas trousers and leggings; and a broad-brimmed felt hat put on over a blue polka-dot handkerchief in such a way that the kerchief hung down, like a havelock, over the nape of his neck. As he cordially shook hands with me there flashed into the field of my mental vision a picture of him as I had seen him last—in full evening dress, making a speech at the Fellowcraft Club in New York, and expressing, in a metaphor almost pictorially graphic, his extremely unfavorable opinion of the novels of Edgar Saltus. In outward appearance there was little resemblance between the Santiago Rough Rider and the orator of the Fellowcraft Club; but the force, vigor, and strength of the personality were so much more striking than the dress in which it happened, for the moment, to be clothed, that there seemed to be really no difference between my latest recollection and my present impression of the man.

We were presented to Colonel (now General) Wood, who seemed to me to be a man of quiet manner but great reserve power, and for twenty minutes we discussed the fight at Guasimas,—which Roosevelt said he would not have missed for the best year in his life,—the road, the campaign, and the latest news from the United States. Then, as it was getting late in the afternoon and we had eight or nine miles to walk before dark, we refreshed ourselves with a hasty lunch of hard bread and water, took a number of letters from officers of the Rough Riders to post at the first opportunity, and started back for the ship.

The Siboney-Santiago road, at that time and for several days thereafter, was comparatively dry and in fairly good condition. It had to be widened a little in some places, and a company or two of soldiers from the Tenth Cavalry were working on it just beyond the Rough Riders' camp; but, as far as we went, loaded army wagons could get over it without the least difficulty. Supplies at the front, nevertheless, were very short. Lieutenant-Colonel Roosevelt told me that his command had only enough hard bread and bacon for that night's supper, and that if more did not come before dark there would be no breakfast for them in the morning. I cannot now remember whether we met a supply-train on our way back to Siboney, or not; but I think not.

At the intersection of the road with the mesa trail, we stopped for a few moments to look over the battle-field of Guasimas. Evidences and traces of the fight, in the shape of cartridge-shells and -clips, bullet-splintered trees, improvised stretchers, and blood-soaked clothes and bandages, were to be seen almost everywhere, and particularly on the trail along which the Rough Riders had advanced. At one spot, in a little hollow or depression of the trail, from which one could see out into an open field about one hundred yards distant, the ground was completely covered with cartridge-shells and -clips from both Mauser and Krag-Jorgensen rifles. A squad of Spaniards had apparently used the hollow as a place of shelter first, and had fired two or three hundred shots from it, strewing the ground with the clips and brass shells of their Mauser cartridges. Then the Rough Riders had evidently driven them out and occupied the hollow themselves, firing two or three hundred more shots, and covering the yellow cartridge-shells of the Mauser rifles with a silvery layer of empty tubes from the Krag-Jorgensens. It looked as if one might pick up a bushel or two of these shells in an area ten or fifteen feet square.

A short distance from the intersection of the trail with the road was a large grave-shaped mound of fresh earth, under which had been buried together eight of the men killed on our side during the fight. There had been no time, apparently, to prepare and put up an inscribed headboard to show who the dead men were, but some of their comrades had carefully collected two or three hundred stones and pebbles—things not easy to find in a tropical jungle—and had laid them close together on the burial-mound in the form of a long cross.

Near this mound, and on the trail leading to it from Siboney, I saw, for the first time, Cuban land-crabs, and formed the opinion, which subsequent experience only confirmed, that they, with the bloody-necked Cuban vultures, are the most disgusting and repellent of all created things. Tarantulas, rattlesnakes, and some lizards are repulsive to the eye and unpleasantly suggestive to the imagination; but the ugliest of them all is not half so uncanny, hideous, and loathsome to me as the Cuban land-crab. It resembles the common marine crab in form, and varies in size from the diameter of a small saucer to that of a large dinner-plate. Instead of being gray or brown, however, like its aquatic relative, it is highly colored in diversified shades of red, scarlet, light

yellow, orange, and black.   Sometimes one tint prevails,
sometimes another, and occasionally all of these colors are
fantastically blended in a single specimen.   The creature
has two long fore claws, or pincers; small eyes, mounted like
round berries on the ends of short stalks or pedicels; and a
mouth that seems to be formed by two horny, beak-like
mandibles. It walks or runs with considerable rapidity in any
direction,—backward, sidewise, or straight ahead,—and is
sure to go in the direction that you least expect. If you
approach one, it throws itself into what seems to be a defensive attitude, raises aloft its long fore claws, looks at
you intently for a moment, and then backs or sidles away on
its posterior legs, gibbering noiselessly at you with the horny
mandibles of its impish mouth, and waving its arms dis-
tractedly in the air like a frightened and hysterical woman
trying to keep off some blood-chilling apparition.

All of these crabs are scavengers by profession and night-
prowlers by habit, and they do not emerge from their lurk-
ing-places in the jungle and make their appearance on the
trails until the sun gets low in the west. Then they come
out by the hundred, if not by the thousand; and as it begins
to grow dark, the still atmosphere of the deep, lonely forest
is filled with the rustling, crackling noise that they make as
they scramble through the bushes or climb over the stiff,
dry blades of the Spanish bayonet. I think it is not an exaggeration to say that at almost any point on the Cuban trail
between Guasimas and Siboney I could stand still for a
moment and count from fifty to one hundred of them, crawling out of the forest and across the path. Lieutenant-
Colonel Roosevelt told me that nothing interfered so much
at first with his sleep in the field as the noise made by these
crabs in the bushes. It is so like the noise that would be
made by a party of guerrillas or bushwhackers, stealing up
to the camp under cover of darkness, that it might well

keep awake even a man who was neither nervous nor imaginative.

Cuban land-crabs, like Cuban vultures, are haunters of battle-fields; but they seek the dead at night, while the vultures drink the eyes and tear off the lips of an unburied corpse in the broad light of day.   On the battle-field of Guasimas, however, while the sun was still above the horizon, I saw, crawling over a little pile of bloody rags, or bandages, a huge crab whose pale, waxy-yellow body suggested the idea that he had been feeding on a yellow-fever corpse and had absorbed its color.   At my approach he backed slowly off the rags, opening and shutting his mouth noiselessly, and waving his fore claws toward me in the air with what seemed like impish intelligence, as if he were saying: "Go away!   What business have you here?   Blood and the dead are mine."

There may be something more repulsive and uncanny than such a performance by a huge corpse-colored land-crab; but, if so, I have never happened to see it.   It made me feel as if I should like to do as the Russian peasant does in similar cases—spit and cross myself.

We reached Siboney about half-past five, and happening to find a boat from the *State of Texas* waiting at the pier, we got on board in time for dinner, after a walk of sixteen or eighteen miles.

CHAPTER X

SIBONEY ON THE EVE OF BATTLE

DURING my absence at the front on Monday, the auxiliary cruiser *Yale*, with two or three regiments of Michigan troops on board, arrived off Siboney, and when I went on deck on Tuesday morning these reinforcements were just beginning to go ashore in a long line of small boats, towed by a steam-launch from one of the war-ships of the blockading fleet.

The landing of troops and supplies on the Cuban coast was the first serious difficulty with which General Shafter had to contend. The little cove at Siboney was wholly unsheltered; there was no wharf or pier at which a steamer might lie; a gale, or even a fresh breeze, from the southeast raised a heavy surf on the strip of sand in front of the village; the water deepened so suddenly and abruptly, at a distance of fifty yards from the shore, that there was practically no anchorage; and all men and stores had to be landed by putting them into small boats and running them up on the beach through the breakers. At Daiquiri, where General Lawton's division disembarked, the situation was a little better, for the reason that the Spanish-American Iron Company had built there a substantial pier, of which the army of invasion could make use. At that place, therefore, General Shafter disembarked a large part of his command, and

unloaded all his wagons, siege-guns, light artillery, etc.   The
mules and horses were put ashore—or rather pitched over-
board with the expectation that they would swim ashore—at
Siboney; but, owing to unskilful management and lack of
guidance, twelve per cent. of the mules—fifty out of four
hundred and fifteen—perished.   Some, instead of making
for the shore, swam directly out to sea until they became
exhausted and sank; while others attempted to land on the
eastern side of the cove, where there was no beach, and were
drowned under the rocks.   Inasmuch as the total number of
draft- and pack-animals loaded at Tampa was wholly inadequate to meet the necessities of such an expedition, the
drowning of twelve per cent. of them, after they had reached
their destination, was a serious and, it seems to me, unnecessary loss.

In the disembarkation of his troops, General Shafter had
the assistance of skilled officers and well-drilled sailors from
the blockading fleet, to say nothing of half a dozen steam-
launches and fifty-two good boats; but when it came to unloading and landing stores, he had to rely on his own men
and his own facilities, and it soon became painfully evident
that they were not equal to the requirements of the situation.   I watched the landing of supplies all day Tuesday, and
formed the opinion that it was disorderly, unskilful, and un-
intelligent.   In the first place, many of the steamers from
which supplies were being taken lay too far from the beach;
and there seemed to be no one who had authority or power
enough to compel them to come nearer.   As a result of this,
the boats and lighters were unable to make as quick and
frequent trips as they might have made if the transports had
been within one hundred yards of the beach, instead of half
a mile away.

In the second place, most of the boats and lighters seemed
to be directed and handled by men who had had little ex-

perience in boating and no experience whatever in landing
through heavy surf.   As a result of this, boats were often
stove against the timbers of the little pier which the engineer
corps had hastily built; while the lighters, instead of being
held by an anchor and stern-line as they went into the breakers, were allowed to swing around into the trough of the sea,
where they either filled and sank, or drifted ashore, broadside to the beach, in such a position that fifty men could
hardly turn them around and get them off.

Finally, the soldiers and Cubans who acted as stevedores,
carrying the boxes from the boats and piling them on the
pier, were not intelligently directed, and, consequently, labored without method or judgment—getting in one another's
way; allowing the pier to become so blocked up with stuff
that nobody could move on it, much less work; and wasting
more energy in talking, shouting, and bossing one another
than they utilized in doing the thing that was to be done.

If I had ever had any doubt with regard to the expediency
of giving to the navy full and absolute control of the army
and its supplies while at sea, such doubt would have been
removed by one day's observation at Siboney.   Army officers,
as a rule, know nothing of water transportation, and cannot
reasonably be expected to know anything about it; and to
put them in charge of transports, lighters, and surf-boats is
almost as inconsiderate as to put a sailor in charge of a farm
and expect him, without any previous training, to run reap-
ing-, binding-, and threshing-machines, take proper care of his
live stock, and get as much out of the soil as an agricultural
expert would.   Every man to his trade; and the landing of
supplies from thirty or forty transports, in small boats, on
an unsheltered, surf-beaten coast, is not the trade of an army
quartermaster.   Lieutenant-Colonel Humphrey and Major
Jacobs undoubtedly did all that they could do, with their
knowledge and experience, and with the limited facilities

that General Shafter had provided for them, to get supplies
ashore; but the results were not gratifying, either to observers at Siboney, or to soldiers at the front.   If officers of
the navy had directed the loading of stores on the transports
at Tampa, and the unloading and landing of them at Daiquiri
and Siboney, there would have been a properly equipped
hospital at the latter place five days sooner than there was;
there would have been forty or fifty more mules in the army's
pack-train; the beach would not have been strewn with the
wrecks of mismanaged boats and lighters; and the transport-
steamers *Alamo, Breakwater, Iroquois, Vigilancia,* and *La
Grande Duchesse* would not have brought back to the United
States hundreds of tons of supplies intended for, and urgently needed by, our soldiers at the front.

On the afternoon of Tuesday, June 28, one of the small
vessels of the mosquito fleet arrived from Guantanamo Bay
with a letter from Captain McCalla in which he said that
General Perez had furnished a pack-train and an escort for
the food that the Red Cross had promised to send to the Guantanamo refugees, and that he would like to have us return
there as soon as possible and land five thousand rations.   As
our hospital work on shore was well under way, and Dr.
Lesser and the nurses had been supplied with everything
that they would need for a day or two, Miss Barton decided
to fill Captain McCalla's requisition at once.   Late Tuesday
evening, therefore, the *State of Texas* left Siboney, and after
a quiet and peaceful run down the coast entered Guantanamo
Bay about six o'clock Wednesday morning.   At half-past six
Captain McCalla came on board to make arrangements for
the landing, and in less than two hours there was a large
lighter alongside, with a steam-launch to tow it to the place
where an officer of General Perez's command was waiting for
it with a pack-train and an escort.   Before noon ten or fifteen
thousand pounds of supplies, consisting principally of beans,

rice, hard bread, and South American jerked beef, had been safely landed on the western side of the entrance to the lower harbor; and as we passed the point, on our return, we saw a large party of Cubans carrying the boxes and barrels up the bank.

We reached Siboney early that evening, drifted and rolled all night on a heavy swell, a mile or two off the coast, and at daybreak on the following morning ran close in to the beach and began landing supplies for several thousand destitute Cuban refugees who had assembled at the little village of Firmeza, three miles back of Siboney in the hills. In getting provisions ashore at Siboney, we encountered precisely the same difficulties that the army had to meet; but we fortunately had with us, as chief of transportation, a man who was familiar with boats and who had had large experience in handling them in circumstances and under conditions similar to those that prevailed on the Cuban coast. In proportion to our facilities, therefore, we got more stuff ashore in a given time than the army quartermasters did, and with fewer accidents. Mr. Warner, I think, was the first man to use, at Siboney, an anchor and a stern-line to prevent a boat or a lighter from broaching to in the surf. It was a simple enough expedient, but nobody, apparently, had thought of it. By dropping an anchor astern, just before the lighter reached the outer edge of the breakers, and then slacking off the line until the boat was near enough so that thirty Cubans could rush into the water, seize it, and run it up on the beach, a landing was effected without difficulty or risk. Then, when the supplies had been unloaded, the stern-anchor line could be used again as a means of pulling the lighter off through the surf into smooth water and preventing it from swinging around broadside to the sea while being launched. The best time for this work was between five and ten o'clock in the morning. After ten o'clock there was almost always a fresh breeze from the southeast, which raised such a surf on the beach that unless the landing of supplies was a matter of extreme urgency it had to be temporarily suspended. We succeeded in getting ashore on Wednesday food enough to satisfy the wants of the refugees at Firmeza, and Mr. Elwell was sent there to superintend its distribution.

Wednesday evening, as there seemed to be no prospect of an immediate engagement at the front, I decided to go to Port Antonio, Jamaica, with Mr. Trumbull White, on the Chicago "Record's" despatch-boat *Hercules*, to post my letters and the letters that had been intrusted to me by Colonel Wood and Lieutenant-Colonel Roosevelt, and to get some articles of camp equipment which I had ordered in New York, but which had failed to reach me before the *State of Texas* sailed from Key West.

We reached Port Antonio at eight o'clock on Thursday, spent the day there, and returned the next night to Siboney. Early Friday morning, as we were approaching the Cuban coast, the captain of the *Hercules* came down into the cabin with the astounding news that the blockading fleet had disappeared. "The jig is up, boys!" he exclaimed excitedly. "They 've taken the city, and the fleet is inside the harbor. I can't see a sign of a ship anywhere along the coast."

We all rushed on deck and gazed with sinking hearts at the long black line of the rampart and the high blue mountains beyond it. If Santiago had been taken in our absence, it would be the cruelest blow that fortune had ever dealt us! Although the sun was still below the horizon, the atmosphere was crystal-clear, and we could see without a glass the step-like outline of Morro Castle, and even the hazy blue smoke rising from the camp-fires on the beach at Siboney; but of the war-ships—the *New York*, the *Brooklyn*, the *Indiana*, and the *Texas*—there was not a sign. I do not know what Mr. White thought,—he seemed to be as cool and imperturbable as ever,—but when I fully realized that the fleet was not there, and drew from that fact the inevitable conclusion that the city had been captured, I was ready to anathematize the British West Indies, Port Antonio, the *Hercules*, and the cruel ill luck which had taken me a hundred miles away at the decisive moment of the Santiago campaign.

As the sun rose over the level plain of the Caribbean, and the swift ocean-going tug bore us nearer and nearer to the dark line of the still distant coast, the captain, who had been sweeping the base of the rampart with a long marine telescope, suddenly shouted: "Aha! I think I can see the *Brooklyn*, boys. It may be all right yet." I looked eagerly toward the position that Commodore Schley's flagship usually occupied on the western side of the harbor entrance, but could see nothing that even suggested the *Brooklyn's* familiar outline. If there were any vessels of the blockading fleet between us and the land, they certainly were off their stations and very close in under the shadow of the land. But the captain's eyesight was better than mine. In five minutes more he announced that he could see the *Brooklyn*, the *New York*, and the *Iowa*. "They're all there," he added after another look, "but some of them seem to be away out of position. The *New York* is off Aguadores, and the *Brooklyn* is half-way down to Aserraderos."

In fifteen minutes more it became apparent to us all that the height of the rampart and the mountains back of it, together with the crystalline clearness of the atmosphere, had led us to underestimate the distance, and that, when we first took alarm at the apparent absence of the blockading fleet, the war-ships were at least fifteen miles away, although the coast did not seem to be five. At such a distance the dull gray hulls of the vessels could hardly be seen, even if they were not below our horizon. With much lighter hearts, but with a feeling, nevertheless, that something of importance had occurred or was about to occur, we ran down alongside the *Iowa*, hailed her through a megaphone, and asked if there was any news. "It's reported that they are fighting over there," replied the officer of the deck, waving his hand toward Santiago, "but we have n't any particulars." There was no smoke rising above the rampart in the direction of the city, we could hear no sound of cannonading, and I was more than half inclined to believe that the report of fighting at the front was premature; but whether this were so or not, the *Iowa*, the *Texas*, the *New York*, and all the warships near us were cleared for action; their officers seemed to be eagerly awaiting orders; Admiral Sampson's flagship was exchanging wigwag flag-signals with a man on the beach beyond the mouth of the Aguadores ravine, and it was perfectly evident that something was expected to happen. Under such circumstances, the thing for us to do was to get back, as speedily as possible, to Siboney. Turning in a great circle around the *Iowa*, we steamed swiftly eastward along the coast, passing the *New York*, the *Suwanee*, and the *Gloucester*, which were lying, cleared for action, close under the walls of the Aguadores fort; exchanging greetings with the New York "Sun's" graceful despatch-boat *Kanapaha*, which came hurrying westward as if bound for some important field of expected activity; and finally rounding to alongside the *State of Texas* in the Siboney cove.

There was nothing in the appearance of the village to indicate that a battle was in progress, or even in anticipation. Boats were going to and fro between the transports and the pier as usual; there was the usual crowd of Cuban ragamuffins and tatterdemalions on the beach, with a sprinkling of soldiers in the streets; everything seemed to be quiet on board the *State of Texas*, and I said to Mr. White, as I bade him good-by, that I did not believe we had missed anything after all.

We soon had evidence, however, that there was an engagement in progress off the coast, if not at the front. Between
nine and ten o'clock in the morning heavy cannonading could
be heard in the direction of Morro Castle, and great clouds
of white smoke began to rise over a projecting point of the
rampart which hid, from our point of view, the mouth of the
Aguadores ravine. Anxious to see what was going on, I persuaded Miss Barton to let the *State of Texas* run out of the
cove and take some position from which we might witness
the bombardment. Getting under way at once, we steamed
out four or five miles in a west-southwest direction to a point
about three miles off Aguadores, from which we could see the
whole line of the coast. A column of infantry—the Thirty-
third Michigan, I think, under command of General Duffield
—had moved westward along the railroad under the rampart
to the mouth of the Aguadores ravine, and was apparently
engaged in attacking the enemy's position there under cover
of Admiral Sampson's guns. We could not clearly follow the
movements of the troops, for the reason that they were hidden, or partially hidden, by the bushes and trees, but we
could see every movement made and every shot fired by the
war-ships. The *Gloucester*, on the western side of the notch,
was knocking to pieces the old stone fort half-way up the
hill; the *New York*, from a position directly in front of the
railroad-bridge, was enfilading the ravine with four- and
eight-inch shells; while the *Suwanee*, completely hidden most
of the time in a great cloud of smoke, was close in to the
mouth of the river, sweeping the whole adjacent region with
a storm of projectiles from her rapid-fire and machine guns.
I do not know whether the old Aguadores fort had any
armament or not. Its sea face had been reduced to a heap
of crumbled masonry before we reached the scene of action,
and I did not afterward see a shot fired from it, nor a single
soldier in or about it. Its offensive power—if it ever had

any—was so completely destroyed that I momentarily expected General Duffield's troops to ford the river above the railroad-bridge and take undisputed possession of it. But the Michigan men were apparently prevented from doing so by the fire from some rifle-pits up the ravine, which the guns of the war-ships could not, or did not, wholly silence. We were not in a position, perhaps, to form a trustworthy judgment with regard to the strength of the Spaniards' defense; but it seemed to me that if the attack had been vigorously made and persistently followed up, the enemy might have been driven from the ravine. Admiral Sampson, in his report of the engagement, says that the Spaniards had no artillery except one small field-piece, which they fired only four or five times, and that not more than fifteen or twenty of them could be seen, at any time, in or about the rifle-pits. General Duffield, on the other hand, reports that they numbered five hundred, and that their artillery shelled the railroad-track and the woods where his troops were until 3 P. M.— about five hours. That their fire was not very destructive sufficiently appears from the fact that, in half a day of more or less continuous skirmishing, General Duffield lost only two men killed and six wounded.

Between three and four o'clock in the afternoon the Michigan troops returned by rail to Siboney; the war-ships withdrew to their blockading stations; and the field, as well as the honors, remained in possession of the Spaniards. After the engagement the *State of Texas* ran close in to the shore, and we saw perhaps a dozen Spanish soldiers standing or walking on the hillside west of the ravine. There may have been more of them in the concealment of the woods; but my impression is that their force was very small, and that General Duffield, with the aid and support of the war-ships, should have been able to clear the ravine and take possession not only of the abandoned fort but of the commanding heights above it.

8

When we got back to Siboney, late in the afternoon, the village was full of rumors of heavy fighting in front of Santiago; and, an hour or two after dark, wounded men, some on foot and some in army wagons, began to arrive at the Siboney hospital from the distant field of battle. As they had all been disabled and sent to the rear in the early part of the day, they could give us no information with regard to the result of the engagement. Many of them had been wounded before they had seen a Spanish intrenchment, or even a Spanish soldier; and all they knew about the fight was that the army had moved forward at daybreak and they themselves had been shot in the woods by an enemy whom they could neither locate nor see.

The Siboney hospital, thanks to the devotion and unwearied energy of Major Lagarde and his assistants, was by this time in fairly good working order. There was a lack of blankets, pillows, and tentage, and the operating facilities, perhaps, were not as ample as they might have been; but in view of the extraordinary difficulties with which the surgeons had had to contend, the results were highly creditable to them, even if not wholly satisfactory to an observer. As fast as the wounded arrived, they walked, or were carried on stretchers, to two or three large tents, pitched end to end and opening into one another, where hospital stewards and nurses placed them on the tables, and the surgeons, some of them stripped naked to the waist, examined their injuries by candlelight, and performed such operations as were necessary to give them relief. They were then taken or led away, and, as far as possible, furnished with blankets and shelter; but as the supply of blankets was very short, and all the available houses and tents were soon filled, the wounded who came in after midnight were laid in a row on the ground and covered with a long strip of canvas. Fortunately, the night was clear, still, and warm, and a nearly full moon made it almost as light as day, so that it was not so cheerless and uncomfortable to lie out on the ground without a blanket as it would have been if the night had been dark and cold, or rainy; but it was bad enough.

Most of our Red Cross surgeons and nurses were assisting in the operating-tents, and I remained on shore until after three o'clock in the morning. There was little that I could do beyond looking up the wounded, who frequently came into the village on foot, after a painful march of ten or twelve miles, and were so weak, hungry, and exhausted that, instead of coming to the hospital, they lay down anywhere in the street or under the wall of a house. Some of these men I found, with the assistance of a friendly and sympathetic Cuban, and had them carried on litters to the operating-tents. All of the wounded who came back from the front that night ought to have had hot tea or coffee, and some such easily digested food as malted milk, as most of them had eaten nothing since the early morning and were worn out with pain and fatigue. But of course no provision had been made for supplying them even with hard bread and water, and when taken from the operating-tables they were simply laid on the ground, to get through the night as best they could without nourishment or drink. We all understand, of course, that, in the oft-quoted words of General Sherman, "war is hell"; but it might be made a little less hellish by adequate preparation for the reception and care of the wounded.

I went off to the *State of Texas* between three and four o'clock, and threw myself into my berth just as day was beginning to break over the hills east of the cove.

CHAPTER XI

THE BATTLES OF CANEY AND SAN JUAN

GENERAL SHAFTER went to the front to take personal command of the army on Wednesday, June 29. At that time the divisions of Generals Kent, Wheeler, and Lawton were encamped on the Siboney-Santiago road, between the high ridge of Sevilla, from which I had seen the city two days before, and a half-ruined house and plantation, two or three miles farther on, known as El Pozo. Most of the troops were in the valley of a small stream which rises on the western slope of the Sevilla watershed, runs for a short distance in the direction of Santiago, and then, after receiving a number of tributaries, turns southward, just beyond the Pozo farm-house, and fal's into the sea through the notch in the rampart at Aguadores. Although the bottom of this valley, in general, was densely wooded, there was a series of grassy openings, or glades, on the northern side of the stream just east of El Pozo, and in one of these openings General Lawton, who led the advance, had established his headquarters.

About three miles due north from El Pozo, and between three and four miles in a northeasterly direction from Santiago, there was a small village called Caney,[1] which, on

[1] I never heard this village called *El* Caney by any Spaniard or any resident of Santiago. Mr. Ramsden, British consul for many years at the latter place, always refers to it in his diary as "Caney," without the definite

116

account of its geographical position, was regarded as a place of considerable strategic importance. It was connected by roads or practicable trails with Santiago on the west, Guantanamo on the east, and El Pozo on the south; and an enemy holding it would not only outflank us on that side as soon as we should pass the Pozo farm-house, but, by means of a rapid cross-march in our rear, might cut or seriously imperil our only line of communication with our base of supplies at Siboney. The fact was well known, furthermore, that there was a strong division of Spanish regulars (about six thousand men) at Guantanamo; and if this division should undertake to reinforce the garrison at Santiago, Caney would be directly on its line of march. In view of these considerations, General Shafter, after a survey of the country from the summit of the hill at El Pozo, determined to seize Caney, and, having thus cut off reinforcements from Guantanamo and protected himself from a flanking movement on the right, advance directly upon the city. The plan was good enough, as far as it went; but General Shafter had made no reconnaissance on the Siboney-Santiago road beyond El Pozo, and was wholly ignorant not only of the strength of the enemy's position there, but of the nature of the country to be traversed. It is true that he had superficially looked over the ground, once, from the top of the Pozo hill; but he could get, in that way, very little accurate knowledge of the topography of the region, and still less of the Spaniards' defensive strength.

Our only possible line of advance, in the center, was the Siboney-Santiago road, which ran, through a dense jungle, down the valley of the Aguadores River, crossed a small stream flowing into that river from the north, then crossed

article, and this was the name given it by every one in Santiago with whom I talked. The use of "El" in connection with Pozo seems to be correct, as Mr. Ramsden invariably calls it, in English, "the Pozo."

the San Juan River, another tributary of the Aguadores, and finally emerged from the forest directly in front of the San Juan heights. The enemy, of course, knew exactly where this road lay, and where it came out of the woods into the open country; and they had so disposed their batteries and rifle-pits that they could not only concentrate their fire upon the lower stretches and the mouth of the road, but sweep with a hail-storm of projectiles the whole margin of the forest where we should have to deploy and form our attacking line. General Shafter had not ascertained these facts by means of a reconnaissance, nor had he, apparently, considered such a state of affairs as a contingency to be guarded against; but Mr. Richard Harding Davis asserts that General Chaffee, commander of a brigade in General Lawton's division, anticipated precisely this situation, and predicted, five days before the battle, that if our men marched down this trail into the open country they would be "piled up so high that they would block the road." He thought that it would be much better to keep away from the road altogether; cut trails parallel with the entire front of the forest and hidden by it, with innumerable little trails leading into the open; and then march the whole army out upon the hills through these trails at the same moment. Whether this suggestion was ever made to the commanding general or not, I do not know; but if it was, it failed to commend itself to his judgment. I refer now—perhaps prematurely —to a state of affairs in our immediate front which was not fully disclosed until much later; but I do so because knowledge of it is absolutely essential to a clear understanding of the way in which the battle of San Juan was fought.

General Shafter's plan of operations, as outlined by Captain Lee, British military attaché, was substantially as follows: General Lawton's division was to attack Caney at daylight, July 1, and was expected to drive the enemy quickly out of that post, which then menaced our right flank. Meanwhile the remainder of the Fifth Corps was to advance along the main trail toward Santiago, pushing back the Spanish outposts, and occupy the line of the San Juan River. There it was to deploy and await Lawton, who, having taken Caney, was to wheel to his left and form up on the right of the main line. All these movements were to be completed by the evening of the 1st, and then the whole army would combine for the assault of San Juan on the 2d.

The advance began on the afternoon of Thursday, June 30. General Lawton's division, accompanied by Capron's battery of four field-guns, marched out on the Caney road, without meeting any opposition, and bivouacked for the night behind a ridge, or hill, about a mile southeast of the village. At the same time the remainder of the corps, consisting of General Wheeler's cavalry division, the division of General Kent, and three batteries of light artillery, moved down the Siboney-Santiago road, and went into camp near the Pozo farm-house. At daybreak on Friday, July 1, both columns were in position, within striking distance of the enemy's intrenched line. As the fighting at Caney was wholly independent of the fighting at San Juan, it will be more convenient to regard the two engagements as separate battles, although they were carried on simultaneously. I shall not attempt, however, to do more than describe the tactics on the two widely separated fields, and briefly state the results.

The defenses of Caney consisted of a strong stone fort on a steep conical hill at the southeastern corner of the village, and four or five substantial log blockhouses, so placed as to command every possible, or at least every practicable, avenue of approach. The blockhouses were connected one with another by deep, narrow trenches; the stone fort was surrounded by a network of outlying rifle-pits; there was a barbed-wire entanglement along the whole eastern front of the enemy's position; and the large trees in the village, as well as the houses and the old stone church, were full of sharp-shooters. The garrison of the place, not including the inhabitants, who, of course, participated to a greater or less extent in the fighting, consisted of three companies of infantry belonging to the San Luis brigade and forty-seven guerrillas—a total force of five hundred and fourteen men. The regulars were armed with the Mauser magazine-rifle, while the guerrillas used a .45-caliber Remington, carrying a large and very destructive brass-jacketed ball. They had neither artillery nor machine-guns, and relied wholly upon their small arms, their rifle-pits, and the great natural strength of their position. The officer in command was Brigadier-General Joaquin Vara del Rey. The attacking force, under direction of General Lawton, consisted of four brigades, numbering about forty-five hundred men, and was made up wholly of regulars with the exception of the Second Massachusetts.

The battle began at half-past six o'clock in the morning. General Chaffee's brigade took up a position six or eight hundred yards from the fort on the eastern side of the village; Ludlow's brigade marched around on the western side, so as to seize the Caney-Santiago road and thus cut off the enemy's escape; while the brigade of General Miles closed in on the south. Capron's battery, from the summit of a hill a little more than a mile southeast of the fort, fired the first shot at 6:35 A. M. Our infantry on General Chaffee's side then opened fire; the Spaniards replied from their fort, blockhouses, and rifle-pits; and the engagement soon became general. For the next three or four hours the battle was little more than a rifle duel at about six hundred yards' range. Capron's battery, from the top of the distant hill, continued to bombard the fort and the village at intervals, but its fire was slow and not very effective. Our infantry, meanwhile, were suffering far more loss than they were able to inflict, for the reason that they could find little or no shelter, while the Spaniards were protected by loopholed walls and deep rifle-pits, and were firing at ranges which had been previously measured and were therefore accurately known.   In spite of their losses, however, our men continued to creep forward, and about eleven o'clock General Chaffee's brigade reached and occupied the crest of a low ridge not more than three hundred yards from the northeastern side of the village. The fire of the Spanish sharp-shooters, at this short range, was very close and accurate, and before noon more than one hundred of General Chaffee's men lay dead or wounded in a sunken road about fifty yards back of the firing line.   The losses in the brigades of Generals Ludlow and Miles, on the western and southern sides of the village, were almost as great, and at 1:30 P. M. the attacking force seemed to be barely holding its own.   At this critical moment, when the chances of success or defeat seemed to be almost evenly balanced, General Lawton received an order from General Shafter to abandon the attack on Caney and hurry to the relief of Generals Kent and Sumner, who were hotly engaged in front of the San Juan heights.   Believing that a retreat at this juncture would be disastrous, and that the demoralizing effect of a repulse at Caney would more than counterbalance the support that he could give the center of the line in front of San Juan, General Lawton disregarded this order and pressed the attack with renewed vigor.   Capron's battery, about this time, got the range of the stone fort, shot away its flagstaff, amid vociferous cheers from our men, and soon began to make great breaches in its massive walls.   General Chaffee, who had been directed to make a final assault on the fort when, in his judgment, the proper time had come, then gave the order to charge; and the Twelfth Infantry, closely followed by several regiments from General Miles's brigade, and the brigade of General Bates, which had just arrived from Siboney, swarmed up the steep slope of the hill, drove the Spaniards out of their rifle-pits, and took the fort by storm. The first man inside its walls was Mr. James Creelman, a war correspondent, who was shot through the shoulder while recovering the Spanish flag. Although the fire from the village and the blockhouses still continued, it gradually slackened, and in less than half an hour the Spaniards who remained alive gave up the struggle and retreated by the northern Santiago road, suffering considerable loss from the fire of General Ludlow's brigade as they passed. At 4 P. M. village, fort, and blockhouses were all in undisputed possession of General Lawton's gallant division. The battle had lasted about nine hours, and in that time seven hundred men had been killed or wounded. Our own loss was four officers and eighty-four men killed, and twenty-four officers and three hundred and thirty-two men wounded; total, four hundred and forty-four. The loss of the Spaniards, as reported by themselves, was two hundred and forty-eight, — about one half their entire strength, — not including inhabitants of the village killed in their houses and in the streets. General Vara del Rey, their commander, was shot through both legs as he stood in the square opposite the village church after the storming of the fort, and then, as his men were placing him on a stretcher, he was instantly killed by a bullet through the head. Our loss, in this obstinately fought battle, was numerically much greater than that of the Spaniards; but their percentage of loss, based on the number of men engaged, was nearly five times as great as ours. When they retreated, they left forty-eight per cent. of their whole force dead or wounded in the intrenchments that they had so gallantly defended, and Lieutenant-Colonel Punet was able to collect and take back to Santiago that night only one hundred and three of the five hundred and fourteen officers and men who originally composed the garrison.

The loss on our side in this engagement was far greater than it probably would have been if General Lawton had had artillery enough to destroy the fort and blockhouses and drive the Spaniards out of their rifle-pits before he pushed forward his infantry; but it was not expected, of course, that the taking of a small and comparatively insignificant village would be so serious and difficult a matter; and as General Shafter had only sixteen light field-guns in all, he doubtless thought that he could not spare more than four for the attack on Caney.

The moral effect of this battle was to give each of the combatants a feeling of sincere respect for the bravery of the other. Our men never doubted, after July 1, that the Spaniards would fight stubbornly—at least, behind intrenchments; while the Spaniards, in turn, were greatly impressed by the dash, impetuosity, and unflinching courage of General Lawton's regulars. A staff-officer of General Vara del Rey said to a correspondent after the battle: "I have never seen anything to equal the courage and dash of those Americans, who, stripped to the waist, offering their naked breasts to our murderous fire, literally threw themselves on our trenches— on the very muzzles of our guns. We had the advantage in position, and mowed them down by the hundreds; but they never retreated or fell back an inch. As one man fell, shot through the heart, another would take his place, with grim determination and unflinching devotion to duty in every line of his face. Their gallantry was heroic." There could hardly be a more generous or a better deserved encomium.

The battle on the Siboney-Santiago road, in the center of our line, began nearly two hours later than the battle at Caney. Grimes's battery, which had taken position on a hill near the Pozo farm-house, opened fire on the heights of San

Juan about eight o'clock. A few moments later the Spaniards, who evidently had the range of the Pozo hill perfectly
from the beginning, returned the fire with shrapnel, killing
two men and wounding a number of others at the first shot,
striking the house at the third, and driving from the hill in
disorder some of the soldiers of the cavalry division who had
been stationed there, as well as a few war correspondents and
non-combatants who had gathered to witness the bombardment.   For three quarters of an hour, or an hour, there was
an artillery duel between Grimes's battery on the Pozo hill and
a Spanish battery situated somewhere on the heights to the
westward.   In this interchange of shots the enemy had all
the advantage, for the reason that the smoke from Grimes's
black powder revealed the position of his guns, while the
smokeless powder of the Spaniards gave no clue to the location of theirs.

About nine o'clock the order was given to advance; and
the divisions of Generals Kent and Wheeler began to move
down the narrow, jungle-skirted trail, toward the open country which was supposed to lie beyond the crossing of the
second stream, under the heights of San Juan.   General
Kent's orders were to move ahead to a green knoll on the
western side of the San Juan River (the second stream), and
there deploy to the left in what was believed to be the margin of the dense forest which covered the bottom of the
valley.   At the same time the cavalry division, which, owing
to the illness of General Wheeler, was temporarily under
command of General Sumner, was directed to advance along
the same trail, cross the San Juan River, deploy to the
right in the margin of the woods, and there await further
orders. The attempt of two divisions to march simultaneously down a forest trail which in places was not more than
twelve feet wide resulted, naturally, in crowding, disorder,
and delay; and when the head of the column, after crossing

the first stream, came within the zone of the enemy's fire, the confusion was greatly increased. The Spaniards, as General Chaffee predicted, had taken the bearing and range of the road, between the first stream and the western edge of the forest, and before the cavalry division reached the ford of the San Juan, on the other side of which it was to deploy and await orders, it was receiving a heavy fire, not only from the batteries and rifle-pits on the San Juan heights, but from hundreds of trees along the trail, in which the enemy had posted sharp-shooters.

So far as I know, riflemen had never before been posted in trees to check the advance of an army through a broken and forest-clad country; but the scheme was a good one, and it was carried out with thoughtful attention to every detail. The sharp-shooters were generally hidden in carefully prepared nests of leaves; some of them had tunics of fresh palm-leaves tied around their bodies from the shoulders down, so that at a little distance they could not be distinguished from the foliage of the trees in which they were concealed; and in a few cases that were reported to me they wore under their leafy tunics double canvas jackets filled with sand and carefully quilted, as a partial protection from bullets. This swarm of tree-men formed the Spanish skirmish-line, and a most dangerous and effective line it was, for the reason that it could be neither seen, driven in, nor dislodged. The hidden marksmen used Mauser rifles with smokeless powder, and although our men heard the reports and were killed or disabled by the projectiles, they had no guide or clue whatever to the location of their assailants. A skirmish-line in thickets or clumps of chaparral on the ground might have been driven back as our army advanced, and thus our rear would have been all the time secure from attack; but a skirmish-line hidden in tree-tops was as dangerous to the rear as to the front, and a soldier pressing forward toward what he sup-

posed to be the enemy's position was just as likely to get a
Mauser bullet in his back as in his breast.   Scores of wounded
men who were brought into the First Division field-hospital
on Friday and Saturday had never seen a Spanish intrenchment, or had even so much as a glimpse of a Spanish soldier.

In spite of the deadly fire to which they were subjected
from front, sides, and rear, our troops pushed on, as rapidly
as the congested state of the trail would permit, toward the
ford of the San Juan River.   The loss which our advance
sustained at this point was greatly increased by the sending
up of an observation balloon, which hung over the road, just
above the trees, and not only attracted the fire of the
Spaniards in front, but served their artillerymen as a target
and a range-finder.   It was an even better firing guide than
the sheets of iron or zinc roofing which they had put up in
some of the openings through which the trail ran; and until
it was finally torn by shrapnel so that it slowly sank into the
forest, the men under and behind it were exactly in the focus
of the converging streams of bullets which it attracted
from all parts of the San Juan heights.   The only useful discovery made by it was the fact that there was a second or
branch trail leading to a lower ford of the San Juan River
which General Kent's division might take, and thus relieve
the crowding on the main road.

Parts of the divisions of Generals Kent and Sumner crossed
the San Juan shortly after noon, and made an attempt to
deploy on its western bank and form in line of battle; but the
jungle was so dense, and the fire which swept the whole margin of the forest between them and the heights of San Juan
was so destructive, that they could do little more than seek
such cover as could be had and await orders.   So far as I
have been able to ascertain, no orders were received at this
critical time by either of the division commanders.   The
narrow road, for a distance of a mile back of the firing line,

was crowded with troops pressing forward to the San Juan ford; General Shafter, at his headquarters two miles in the rear, had little knowledge of the situation, and no adequate means of getting orders to his subordinates at the front; and meanwhile our advanced line, almost lost in the jungle, was being decimated by a fire which the men could not effectively return, and which it was impossible long to endure. Exactly what happened at this turning-point of the battle, who took the lead, and what orders were given, I do not certainly know; but the troops nearest the edge of the forest, including the Rough Riders, two regiments of General Hawkins's brigade (the Sixth and Sixteenth), a few men from the Seventy-first New York under Captain Rafferty, and perhaps squads or fragments of three or four other commands, suddenly broke from cover, as if moved by a general spontaneous impulse, and, with Colonel Roosevelt and General Hawkins as their most conspicuous, if not their foremost, leaders, charged "Kettle Hill" and the heights of San Juan. The advancing line, at first, looked very weak and thin; but it was equal to its task. In less than fifteen minutes it had reached the crest, and was driving the Spaniards along it toward the blockhouse, and down the slope behind it into the next valley. With the aid of the Ninth, Thirteenth, and Twenty-fourth Infantry, and the Gatling-gun battery of Lieutenant Parker, which supported the charging line by enfilading the enemy's trenches from a position on the left, the summit of the long ridge was soon cleared, the blockhouse captured, and the battle won before two o'clock in the afternoon.

Whether General Sumner or General Kent directly and personally ordered this charge or not, I cannot say; but from statements made to me by officers and men who participated in it, I am inclined to believe that it really was—as it has since been called—a "great popular movement," the credit for which belongs chiefly to the regimental and company officers and their men. That General Shafter had nothing to do with it is evident. He might have ordered it if he had been there; but he was not there. One of the wounded men in the field-hospital told me a story of a sergeant in one of the colored regiments, who was lying, with his comrades, in the woods, under the hot fire from the San Juan heights. Getting no order to advance, and tiring of the inaction, he finally sprang to his feet and rushed out into the open, shouting to the men of his company: "Come on, boys! Let's knock h—l out of the blankety-blanks!" whereupon the whole regiment rose like a single man, and started, at a dead run, for the hill. The story is doubtless apocryphal, but it will serve as an illustration of the way in which the charge up the slope of San Juan may have originated. Our men in the edge of the woods, in the bushes, and in the grain-fields had perhaps become so tired of inaction, and so exasperated by the deadly fire which was picking them off, one by one, as they lay, that they were ready for any desperate venture; and when somebody—no matter who—started forward, or said, "Come on, boys!" they simply rose en masse and charged. I cannot find, in the official reports of the engagement, any record of a definite order by any general officer to storm the heights; but the men were just in the mood for such a movement, and either with orders or without orders they charged up the hill, in the face of a tremendous fire from batteries, trenches, and blockhouses, and, in the words of an English officer, quoted by General Breckenridge in his testimony before the Investigating Commission, they not only covered themselves with glory, but extricated their corps commander "from a devil of a fix."

When the divisions of Generals Kent and Wheeler had been distributed along the crest of the San Juan ridge, the line looked too weak and thin to hold the position; but Skobeleff

once said that a position carried by attack can be held, even
if seventy-five per cent. of the attacking force have perished;
and there was no doubt in the minds of the regulars and the
Rough Riders that there were enough of them left not only
to hold San Juan, but to take the city.   Mr. Ramsden, British
consul in Santiago, says, in his diary, that the Spaniards were
so disheartened by their defeat that "if the Americans had
followed up their advantage and rushed the town, they would
have carried it."   But our men were too much exhausted by
the heat, and by their floundering in the jungle, to fight another battle that day.   When the firing ceased they had to
pick up the wounded and bury the dead, and then they spent
a large part of the night in erecting breastworks, digging
trenches, and making preparations for a counter-attack.

CHAPTER XII

THE FIELD-HOSPITAL

ON the morning of Friday, July 1, Dr. Egan and I, with three Cuban soldiers put at our service by General Castillo, set out on foot for the front, carrying on our backs or in our hands such medicines and hospital supplies as we thought would be most needed by the wounded, as well as hammocks, blankets, cooking-utensils, and four or five days' rations for ourselves. The march was a long and tiresome one, and it was after noon before we reached the glade, or opening, near the Pozo house which had been selected as the site for the first and only field-hospital of the Fifth Army-Corps. We reported at once to Major Wood, chief surgeon of the First Division, who gave us a hearty welcome and at once granted our request to be set at work. The second day's battle was then in progress; the booming of cannon and the rattle of Krag-Jorgensens could be plainly heard a short distance in advance, and wounded men by the score were coming back in army wagons from the firing line.

The First Division hospital of the Fifth Army-Corps was established in the field, about three miles east of Santiago, Wednesday, June 29. At that time it was in advance of the whole army, and had no other protection than a line of pickets thrown out toward the enemy's intrenchments. The site of the camp was a large, partly open glade, or field, on the floor

130

of a wooded valley, which was bounded on the northeast, at a distance of three miles, by a range of mountains, and which extended to within a mile of Santiago. Through this valley ran the Siboney-Santiago road, nearly parallel with a brook which had its source in the mountains to the northward, and after being joined by a number of other brooks coming from the same direction, fell into the sea through a notch in the coast rampart three or four miles east of Morro Castle. The glade, or field, in which the hospital camp stood was one of a series of similar glades stretching away to the northeast toward the base of the mountains, and resembling a little in outline and topographical arrangement the openings known as "barrens" in the forests of Nova Scotia. In every other direction except the one taken by this line of glades the camp was bounded by a dense tropical jungle through which the Siboney-Santiago road had been cut. The opening occupied by the hospital camp was covered with a dense growth of high wild grass, shaded here and there by small clumps of piñon-bushes, with a few larger trees of kinds to me unknown. South and southwest of the camp lay a tropical forest which I did not undertake to explore, but which our pickets said was so wild and so tangled with vines and creepers as to be almost impenetrable. The site of the camp between the road and the brook was well chosen, and it was, perhaps, as satisfactory a place for a hospital as could have been found in that vicinity.

The hospital, when I arrived, consisted of three large tents for operating-tables, pharmacy, dispensary, etc.; another of similar dimensions for wounded officers; half a dozen small wall-tents for wounded soldiers; and a lot of "dog-kennels," or low shelter-tents, for the hospital stewards, litter-bearers, and other attendants. I do not know how many ambulances the hospital had for the transportation of wounded from the battle-line, but I saw only two, and was informed by Dr. God-

frey that only three had been brought from Tampa. Fifty
or more had been sent to that port for the use of the Fifth
Army-Corps, but had been left there, by direct order of General Shafter, when the expedition sailed.

The hospital staff at the beginning of the first day's battle
consisted of five surgeons: namely, Major M. W. Wood, chief
surgeon of the First Division; Major R. W. Johnson, in command of the First Division hospital; Dr. Guy C. Godfrey,
Dr. H. P. Jones, and Dr. F. J. Combe.

The resources and supplies of the hospital, outside of
instruments, operating-tables, and medicines, were very
limited.   There was tent-shelter for only about one hundred
wounded men; there were no cots, hammocks, mattresses,
rubber blankets, or pillows for sick or injured soldiers; the
supply of woolen army blankets was very short and was soon
exhausted; and there was no clothing at all except two or
three dozen shirts.   In the form of hospital food for sick or
wounded men there was nothing except a few jars of beef
extract, malted milk, etc., bought in the United States by
Major Wood, taken to the field in his own private baggage,
and held in reserve for desperate cases.

Such was the equipment of the only field-hospital in Cuba
when the attack on Santiago began.   That it was wretch-
edly incomplete and inadequate I hardly need say, but the
responsibility for the incompleteness and inadequacy cannot
be laid upon the field force.   They took to the hospital camp
from the steamers everything that they could possibly get
transportation for.   There was only one line of very bad road
from Daiquiri and Siboney to the front, and along that line
had to be carried, with an utterly insufficient train of mules
and wagons, all the food and ammunition needed by an
advancing army of more than sixteen thousand men.   In
loading the mules and wagons preference was given to stores
and supplies that could be used in killing Spanish soldiers

rather than to stores and supplies that would be needed in caring for our own, and the result was the dreadful and heartrending state of affairs in that hospital at the end of the second day's fight. If there was anything more terrible in our Civil War, I am glad that I was not there to see it.

The battle before Santiago began very early on Friday morning, July 1, and the wounded, most of whom had received first aid at bandaging-stations just back of the firing line, reached the hospital in small numbers as early as nine o'clock. As the hot tropical day advanced, the numbers constantly and rapidly increased until, at nightfall, long rows of wounded were lying on the grass in front of the operating-tents, without awnings or shelter, awaiting examination and treatment. The small force of field-surgeons worked heroically and with a devotion that I have never seen surpassed; but they were completely overwhelmed by the great bloody wave of human agony that rolled back in ever-increasing volume from the battle-line. They stood at the operating-tables, wholly without sleep, and almost without rest or food, for twenty-one consecutive hours; and yet, in spite of their tremendous exertions, hundreds of seriously or dangerously wounded men lay on the ground for hours, many of them half naked, and nearly all without shelter from the blazing tropical sun in the daytime, or the damp, chilly dew at night. No organized or systematic provision had been made for feeding them or giving them drink, and many a poor fellow had not tasted food or water for twelve hours, and had been exposed during all that time to the almost intolerable glare of the sun. I saw a soldier of the Tenth Cavalry, who had been shot through the body, lie on the ground in front of the operating-tent for at least three hours, naked to the waist, and exposed to sunshine in which I could hardly hold my hand. I speak of this particular soldier, not because he was an exception, but rather because he exhibited such magnificent fortitude and self-control. Although he must have been suffering terrible agony, he lay there for three hours without a murmur or a complaint, and, so far as I could see, without change of countenance, until his turn came and he was lifted upon the operating-table.

At sunset the five surgeons had operated upon and dressed the wounds of one hundred and fifty-four men. As night advanced and the wounded came in more rapidly, no count or record of the operations was made or attempted. Late in the evening of Friday, division and regimental surgeons began to come back to the hospital from the front, and the operating force was increased to ten. More tables were set out in front of the tents, and the surgeons worked at them all night, partly by moonlight and partly by the dim light of flaring candles held in the hands of stewards and attendants. Fortunately, the weather was clear and still, and the moon nearly full. There were no lanterns, apparently, in the camp,—at least, I saw none in use outside of the operating-tent,—and if the night had been dark, windy, or rainy, four fifths of the wounded would have had no help or surgical treatment whatever until the next day. All the operations outside of a single tent were performed by the dim light of one unsheltered and flaring candle, or at most two. More than once even the candles were extinguished for fear that they would draw the fire of Spanish sharp-shooters who were posted in trees south of the camp, and who exchanged shots with our pickets at intervals throughout the night. These cold-blooded and merciless guerrillas fired all day Friday at our ambulances and at our wounded as they were brought back from the battle-line, and killed two of our Red Cross men. There was good reason to fear, therefore, that they would fire into the hospital. It required some nerve on the part of our surgeons to stand beside operating-tables all night with their backs to a dark tropical jungle out of which came at intervals the sharp reports of guerrillas' rifles. But there was not a sign of hesitation or fear. Finding that they could not work satisfactorily by moonlight, brilliant although it was, they relighted their candles and took the risk. Before daybreak on Saturday morning they had performed more than three hundred operations, and then, as the wounded had ceased to come in, and all cases requiring immediate attention had been disposed of, they retired to their tents for a little rest. The five men who composed the original hospital force had worked incessantly for twenty-one hours.

Of course the wounded who had been operated upon, or the greater part of them, had to lie out all night on the water-soaked ground; and in order to appreciate the suffering they endured the reader must try to imagine the conditions and the environment. It rained in torrents there almost every afternoon for a period of from ten minutes to half an hour, and the ground, therefore, was usually water-soaked and soft. All the time that it did not rain the sun shone with a fierceness of heat that I have seldom seen equaled, and yet at night it grew cool and damp so rapidly as to necessitate the putting on of thicker clothing or a light overcoat. Many of the wounded soldiers, who were brought to the hospital from a distance of three miles in a jolting ambulance or army wagon, had lost their upper clothing at the bandaging-stations just back of the battle-line, where the field-surgeons had stripped them in order to examine or treat their wounds. They arrived there, consequently, half naked and without either rubber or woolen blankets; and as the very limited hospital supply of shirts and blankets had been exhausted, there was nothing to clothe or cover them with. The tents set apart for wounded soldiers were already full to overflowing, and all that a litter-squad could do with a man when they lifted him from the operating-table on Friday

night was to carry him away and lay him down, half naked
as he was, on the water-soaked ground under the stars.
Weak and shaken from agony under the surgeon's knife and
probe, there he had to lie in the high, wet grass, with no one
to look after him, no one to give him food and water if he
needed them, no blanket over him, and no pillow under his
head. What he suffered in the long hours of the damp,
chilly night I know because I saw him, and scores more like
him; but the reader, who can get an idea of it only through
the medium of words, can hardly imagine it.

When the sun rose Saturday morning, the sufferings of
the wounded who had lain out all night in the grass were
intensified rather than relieved, because with sunshine came
intense heat, thirst, and surgical fever. An attempt was
made to protect some of them by making awnings and
thatched roofs of bushes and poles; but about seven o'clock
ambulances and wagons loaded with wounded began again
to arrive from the battle-line, and the whole hospital force
turned its attention to them, leaving the suffering men in the
grass to the care of the camp cooks and a few slightly
wounded soldiers, who, although in pain themselves, could
still hobble about carrying hard bread and water to their
completely disabled and gasping comrades.

The scenes of Saturday were like those of the previous day,
but with added details of misery and horror. Many of the
wounded, brought in from the extreme right flank of the army
at Caney, had had nothing to eat or drink in more than twenty-
four hours, and were in a state of extreme exhaustion. Some,
who had been shot through the mouth or neck, were unable
to swallow, and we had to push a rubber tube down through
the bloody froth that filled their throats, and pour water into
their stomachs through that; some lay on the ground with
swollen bellies, suffering acutely from stricture of the urinary
passage and distention of the bladder caused by a gunshot

wound; some were paralyzed from the neck down or the waist down as a result of injury to the spine; some were delirious from thirst, fever, and exposure to the sun; and some were in a state of unconsciousness, coma, or collapse, and made no reply or sign of life when I offered them water or bread. They were all placed on the ground in a long, closely packed row as they came in; a few pieces of shelter-tenting were stretched over them to protect them a little from the sun, and there they lay for two, three, and sometimes four hours before the surgeons could even examine their injuries. A more splendid exhibition of patient, uncomplaining fortitude and heroic self-control than that presented by these wounded men the world has never seen.   Many of them, as appeared from their chalky faces, gasping breath, and bloody vomiting, were in the last extremity of mortal agony; but I did not hear a groan, a murmur, or a complaint once an hour.   Occasionally a trooper under the knife of the surgeon would swear, or a beardless Cuban boy would shriek and cry, "Oh, my mother, my mother!" as the surgeons reduced a compound fracture of the femur and put his leg in splints; but from the long row of wounded on the ground there came no sound or sign of weakness.   They were suffering,—some of them were dying,—but they were strong.   Many a man whose mouth was so dry and parched with thirst that he could hardly articulate would insist on my giving water first, not to him, when it was his turn, but to some comrade who was more badly hurt or had suffered longer.   Intense pain and the fear of impending death are supposed to bring out the selfish, animal characteristics of man; but they do not in the higher type of man.   Not a single American soldier, in all my experience in that hospital, ever asked to be examined or treated out of his regular turn on account of the severity, painful nature, or critical state of his wound.   On the contrary, they repeatedly gave way to one another, saying:

"Take this one first—he's shot through the body.   I've only got a smashed foot, and I can wait."   Even the courtesies of life were not forgotten or neglected in that valley of the shadow of death.   If a man could speak at all, he always said, "Thank you," or "I thank you very much," when I gave him hard bread or water.   One beardless youth who had been shot through the throat, and who told me in a husky whisper that he had had no water in thirty-six hours, tried to take a swallow when I lifted his head.   He strangled, coughed up a little bloody froth, and then whispered: "It's no use; I can't.   Never mind!"   Our Dr. Egan afterward gave him water through a stomach-tube.   If there was any weakness or selfishness, or behavior not up to the highest level of heroic manhood, among the wounded American soldiers in that hospital during those three terrible days, I failed to see it.   As one of the army surgeons said to me, with the tears very near his eyes: "When I look at those fellows and see what they stand, I am proud of being an American, and I glory in the stock.   The world has nothing finer."

It was the splendid courage and fortitude of the men that made their suffering so hard to see.   As the row of prostrate bodies on the ground grew longer and longer Saturday afternoon and evening, the emotional strain of the situation became almost unbearable, and I would have exchanged all the knowledge and ability I possessed for the knowledge and skill even of a hospital steward, so that I might do something more than carry around food and water to those suffering, uncomplaining American soldiers.

Late Saturday afternoon there was a heavy tropical shower, which drenched not only the wounded who were awaiting examination in front of the operating-tents, but also the men who had been operated upon and carried away into the long grass.   I doubt, however, whether it made their condition any worse—at least for a time. Most of them had been exposed for hours to a tropical sun, and the rain must have given them, at first, a feeling of coolness and relief.

As the sun set and darkness settled down upon the camp after the short tropical twilight, candles were again lighted around the operating-tables, and the surgeons worked on without intermission and without rest. The rattle of rifles and machine-guns and the booming of artillery along the line of battle died away into an occasional sputter after dark; the full moon rose into a cloudless sky, and the stillness of the jungle south of the camp was broken only by an occasional shot from a sentry or from a Spanish sharp-shooter hidden in a tree. Around the operating-tables there was a sound of half-audible conversation as the surgeons gave directions to their assistants or discussed the injuries of the men upon whom they were at work, and now and then a peremptory call for "Litter-squad here!" showed that another man was about to be brought to the operating-table, or carried from it into the field and laid on the ground.

At midnight Saturday the number of wounded men that had been brought into the hospital camp was about eight hundred. All that could walk, after their wounds had been dressed, and all that could bear transportation to the sea-coast in an army wagon, were sent to Siboney to be put on board the hospital steamers and transports. There remained in the camp several hundred who were so severely injured that they could not possibly be moved, and these were carried to the eastern end of the field and laid on the ground in the high, wet grass. I cannot imagine anything more cruelly barbarous than to bring a severely wounded man back four or five miles to the hospital in a crowded, jolting army wagon, let him lie from two to four hours with hardly any protection from the blazing sunshine in the daytime or the drenching dew at night, rack him with agony on the operating-table, and then carry him away, weak and helpless, put him on the water-soaked ground, without shelter, blanket, pillow, food, or drink, and leave him there to suffer alone all night. And yet I saw this done with scores, if not hundreds, of men as brave and heroic as any that ever stood in a battle-line. It might not have been so,—it ought not to have been so,—but so it was; and in that hospital there were no means whatever of preventing it. The force of surgeons and hospital stewards immediately available was altogether too small to attend properly to the great number of wounded thrown suddenly upon their hands, and no men could be spared to look after the wretched and suffering soldiers in the grass whose wounds had been treated, when there were a hundred more who had not even been looked at in twenty-four hours, and who were lying in a long, closely packed row on the ground, awaiting their turns at the operating-tables. When a litter-squad had carried a man away into the bushes, they had to leave him there and hurry back to put another sufferer on a table or bring another from an ambulance or army wagon to the operating-line. Instead of the force of five surgeons and about twenty stewards and attendants with which the hospital began work on Friday, there should have been a force of fifty surgeons and at least two hundred stewards, attendants, and stretcher-bearers, so that they might have been divided into two watches, or reliefs, working and resting alternately. As it was on Friday, five surgeons and twenty attendants had to take care of the wounded from three whole divisions. They were reinforced by five more surgeons and perhaps twenty more attendants Friday evening, but even this force was so insufficient and inadequate that at midnight on Saturday one of the highest medical officers in the camp said to me: "This department is in a state of complete collapse."

In nothing were the weakness and imperfect equipment of the hospital more apparent than in the provision made—or rather the lack of provision—for the care of wounded after their wounds had been dressed. It seems to have been expected that, when injured men were brought back from the battle-line, their blankets, canteens, and rations would be brought with them; but in seventy-five per cent. of the cases this was not done, and it was unreasonable under the circumstances to expect that it would be done. The men did not go into action carrying their blankets and rations; on the contrary, most of them left all unnecessary impedimenta in their camps and went into the fight as lightly clad as possible, often stripped naked to the waist. When they were shot, their comrades picked them up and carried them to the rear just as they were. There was no time to inquire for their personal belongings or to send to their camps for their blankets; and they came back to the hospital not only without blankets or ponchos, but often hatless, shirtless, and in trousers ripped up by surgeon's scissors. Some of them had empty canteens, but I did not see one who had food. Ample provision should have been made in this hospital for clothing, feeding, and supplying the wants of wounded men brought back in this destitute condition; but such provision as was made proved to be wholly inadequate. The few dozen shirts and blankets that the hospital contained were soon distributed, and then the wounded men were taken from the operating-tables and laid on the ground in the outskirts of the camp in the same state, as regards clothing and bedding, that they were in when picked up on the battle-field. For feeding them no arrangements whatever had been made, and, indeed, there was no food in the hospital suited to their requirements. Our Red Cross surgeon, Dr. Egan, and I brought in a few bottles of malted milk, maltine, beef extract, limes, etc., but as we could not get transportation for a single pound of stuff and had to march in twelve miles over a bad road, we could not bring much, and our limited

supply of invalid food, although administered only in desperate cases, was exhausted in two or three hours.

Major Wood, who superintended the bringing in and disposition of the wounded, did everything that was possible to
make them comfortable, and worked day and night with tire-
less energy and devotion; but there was very little that could
be done with the resources at his command.

The second day's battle in front of Santiago consisted,
generally speaking, of a series of attempts on the part of
the Spaniards to drive our troops from the positions which
they had taken by assault on Friday. The firing continued
throughout the day, and at times was very heavy; but just
before sunset it died away to a faint sputter and crackle of
rifles, and at dark ceased altogether. The moon rose in an
unclouded sky over the dark tree-tops east of the camp; the
crickets began to chirp in the thicket across the brook;
sounds like the rapid shaking of a billiard-ball in a resonant
wooden box came from nocturnal birds or tree-toads hidden
in the depth of the forest; and the teeming life of the tropical wilderness, frightened into silence for a time by the
uproar of battle, took courage from the stillness of night,
and manifested its presence by chirps, croaks, and queer,
unfamiliar cries in all parts of the encircling jungle.

About ten o'clock the stillness was broken by the boom of
a heavy gun at the front, followed instantly by the crash and
rattle of infantry fire, which grew heavier and heavier, and
extended farther and farther to the north and south, until
it seemed to come from all parts of our intrenched line on
the crest of the San Juan ridge. For nearly half an hour
the rattle and sputter of rifles, the drumming of machine-
guns, and the intermittent thunder of artillery filled the air
from the outskirts of Santiago to the hospital camp, drowning the murmur of the rippling brook, and silencing again
the crickets, birds, and tree-toads in the jungle beyond
it. Then the uproar ceased, almost as suddenly as it had

begun; the stillness of night settled down again upon the lonely tropical wilderness; and if I had not been able to hear the voices of the surgeons as they consulted over an operating-table, and an occasional shot from a picket or a sharpshooter in the forest, I should not have imagined that there was an army or a battle-field within a hundred miles. From the wounded who came back from the firing line an hour or two later we learned that the enemy made an attempt, about ten o'clock, to recapture the San Juan heights, but were repulsed with heavy loss.

Saturday's fighting did not materially change the relative positions of the combatants, but it proved conclusively that we could hold the San Juan ridge against any attacking force that the Spaniards could muster. Why, after a demonstration of this fact, General Shafter should have been so discouraged as to "seriously consider the advisability of falling back to a position five miles in the rear," I do not know. Our losses in the fighting at Caney and San Juan were only two hundred and thirty-nine men killed and thirteen hundred and sixty-three wounded, yet General Shafter was so disheartened that he not only thought of retreating to a position five miles in the rear, but seems to have been upon the point of surrendering the command of the army to General Breckenridge. Ill health, doubtless, had much to do with this feeling of discouragement. It certainly was not warranted by anything that one could see at the end of the second day's fight. We had taken every position that we had attacked; we had lost only ten per cent. of our available force; and we were strongly intrenched on the crest of a high hill less than a mile and a half from the eastern boundary of the city. After General Lawton's division and the brigade of General Bates had reinforced Generals Kent and Wheeler at San Juan, there was very little reason to fear that the Spaniards would drive us from our position.

The fighting of all our soldiers, both at Caney and at San

Juan, was daring and gallant in the extreme; but I cannot refrain from calling particular attention to the splendid behavior of the colored troops. It is the testimony of all who saw them under fire that they fought with the utmost courage, coolness, and determination, and Colonel Roosevelt said to a squad of them in the trenches, in my presence, that he never expected to have, and could not ask to have, better men beside him in a hard fight. If soldiers come up to Colonel Roosevelt's standard of courage, their friends have no reason to feel ashamed of them. His commendation is equivalent to a medal of honor for conspicuous gallantry, because, in the slang of the camp, he himself is "a fighter from 'way back." I can testify, furthermore, from my own personal observation in the field-hospital of the Fifth Army-Corps Saturday and Saturday night, that the colored regulars who were brought in there displayed extraordinary fortitude and self-control. There were a great many of them, but I cannot remember to have heard a groan or a complaint from a single man. I asked one of them whether any of his comrades showed signs of fear when they went into action. "No," he replied, with a grin, "not egzactly; two or three of 'em looked kindo' squandered just at first, but they mighty soon braced up."

Among the volunteer regiments that were hotly engaged and lost heavily in Friday's battle were the Seventy-first New York and the Second Massachusetts. Both were armed with Springfield rifles, and this put them at a great disadvantage as compared with the regulars, all of whom used Krag-Jorgensen rifles or carbines with smokeless powder. In a wooded and chaparral-covered country like that around Santiago, where it was so easy to find concealment and so difficult to see troops at a distance, the use of smokeless powder was of the utmost possible importance. A body of men might be perfectly hidden in woods or chaparral within five hun-

dred yards of the enemy's intrenchments, and if they used
smokeless powder they might fire from there for half an hour
without being seen or getting a return shot; but if they were
armed with Springfields, the smoke from their very first volley
revealed to the enemy their exact position, and the chaparral
that concealed them was torn to pieces by a hail-storm of
projectiles from Mausers and machine-guns. It was cruel
and unreasonable to ask men to go into action, in such a field,
with rifles that could be used only with common powder. Our
men might as well have been required to hoist above the
bushes and chaparral a big flag emblazoned with the words,
"Here we are!" Dr. Hitchcock, surgeon of the Second
Massachusetts, told me that again and again, when they
were lying concealed in dense scrub beside a regiment of
regulars, the latter would fire for twenty minutes without
attracting a single return shot from the enemy's line; but
the moment the men of the Second Massachusetts began
to use their Springfields, and the smoke rose above the
bushes, the Spaniards would concentrate their fire upon the
spot, and kill or wound a dozen men in as many minutes. It
is to be hoped that our government will not send any more
troops abroad with these antiquated guns. They were good
enough in their day, but they are peculiarly unsuited to the
conditions of warfare in a tropical field.

Wounded men from the front continued to come into the
hospital camp on Saturday until long after midnight, and the
exhausted surgeons worked at the operating-tables by candlelight until 3 A. M. I noticed, carrying stretchers and looking
after the wounded, two or three volunteer assistants from
civil life, among them Mr. Brewer of Pittsburg, who died of
yellow fever a few days later at Siboney.

Worn out by sleeplessness, fatigue, and the emotional
strain of two nights and a day of field-hospital experience, I
stretched my hammock between two trees, about three o'clock
10

in the morning, crawled into it, and slept, for two or three hours, the dead, dreamless sleep of complete exhaustion. Dr. Egan, I think, did not lie down at all. After all the other surgeons had gone to their tents, he wandered about the camp, looking after the wounded who lay shivering here and there on the bare, wet ground, and giving them, with medicines, stomach-tube, and catheter, such relief as he could. Soon after sunrise I awoke, and after a hasty breakfast began carrying around food and water. I shall not attempt to describe fully the terrible and heartrending experience of that morning; but two or three of the scenes that I was compelled to witness seem, even now, to be etched on my memory in lines of blood. About nine o'clock, for example, I went into a small wall-tent which sheltered a dozen or more dangerously wounded Spaniards and Cuban insurgents. Everything that I saw there was shocking. On the right-hand side of the tent, face downward and partly buried in the water-soaked, oozy ground, lay a half-naked Cuban boy, nineteen or twenty years of age, who had died in the night. He had been wounded in the head and at some time during the long hours of darkness between sunset and dawn the bandage had partly slipped off, and hemorrhage had begun. The blood had run down on his neck and shoulders, coagulating and stiffening as it flowed, until it had formed a large, red, spongy mass around his neck and on his naked back between the shoulder-blades. This, with the coal-black hair, the chalky face partly buried in mud, and the distorted, agonized attitude of the half-nude body, made one of the most ghastly pictures I had ever seen. There was already a stench of decomposition in the hot air of the tent, and the coagulated blood on the half-naked corpse, as well as the bloody bandage around its head, was swarming with noisy flies. Just beyond this terrible object, and looking directly at it, was another young Cuban who had been shot through the body, and who was half crouching, half kneeling, on the ground, with his hands pressed to his loins. He was deadly pale, had evidently been in torment all night, and was crying, over and over again, in a low, agonized tone, "Oh, my mother, my mother, my mother!" as he looked with distracted eyes at the bloody, half-naked body of his dead comrade and saw in it his own impending fate. The stench, the buzzing flies, the half-dried blood, the groans, and the cries of "O, mi madre!" "O Jesu!" from the half-naked wretches lying in two rows on the bare, muddy ground, came as near making an inferno as anything one is ever likely to see.

In another tent, a short distance away, I found a smooth-faced American soldier about thirty years of age, who had been shot in the head, and also wounded by a fragment of a shell in the body. He was naked to the waist, and his whole right side, from the armpit to the hip, had turned a purplish-blue color from the bruising blow of the shell. Blood had run down from under the bandage around his head, and had then dried, completely covering his swollen face and closed eyelids with a dull-red mask. On this had settled a swarm of flies, which he was too weak to brush away, or in too much pain to notice. I thought, at first, that he was dead; but when I spoke to him and offered him water, he opened his bloodshot, fly-encircled eyes, looked at me for a moment in a dull, agonized way, and then closed them and faintly shook his head. Whether he lived or died, I do not know. When I next visited the tent he was gone.

As soon as possible after my arrival at the hospital I had obtained an order from Lieutenant-Colonel Pope, chief surgeon of the Fifth Army-Corps, for wagons, and on Saturday afternoon I telephoned Miss Barton from General Shafter's headquarters to send us blankets, clothing, malted milk, beef extract, tents, tent-flies, and such other things as were most urgently needed. Sunday afternoon, less than twenty-four hours after my message reached her, she rode into the hospital camp in an army wagon, with Mrs. Gardner, Dr. Gardner, Dr. Hubbell, and Mr. McDowell. They brought with them a wagon-load of supplies, including everything necessary for a small Red Cross emergency station, and in less than two hours they were refreshing all the wounded men in the camp with corn-meal gruel, hot malted milk, beef extract, coffee, and a beverage known as "Red Cross cider," made by stewing dried apples or prunes in a large quantity of water, and then pouring off the water, adding to it the juice of half a dozen lemons or limes, and setting it into the brook in closed vessels to cool. After that time no sick or wounded man in the camp, I think, ever suffered for want of suitable food and drink.

On Monday Miss Barton and Dr. Hubbell went back to the steamer at Siboney for additional supplies, and in twenty-four hours more we had blankets, pillows, and hospital delicacies enough to meet all demands. We should have had them there before the battle began, if we could have obtained transportation for them from the sea-coast. As fast as possible the wounded were taken in army wagons from the field-hospital to Siboney, where they were put on board the transports, and at eight o'clock on Tuesday evening Major Johnson was able to report to Major Wood that every wounded man left in the hospital was in a tent, with a rubber poncho or tarpaulin under him and a blanket over him.

In spite of unfavorable conditions, the percentage of recoveries among the wounded treated in this hospital was much greater than in any other war in which the United States has ever been engaged. This was due partly to improved antiseptic methods of treatment, and partly to the nature of the wound made by the Mauser bullet. In most cases this wound was a small, clean perforation, with very little shattering or mangling, and required only antiseptic bandaging and care. All abdominal operations that were attempted in the field resulted in death, and none were performed after the first day, as the great heat and dampness, together with the difficulty of giving the patients proper nursing and care, made recovery next to impossible.

CHAPTER XIII

SIBONEY DURING THE ARMISTICE

O N the morning of July 3, General Shafter, who had recovered confidence, demanded the immediate surrender of Santiago, threatening, in case of refusal, to bombard the
city; and negotiations under a flag of truce continued thereafter for a period of ten days. Meanwhile, on the evening
of Friday, July 8, Miss Barton, Dr. Egan, Dr. Hubbell, and
I returned to the *State of Texas* to meet Mrs. J. Addison
Porter, wife of the President's secretary, who had just arrived
on the hospital steamer *Relief*, and to get some ice and other
hospital supplies of which we were in need. We left the field-
hospital in an army wagon about seven o'clock and reached
Siboney soon after ten. The surf raised by a strong south-
easterly wind was rolling so high on the strip of beach behind
which the village stood that we could not get off on board
the *State of Texas*, nor even communicate with her. It was
extremely tantalizing to us, tired, hungry, and camp-soiled
as we were, to see the lights of our steamer only a quarter
of a mile away, to know that almost within reach were a cool
bath, a good supper, a clean bed, and all the comforts, if not
the luxuries, of life, and yet to feel that, so far as we were
concerned, they were as unattainable as if the ship were in
the Bay of San Francisco.

Siboney at that time was a wretched little hamlet containing only ten or fifteen abandoned and incredibly dirty Spanish houses, most of which were in use either as hospitals or
for government offices.   None of them contained sleeping
accommodations, even of the most primitive kind; all of
them were crowded; and if one arrived in the village, as we
did, at a late hour of the night, there was nothing to be done
but bivouac somewhere on the dirty, flea-infested floor of an
open piazza, or lie out on the ground.   One of the largest
and most commodious buildings in the village, a one-story
house with a high front stoop or porch, had been used,
apparently, during the Spanish occupation of the place, as a
store or shop.   At the time of our return from the front it
sheltered the "United States Post-Office, Military Station
No. 1," which had been transferred from Daiquiri to Siboney
two or three days before.   In front of this building our army
wagon stopped, and we men went in to inquire for mail and
to see if we could find a decently clean place for Miss Barton
to sleep.   She was quite ready to bivouac in the army wagon;
but we hoped to get something better for her.   Mr. Brewer,
the postmaster, whom I had met in one of my lecture trips
through the West and more recently in the field, received us
cordially, and at once offered Miss Barton his own cot, in a
room that had not yet been cleaned or swept, back of the
general delivery department.   By the light of a single candle
it seemed to be a gloomy, dirty, and barn-like apartment; but
the cot was the only thing in the shape of a bed that I had
seen in Siboney, outside of the hospitals, and we accepted it
for Miss Barton with grateful hearts.   The employees of the
post-office were all sleeping in camp-chairs or on the counters
and floors.   Where Mr. Brewer went when he had given his
own bed to Miss Barton, I do not know.   I left her writing
orders and telegrams by the light of a flaring, guttering
candle at about eleven o'clock, and went out on the piazza to

take a more careful survey of the premises and make up my mind where I would sleep.

Lying across the high stoop was a long white object, which appeared, in the darkness, to be a woman in her nightgown, with her head raised a little on the sill of a disused door. I stepped over her once in going down-stairs to the street, and wondered what calamity of war had reduced a woman to the necessity of sleeping in such a place and in circumstances of such hardship and privation. I was just discussing with Dr. Hubbell the possibility of getting the United States Signal Corps man in the telegraph office to signal our steamer for a boat, regardless of the high surf, when the long white figure on the floor rose, with an unmistakably masculine grunt, and remarked, with a slight English accent, that he did not think there was any possibility of getting off to a ship in a small boat, inasmuch as he had been trying for twenty-four hours to get on board of his own vessel and had not succeeded yet. The figure proved to be that of Lord Alfred Paget, naval observer for the British government, and what I had taken in the darkness for the white gown of a woman was his white-duck uniform. After discussing the situation for a few moments, and declaring discontentedly that our engineer corps had had time enough to build six piers and yet had not finished one, he lay down on the floor again, without blanket, pillow, or overcoat, rested his head on the sill of the disused door, and apparently went to sleep, while I debated in my mind the question whether I had better sleep with him on the floor of the piazza, and take the chance of getting yellow fever from a possibly infected building, or lie out on the ground, where I might be stepped on by prowling Cuban refugees, or run over by a mule-team coming in from the front. I finally decided that sleeping accommodations which were good enough for Lord Alfred were good enough for me, and, just as the moon was rising

over the high, rocky rampart east of the village, I rolled
myself up in my blanket and lay down on the floor against
the piazza rail.   Dr. Hubbell slept on the counter of the
money-order division of the post-office, while Dr. Egan, without blanket or pillow, stretched himself out on the dirty
planks below.

We were all up at daybreak, and making my toilet by
tightening my belt and putting on my mud-spattered pith
helmet, I went down to the water's edge to try to find some
means of communicating with the ship.   During my absence
at the front there had evidently been strong winds and heavy
seas, for the strip of beach was covered with the wrecks of
lighters which had been smashed while trying to land supplies
in the surf, and a large steam lighter-launch, loaded with
twenty tons or more of hard bread, beans, etc., was lying on
the bottom, half submerged, about fifty yards from shore, with
the sea breaking over her.   The small temporary pier at
which I landed when I went to the front had been completely
demolished and swept away, but another stronger one was in
process of construction.

The most serious embarrassments with which the army of
invasion had to contend after it reached the coast and began
its march on Santiago were: first, the extreme difficulty of
landing supplies in a place like Siboney, where there was
neither pier nor shelter, and where the beach was lashed a
large part of the time by a high and dangerous surf; and,
second, the difficulty of getting such supplies to the front over
a single line of very bad road, with an insufficient number of
mules and army wagons.   If these two difficulties had been
foreseen and provided for there would not have been so many
smashed lighters and launches on the beach, and the soldiers
at the front would not have lived so much of the time on
short rations, nor have been compelled to boil water and cook
their rations in coffee-cups and tomato-cans, as they had to do

throughout the campaign. The difficulty of landing supplies on that exposed and surf-beaten coast might have been anticipated, it seems to me, and provided for. The war-ships of Sampson's and Schley's fleets were there long before General Shafter's army left Tampa, and their commanders must have seen, I think, that to get supplies ashore through the surf at any point between Santiago and Guantanamo Bay would be extremely difficult and hazardous, and would proba-bly require the use of special engineering devices and appli-ances. The prevailing winds there are from the east and southeast, and from such winds the little indentations of the coast at Siboney and Daiquiri afforded no protection what-ever. A strong breeze raised a sea which might amount to nothing outside, but which was very troublesome, if not dangerous, to loaded boats and lighters as soon as they reached the line where it began to break in surf. The water was very deep close to shore; it was difficult, therefore, to construct a pier of any great length; and even if there had been a long and solid pier, small boats and lighters could not have discharged cargo upon it with any safety while they were being tossed up and down and dashed against it by a heavy sea.

I do not pretend to be an expert in such matters, but in watching the landing of supplies here, both from our own steamer and from the army transports, it seemed to me that what is known, I believe, as a "cable hoist" might have been used to advantage if it had been provided in time. It is a contrivance resembling the cable and car employed by life-saving crews on our coasts to bring shipwrecked sailors ashore under similar conditions; or, to use a comparison that is more familiar, it is a reproduction on a large scale of the traveling cash-boxes on wires used in large department stores. If a suitable transport had been anchored outside the line of surf, fifty or seventy-five yards from the beach, and a steel cable stretched from it to a strong mast on shore, I do not see any reason why cargo might not have been carried over the cable in a suspended car or cars with much greater rapidity and safety than it was carried in lighters. Such devices are used, I think, at several points on the western coast of South America for putting guano and phosphates on board of vessels where communication with the shore is hazardous and uncertain on account of swell or surf.

The second difficulty, namely, that of transportation to the front, might have been avoided by taking to Cuba a larger number of wagons and mules. Our army before Santiago suffered for want of a great many things that the soldiers had with them on the transports, but that were not landed and carried promptly forward. Among such things were large tents, rubber blankets, camp-kettles, and large cooking-utensils generally. "What's the use of telling us to drink only boiled water," said an officer of the Seventh Infantry to me, "when we have n't anything bigger than a coffee-cup or an old tomato-can to boil it in, or to keep it in after it has been boiled? They tell us also that we must sleep in hammocks, not get wet if we can help it, and change our under-clothes whenever we do get wet. That's all very well, but there is n't a hammock in my company. I have n't any rubber blanket or spare underclothes myself, and I don't believe any of my soldiers have. They made us leave at Tampa everything that we could possibly dispense with, and then, when we got here, they did n't land and send with us even the indispensable things that we had on the transports."

The complaint of the officer was a perfectly just one, and I heard many more like it. The insufficient and inadequate provision for the care and feeding of the wounded at the field-hospital of the Fifth Army-Corps, which I have tried to describe in the preceding chapter, was due largely to the inability of General Shafter's commissaries and quartermasters to cope successfully with the two great difficulties above indicated, namely, landing from the steamers and transportation to the front. The hospital corps had supplies on the vessels at Siboney, but as everything could not possibly be landed and carried forward at once, preference was given to ammunition and rations for able-bodied soldiers rather than to tents, blankets, and invalid food for the wounded. I do not mean to be understood as saying that the hospital-corps men had even on the transports everything that they needed in order to enable them to take proper care of the eight hundred or one thousand wounded who were thrown on their hands in the course of forty-eight hours. I do not know whether they had or not. Neither do I mean to say that the commissaries and quartermasters did not do all that they possibly could to land and forward supplies of all kinds. I mean only that, as a result of our inability to surmount difficulties promptly, our army at the front was not properly equipped and our wounded were not adequately cared for.

The hospital corps and quartermaster's and commissary departments of the army, however, were not alone in their failure to anticipate and fully provide for these difficulties. The Red Cross itself was in no better case. There was perhaps more excuse for us, because when we fitted out we did not know where the army was going nor what it proposed to do, and we had been assured by the surgeon-general and by General Shafter that, so far as the care of sick and wounded soldiers was concerned, our services would not be required. We expected, however, that they would be, and could we have known in what field and under what conditions our army was going to move and fight, we should probably have had, in some directions, a better, or at least a more suitable, equipment. If we had had at Siboney on June 26 half a dozen army wagons, an equal number of saddle-horses, and forty or fifty mules of our own, we should have been in much better condition than we were to cope with the difficulties of the situation. But for the assistance of the army, which helped us out with transportation, notwithstanding its own limited resources, we should not have been able to establish a Red Cross station at the front in time to coöperate with the hospital corps after the battle of July 1–2, nor should we have been able to send food to the fifteen thousand refugees from Santiago who fled, hungry and destitute, to the right wing of our army at Caney when General Shafter threatened to bombard the city. For the opportunity to get into the field we were indebted to the general in command, to his hospital corps, and to the officers of his army; and we desire most gratefully to acknowledge and thank them for the helping hand that they extended to us when we had virtually no transportation whatever of our own.

When we returned to the *State of Texas* on July 9, the situation, so far as Red Cross relief-work on the southeastern coast of Cuba is concerned, was briefly as follows: We had a station in the field-hospital of the Fifth Army-Corps at the front, and a hospital of our own in Siboney, with twenty-five beds attended by six trained nurses under direction of Dr. Lesser. We also had entire charge of one ward of thirty beds in the general hospital directed by General Lagarde. We were feeding refugees at several points on a line extending east and west nearly sixty miles from the right wing of our army at Caney to the naval station at Guantanamo Bay, and at the latter place we had landed fifteen thousand rations to be distributed under the general direction of Captain McCalla, of the cruiser *Marblehead*, and General Perez, commanding the Cuban forces in the Guantanamo district. To the refugees from Santiago at Caney—about fifteen thousand in number and mostly women and children —we had forwarded, chiefly in army wagons furnished by General Shafter, six or eight tons of food, and were sending more as fast as we could land it in lighters through the surf. Mr. Elwell, of Miss Barton's staff, was taking care of two or three thousand refugees at Firmeza, a small village in the hills back of Siboney, and we hoped soon to enter the harbor of Santiago, discharge the cargo of the *State of Texas* at a pier, assort it in a warehouse, and prosecute the work of relief upon a more extensive scale. Our sanguine anticipations, however, were not to be realized as soon as we hoped they would be, and our relief-work was practically suspended on July 10, as the result of an outbreak of yellow fever.

The circumstances in which this fever first made its appearance were as follows: When the army landed at Siboney it found there a dirty little Cuban village of from twelve to twenty deserted houses, situated at the bottom of a wedge-shaped cleft in the long, rocky rampart which forms the coast-line between Siboney and Morro Castle, and at the mouth of a low, swampy, malarious ravine or valley extending back into the foot-hills, and opening upon the sea through the notch. The site of the village, from a sanitary point of view, was a very bad one, not only because it was low and confined, but because in the valley immediately back of it there were a number of stagnant, foul-smelling ponds and pools, half overgrown with rank tropical vegetation, and so full of decaying organic matter that when I passed them for the first time on my way to the front I instinctively held my breath as much as possible because the very air from them seemed poisonous. The houses of the village, as a result of long neglect, had become as objectionable from a sanitary point of view as the location in which they stood. They were rather large, well-built, one-story frame houses with zinc roofs, and were erected, if I mistake not, by the Spanish-American Iron Company for the accommodation of its native employees. Originally they must have been very commodious and comfortable buildings, but through the neglect and untidiness of their later occupants they had become so dirty that no self-respecting human being would be willing to live in them.

Such were the village and the houses of Siboney when the army landed there on June 23. In view of the nature of the Cuban climate during the rainy season, and the danger of infection from abandoned houses whose history was entirely unknown, and within whose walls there might have been yellow fever, it was obviously somebody's duty not only to clean up the place as far as possible, but to decide whether the houses should be burned to the ground as probable sources of infection, or, on the other hand, washed out, fumigated, and used. The surgeons of the blockading fleet recommended that the buildings be destroyed, for the reason that if Siboney were to be the army's base of supplies it would be imprudent to run the risk of infection by allowing them to be used. Instead of acting upon this advice, however, the army officers in command at Siboney not only allowed the houses to be occupied from the very first, but put men into them without either disinfecting them or cleaning their dirty floors. Chlorid of lime was not used anywhere, and the foul privies immediately back of and adjoining the houses were permitted to stand in the condition in which they were found, so that the daily rains washed the excrement from them down under the floors to saturate further the already contaminated soil.

When we returned from the front on July 9, we found the condition of the village worse than ever. No attempt, apparently, had been made to clean or disinfect it; no sanitary precautions had been taken or health regulations enforced; hundreds of incredibly dirty and ragged Cubans —some of them employed in discharging the government transports and some of them merely loafers, camp-followers, and thieves—thronged the beach, evacuating their bowels in the bushes and throwing remnants of food about on the ground to rot in the hot sunshine; there was a dead and decomposing mule in one of the stagnant pools behind the village, and the whole place stank. If, under such conditions, an epidemic of fever had not broken out, it would have been so strange as to border on the miraculous. Nature alone would probably have brought it about, but when nature and man coöperated the result was certain. On July 8 the army surgeons reported three cases of yellow fever among the sick in the abandoned Spanish houses on shore. On the 10th the number of cases had increased to thirty, and included Dr. Lesser, chief surgeon of the Red Cross, and his wife, two Red Cross nurses, and Mrs. Trumbull White, wife of the correspondent of the Chicago "Record," who had been working as a nurse in the Red Cross hospital.

On the 11th General Miles arrived from Washington, and on ascertaining the state of affairs ordered the burning of every house in the village. I doubt very much whether this step was necessary or judicious, for the reason that it was taken too late. If there was any reason to believe, when the army first began to disembark at Siboney, that the houses of the village were likely to become sources of infection, they should have been burned or fumigated at once. To burn them after they had set yellow fever afloat in that malarious and polluted atmosphere was like locking the stable door after the horse has been stolen. But it is very questionable whether they should have been burned at any time. In a country like eastern Cuba, where at intervals of two or three days throughout the wet season there is a tropical downpour of rain which deluges the ground and beats through the most closely woven tent, a house with a tight zinc roof and a dry floor is a most valuable possession, and it should not be destroyed if there is any way of disinfecting it and making it a safe place of human habitation. All the evidence obtainable in Santi-

ago was to the effect that these houses were not infected
with yellow fever; but even if they had been, it was quite
possible, I think, to save them and make them useful.   If,
when the army landed, the best of the buildings had been
thoroughly cleaned and then fumigated by shutting them
up tightly and burning sulphur and other suitable chemical
substances in them, the disease-germs that they contained
might have been destroyed.   Convict barges saturated with
the germs of smallpox, typhus, dysentery, and all sorts of
infectious and contagious diseases are treated in this way
in Siberia, and there is no reason why houses should not be
so purified in Cuba.   General Miles and his chief surgeon
decided, however, that the whole village should be burned,
and burned it was.   The postal, telegraph, and signal-service
officers were turned out of their quarters and put into tents;
a yellow-fever camp was established in the hills about two
miles north of Siboney; more hospital tents and tent-flies
were pitched along the sea-coast west of the notch; and as
fast as sick and wounded soldiers could be removed from the
condemned houses and put under canvas or sent to the
yellow-fever camp, the houses were destroyed.

In view of the fact that yellow fever had made its appearance in the army before Santiago as well as at Siboney,
Miss Barton, acting under the advice and direction of Major
Wood, chief surgeon of the First Division hospital, abandoned the Red Cross station at the front, brought all its
equipment and supplies back to the sea-coast, and put them
again on board the *State of Texas*.   She also decided not to
allow fever-stricken employees of the Red Cross to be cared
for on board the steamer, and Dr. and Mrs. Lesser and two
nurses were therefore carried on their cots to a railroad-train
and transported to the yellow-fever camp two miles away.
I went through the fever hospital where they lay just before
they were removed, and made up my mind—very ignorantly

11

and presumptuously, perhaps—that neither they nor any of the patients whom I saw had yellow fever, either in a mild form or in any form whatever. They seemed to me to have nothing more than calenture, brought on by overwork, a malarious atmosphere, and a bad sanitary environment. Mrs. White, who was also said to have yellow fever, recovered in three days, just in time to escape being sent to the yellow-fever camp with Dr. and Mrs. Lesser. I have no doubt that there were some yellow-fever cases among the sick who were sent to the camp at the time when the village of Siboney was burned, but I did not happen to see any of them, and it is the opinion of many persons who are far better qualified to judge than I, that yellow-fever cases and calenture cases were lumped together without much discrimination, and that the latter greatly outnumbered the former.

On July 15 the number of so-called yellow-fever cases exceeded one hundred, and the most energetic measures were being taken by the medical authorities on shore to prevent the further spread of the disease. Everything that could possibly hold or transmit infection was burned, including my blankets, mackintosh-cape, etc., which I had accidentally left in the post-office overnight, as well as all the baggage and personal effects of the postal clerks. Mr. Brewer, the postmaster, died of the fever, Mr. Kempner, the assistant postmaster, was reduced to sleeping in a camp-chair out of doors without overcoat or blanket, and the telegraph and telephone operators worked night and day in a damp, badly ventilated tent, with their feet literally in pools of mud and water.

On July 15 we heard at Siboney that Santiago had surrendered, and on the following day we steamed down to the mouth of Santiago harbor, with a faint hope that we might be permitted to enter. Admiral Sampson, however, informed us that the surrender, although agreed upon, had not yet taken place, and that it would be impossible for us to enter the harbor until after Morro Castle and the shore batteries had been evacuated.   We then sailed for Guantanamo Bay, with the intention of landing more supplies for the refugees in that district; but inasmuch as we had been lying in the fever-infected port of Siboney, Captain McCalla, who came out to the mouth of the bay in a steam-launch to meet us, refused to take the supplies, and would not let us communicate with the shore.   On the night of July 16, therefore, we returned to Siboney, and at noon on the 17th we were again off Morro Castle, waiting for an opportunity to enter the harbor.

CHAPTER XIV

ENTERING SANTIAGO HARBOR

AS soon as possible after our return from Guantanamo, Miss Barton sent a note to Admiral Sampson, on board the flagship *New York*, saying that, as the inhabitants of the city were reported to be in a starving condition, she hoped that food would be allowed to go in with the forces. The admiral promptly replied: "The food shall enter in advance of the forces; you may go in this afternoon." Almost any other naval commander, after destroying a hostile fleet and reducing all the batteries that defended a hostile city, would have wished to crown his victory and enjoy his triumph by entering the harbor in advance of all other vessels and on one of his own ships of war; but Admiral Sampson, with the modesty and generosity characteristic of a great and noble nature, waived his right to be the first to enter the city, and sent in the *State of Texas*, flying the flag of the Red Cross and carrying food and relief for the wounded, the starving, and the dying.

An officer from the *New York* had been at work all day locating and removing the submarine mines in the narrow part of the channel just north of Morro Castle; but there were still four that had not been exploded. As they were electrical mines, however, and as the cables connecting them with the shore had been cut, they were no longer dangerous, and there was nothing to prevent the entrance of the *State of Texas* except the narrowness of the unobstructed part of the channel.   The collier *Merrimac,* sunk by Lieutenant Hobson and his men, was not in a position to interfere seriously with navigation.   Cervera's fleet ran out without any serious trouble on the western side of her, and there was no reason why Admiral Sampson, if he decided to force an entrance, should not run in, following the same course.   In order to prevent this, the Spaniards, on the night of July 4, attempted to sink the old war-ship *Reina Mercedes* in such a position that she would close the channel at a point where it is very narrow, between the *Merrimac* and the entrance to the harbor.   The ships of the blockading fleet, however, saw her coming out about midnight, turned their big guns upon her, and sank her with six- and eight-inch projectiles before she could get into position.   She drifted around parallel with the shore, and lay half submerged on the eastern side of the channel, about one hundred and fifty yards from the entrance and three hundred or three hundred and fifty yards from the *Merrimac.*

At four o'clock Admiral Sampson sent Lieutenant Capehart on board the *State of Texas* to give Captain Young all necessary information with regard to the channel and the mines, and a few moments later, under the guidance of a Cuban pilot, we steamed slowly in under the gray, frowning battlements of Morro Castle.   As we approached it I had an opportunity to see, for the first time, the nature and extent of the damage done to it by the guns of Admiral Sampson's fleet, and I was glad to find that, although it had been somewhat battered on its southern or sea face, its architectural picturesqueness had not been destroyed or even seriously impaired.   To an observer looking at it from the south, it has, in general outline, the appearance of three huge cubes or rectangular masses of gray masonry, put together in such a way that the largest cube occupies the crest of the bold, almost precipitous bluff which forms the eastern side of the entrance to the harbor, while the other two descend from it in colossal steps of diminishing size toward an escarpment in the hillside seventy-five or a hundred feet below, where appear five or six square, grated doors, leading, apparently, to a row of subterranean ammunition-vaults. Underneath the escarpment is a zigzag flight of steps, screened at exposed points by what seem to be comparatively recent walls, or curtains of masonry, much lighter in color than the walls of the castle itself. Still lower down, at the base of the bluff, are two or three huge, dark caves into which the swell of the Caribbean Sea rolls with a dull, reverberating roar. The height of the castle above the water appears to be one hundred and fifty or two hundred feet. There are very few embrasures, or port-holes, in the gray, lichen-stained walls of the old fortification, and, so far as I could see, it had no armament whatever except two or three guns mounted en barbette on the parapet of the uppermost cube, or bastion.

As a defensive work the Morro Castle of Santiago has no importance or significance whatever, and its complete destruction would not have made it any easier for Admiral Sampson to force an entrance to the harbor. It is the oldest Morro, however, in Cuba; and as a relic of the past, and an interesting and attractive feature in a landscape already picturesque, it has the highest possible value, and I am more than glad that it was not destroyed. There was no reason, really, for bombarding it at all, because it was perfectly harmless. The defenses of Santiago that were really dangerous and effective were the submarine mines in the channel and the earthwork batteries east and west of the entrance to the harbor. Morro was huge, formidable-looking, and impressive to the eye and the imagination, but the horizontal reddish streaks of freshly turned earth along the crests of the hills east and west of it had ten times its offensive power. I saw the last Spanish soldier leave the castle at noon on Sunday, and when we passed it, soon after four o'clock, its flag was gone, its walls were deserted, and buzzards were soaring in circles about its little corner turrets.

About one hundred and fifty yards inside the entrance to the harbor we passed the wreck of the *Reina Mercedes*, lying close to the shore, on the right-hand side of the channel, with her port rail under water and her masts sloping at an angle of forty-five degrees to the westward. Two brass-bound sea-chests and a pile of signal-flags were lying on her deck aft, and she had not been touched, apparently, since she was sunk by the guns of our battle-ships on the night of July 4.

Three hundred or three hundred and fifty yards farther in we passed what the sailors of the fleet call "Hobson's choice," the steam-collier *Merrimac*. She lay in deep water, about midway from shore to shore, and all that could be seen of her were the tops of her masts and about two feet of her smoke-stack. If the channel were narrow and were in the middle of the passage, she would have blocked it completely; but apparently it is wider than her length, and vessels draw-ing twenty feet or more of water could go around her with-out touching bottom. It is a little remarkable that both combatants should have tried to obstruct this channel and that neither should have succeeded. The location chosen by the Spaniards seemed to me to be a better one than that selected by Hobson; but it is so near the mouth of the har-bor that the chance of reaching it with a vessel in the glare of our search-lights and under the fire of our guns was a very slight one. The *Reina Mercedes* reached it, but was disabled before she could get into position.[1]

1 The point where the *Merrimac* was sunk was not the point selected by Lieutenant Hobson, who aimed to sink her farther out, and more nearly in the position reached by the *Reina Mercedes*, but was prevented from doing so, as described in his article in "The Century" for January, 1899.—EDITOR.

Beyond the *Merrimac* the entrance to the harbor widens a little, but the shores continue high and steep for a distance of a mile or more.   At intervals of a few hundred yards, however, beautiful deep coves run back into the high land on either side, and at the head of every one the eye catches a glimpse of a little settlement of half a dozen houses with red-tiled roofs, or a country villa shaded by palms and half hidden in shrubbery and flowers.   One does not often see, in the tropics or elsewhere, a harbor entrance that is more striking and picturesque than the watery gateway which leads from the ocean to the spacious upper bay of Santiago. It does not look like an inlet of the sea, but suggests rather a tranquil, winding river, shut in by high, steep ramparts of greenery, with here and there an opening to a beautiful lateral cove, where the dark masses of chaparral are relieved by clumps of graceful, white-stemmed palms and lighted up by the solid sheets of bright-red flowers which hide the foliage of the *flamboyam*, or flame-tree.

As ours was the first vessel that had entered the harbor in nearly two months, and as we were flying the Red Cross flag, our arrival naturally caused great excitement in all the little settlements and at all the villas along the shores. Men, women, and children ran down to the water's edge, waving their hats and handkerchiefs or brandishing their arms in joyous welcome, and even old, gray-haired, and feeble women, who could not get as far as the shore, stood in front of their little houses, now gazing at us in half-incredulous amazement, and then crossing themselves devoutly with bowed heads, as if thanking God that siege and starvation were over and help and food at hand.

About half-way between Morro Castle and Santiago there is a high, bare, flat-topped hill, or mesa, called the Behia, on which there is a signal-station with a mast for the display of flags.   Just before this hill is reached the channel widens, and, as the steamer rounds a high, bold promontory, the beautiful upper bay comes into view, like a great placid lake framed in a magnificent amphitheater of mountains, with a fringe of cocoanut-palms here and there to break the level shore-line, and a few splashes of vivid red where flame-trees stand out in brilliant relief against the varied green of the mountain background. Two miles away, on the eastern side of the harbor, appeared the city of Santiago—a sloping expanse of red-tiled roofs, green mango-trees, and twin-belfried Spanish churches, rising from the water's edge to the crest of a range of low hills which bound the bay on that side. A week or ten days earlier I had seen the town from the rifle-pits of the Rough Riders at the front of our army; but its appearance from the harbor was so different that I could hardly recognize it as the same place. Seen from the intrenched hill occupied by General Wheeler's brigade, it appeared to consist mainly of barracks, hospitals, and shed-like buildings flying the flag of the Red Cross, and had no beauty or picturesqueness whatever; but from the water it seemed to be rather an interesting and attractive Spanish-American town.

As we entered the upper bay and caught sight of the city, some of our Red Cross nurses who were standing with Miss Barton in a little group at the bow of the steamer felt impelled to give expression to their feelings in some way, and, acting upon a sudden impulse and without premeditation, they began to sing in unison "Praise God, from whom all blessings flow." Never before, probably, had the doxology been heard on the waters of Santiago harbor, and it must have been more welcome music to the crowds assembling on shore than the thunder of Admiral Sampson's cannon and the jarring rattle of machine-guns from the advance line of our army. The doxology was followed by "My country, 't is of thee," in which the whole ship's company joined with a thrill of patriotic pride; and to this music the *State of Texas* glided swiftly up the harbor to her anchorage. It was then about half-past five. The daily afternoon thunder-shower had just passed over the city, and its shadow still lay heavy on the splendid group of peaks west of the bay; but the light-green slopes of the grassy mountains to the eastward, as well as the red roofs and gray church steeples of the city, were bathed in the warm yellow light of the sinking sun.

Before we had fairly come to anchor, a great crowd had assembled on the pier nearest to us, and in less than five minutes half a dozen small boats were alongside, filled with people anxious to know whether we had brought food and when we would begin to distribute it. Many of them said that they had not tasted bread in weeks, and all agreed that there was nothing to eat in the city except rice, and very little of that. We told them that we should begin discharging the cargo of the *State of Texas* early on the following morning and should be in a position to feed ten thousand people within the next twenty-four hours. The normal population of the city at that time was about fifty thousand, but a large part of it had fled to Caney and other suburban villages to escape the bombardment, and more than half the houses were closed and deserted. General Shafter had entered the city with a single regiment—the Ninth Infantry—at noon, and had raised the American flag over the palace of the Spanish governor.

CHAPTER XV

THE CAPTURED CITY

WE lay at anchor all Sunday night off the foot of the street known as Calle Baja de la Marina, and early on Monday morning steamed up to the most spacious and convenient pier in the city, made fast our lines, and began to discharge cargo. The dock and warehouse facilities of Santiago are fairly good. They are not so extensive as those of an American seaport of equal importance, but so far as they go they leave little to be desired. The pier at which the *State of Texas* lay was spacious and well built; an iron tramway ran from it to the customs warehouse, and, with the help of one hundred stevedores, Mr. Warner, of Miss Barton's staff, found it possible to unload and store from three hundred and twenty-five to three hundred and fifty tons of foodstuffs per day. As soon as the steamer had made fast her lines a great crowd of forlorn-looking men and children, clothed in the loose, dirty white-cotton shirts and trousers and battered straw hats which make up the costume of the lower classes, assembled on the pier to stare at the newcomers and watch the unloading of the ship. They were of all ages and complexions, from coal-black, grizzle-headed old negroes leaning on canes to half-starved and half-naked Cuban children, whose tallowy faces and distended abdomens were unmistakable evidences of fever and famine. They were not, as

171

a rule, emaciated, nor did they seem to be in the last stages
of starvation; but the eagerness with which they crowded
about the open ports of the steamer, and watched the bags
of beans, rice, and corn-meal as they were brought out by the
stevedores and placed on the little flat-cars of the tramway,
showed that at least they were desperately hungry.   Now
and then a few beans, or a few grains of rice, would escape
from one of the bags through a small rip or tear, and in an
instant half a dozen little children would be scrambling for
them, collecting them carefully one by one, and putting them
into their hats or tying them up in their shirt-tails and the
hems of their tattered frocks.   In one instance half a bushel
or more of corn-meal escaped from a torn bag and lay in a
heap on the dirty pier.   One of the prowling Cuban boys
espied it, gathered up a hatful of it, and then looked around
for something in which he could put the remainder.   Failing
to see anything that could be utilized as a receptacle, he
seemed for a moment to be in despair; but presently a bright
thought flashed into his mind, and was reflected in his thin,
eager, street-Arab face.   Taking out of his pocket two bits
of dirty string, he tied his loose cotton trousers tightly around
his ankles, and then, unbuttoning his waist-band, he began
scooping up the corn-meal from the filthy planks and shoveling it into his baggy breeches.   Five minutes later he wad-
dled off the pier in triumph, looking, so far as his legs were
concerned, like a big, badly stuffed sawdust doll, or a half-
starved gamin suffering from elephantiasis.

   As the day advanced, the number of men and children who
crowded about the steamer watching for opportunities to
pilfer or pick up food became so great that it was necessary
to clear the pier and put a guard of soldiers there to exclude
the public altogether.   Then the hungry people formed in a
dense mass in the street opposite the steamer, and stood there
in the blazing sunshine for hours, watching the little flat-cars

loaded with provisions as they were rolled past to the warehouse. From an English cable-operator, who came down to the pier, we learned that for weeks there had been nothing in the city to eat except rice, and that the supply even of that was limited. Hard-bread crackers had sold as high as one dollar apiece and canned meat at four dollars a can, and many well-to-do families had not tasted bread, meat, or milk in more than a month.

Although there was said to be little or no yellow fever in Santiago, the captain of the *State of Texas* decided to quarantine the steamer against the shore, and gave notice to all on board that if any person left the ship he could not return to it. This made going ashore a serious matter, because there was virtually nothing to eat in the city, and no place for a stranger to stay, and if one cut loose from the steamer he might find himself without shelter and without any means whatever of subsistence. We had on board, fortunately, a young American named Elwell, who had lived several years in Santiago, and was well acquainted not only with its resources, but with a large number of its citizens. He said that there was a club there known as the Anglo-American Club, organized and supported by the foreign merchants of the city and the English cable-operators. Of this club he was one of the organizers and charter members, and although it had been closed during the blockade and siege, it would probably be reopened at once, and with an introduction from him I could get a room in it. He doubted whether the steward could give me anything to eat, but I could take food enough with me to last for a day or two, and as soon as possible arrangements would be made to supply the club with provisions from the *State of Texas*. Encouraged by this statement of the possibilities, I decided on Tuesday morning to abandon the steamer and trust myself to the tender mercies of the city and the Anglo-American Club. Hastily packing up a couple of hand-bags, and hiring a ragged, dirty Cuban to carry them and act in the capacity of guide, I left the ship, elbowed my way through the crowd of people at the head of the pier, and entered one of the narrow, ill-paved, and incredibly dirty streets which lead upward from the water-front to the higher part of the city.

The first impression made by Santiago upon the newcomer in July, 1898, was one of dirt, disorder, and neglect. It always had the reputation of being the dirtiest city in Cuba, and at the time of the surrender it was at its worst. I hardly know how to give an adequate idea of it to one who is not familiar with Spanish-American cities and architecture, but I will try. In the first place, the site of the city is the slope of a hill which falls rather steeply to the water on the eastern side of the bay. The most important streets, such as Enramadas and Calle Baja de la Marina, extend up and down the slope at right angles to the water-front, and are crossed at fairly regular intervals by narrower streets or alleys running horizontally along the hillside, following its contour and dipping down here and there into the gullies or ravines which stretch from the crest of the hill to the shore of the bay. As a result of the natural configuration of the ground there is hardly a street in the city that is even approximately level except the wide boulevard which forms the water-front. The east and west streets climb a rather steep grade from this boulevard to the crest of the elevation, and the north and south streets run up and down over the ridges and into the gullies of the undulating slope, so that wherever one goes one finds one's self either ascending or descending a hill. The widest streets in the city—exclusive of the Cristina Boulevard—are hardly more than thirty feet from curb to curb, and the narrowest do not exceed fifteen. The pavements at the time of my visit were made of unbroken stones and rocks from the size of one's fist to the size of a bushel-basket; the sidewalks averaged from two to three and a half feet in width, and the gutters were open drains, broken here and there by holes and pockets filled with decaying garbage and dirty, foul-smelling water. Piles of mango-skins, ashes, old bones, filthy rags, dung, and kitchen refuse of all sorts lay here and there on the broken and neglected pavements, poisoning the air with foul exhalations and affording sustenance to hundreds of buzzards and myriads of flies; little rills of foul, discolored water trickled into the open gutters at intervals from the kitchens and cesspools of the adjoining houses; every hole and crevice in the uneven pavement was filled with rotting organic matter washed down from the higher levels by the frequent rains, and when the sea-breeze died away at night the whole atmosphere of the city seemed to be pervaded by a sickly, indescribable odor of corruption and decay. I had expected, as a matter of course, to find Santiago in bad sanitary condition, but I must confess that I felt a little sinking of the heart when I first breathed that polluted air and realized that for me there was no return to the ship and that I must henceforth eat, work, and sleep in that fever-breeding environment. In a long and tolerably varied experience in Russia, the Caucasus, Asia Minor, and European Turkey, I have never seen streets so filthy as in some parts of this Cuban city, nor have I ever encountered such a variety of abominable stenches as I met with in the course of my short walk from the steamer to the Anglo-American Club.

The houses and shops which stood along these narrow, dirty streets were generally one story in height, with red-tiled roofs, high, blank walls of stuccoed or plastered brick covered with a calcimine wash of pale blue or dirty yellow, large, heavy plank doors, and equally large, unglazed windows protected by prison gratings of iron bars and closed with tight inner shutters. There were no trees in the streets, —

at least, in the business part of the city,—no yards in front
of the houses, no shop-windows for the display of goods, and
no windows of glass even in the best private houses.   I
cannot remember to have seen a pane of window-glass in
this part of Cuba.   The windows of both shops and houses
were mere rectangular openings in the wall, six feet by ten
or twelve feet in size, filled with heavy iron gratings or protected by ornamental metal scrollwork embedded all around
in the solid masonry.   These barred windows, with the heavy
plank doors, thick stuccoed walls, and complete absence of
architectural ornament, made the narrow, muddy streets look
almost as gloomy and forbidding as if they were shut in by
long rows of Russian prisons.   The natural gloominess of
the city, due to the narrowness of the streets and the character of the architecture, was heightened at the time of the
surrender by the absence of a large part of the population
and the consequent shutting up of more than half the houses.
Thousands of men, women, and children had fled to Caney
and other suburban villages to escape the bombardment, and
the long rows of closed and empty houses in some of the
streets suggested a city stricken by pestilence and abandoned.
At the time when we landed there was not a shop or a store
open in any part of Santiago.   Here and there one might
see a colored woman peering out through the grated window
of a private house, or two or three naked children with tallowy complexions and swollen abdomens playing in the
muddy gutter, but as a rule the houses were shut and barred
and the streets deserted.

The first pleasant impression that I received in Santiago
was made by the Anglo-American Club.   It was situated on
a narrow, dirty street behind the Spanish theater, in a very
low, disreputable part of the city, and did not impress me,
at first sight, as being likely to afford even the ordinary
necessaries and comforts of life, much less the luxuries and

conveniences suggested to the mind of a city man by the word "club." But external appearance in a Spanish-American city is often deceptive, and it was so in this case. Opposite the rear or stage entrance of the theater, where half a dozen soldiers of the Ninth Infantry were cooking breakfast in the street, my ragged Cuban guide turned into a dark vaulted passage which looked as if it might be one of the approaches to a jail. "It can't be possible," I said to myself, "that this damp, gloomy tunnel is the entrance to a club; the guide must have misunderstood the directions given him."

But the guide was right. At a distance of thirty-five or forty feet from the street the vaulted passage opened into a paved patio, or court,—a sort of large, square well, —in the center of which stood a green, thrifty, broad-leaved banana-tree, fifteen or twenty feet in height. From the corners of this court, on the side opposite the street entrance, two broad flights of steps led up to what seemed to be a hanging garden of greenery and flowers, shut in on all sides by piazzas and galleries. Climbing one of these flights of steps, I found myself in a second and higher patio, shaded by large mango- and mamonilla-trees, brightened by borders of flowering shrubs and plants, and filled with the fragrance of roses, geraniums, and pomegranate blossoms. The transition from the heat, filth, and sickening odors of the narrow street to the seclusion and shady coolness of this flower-scented patio was as delightful as it was sudden and unexpected. I could hardly have been more surprised if I had entered what I supposed to be a Siberian forwarding prison, and found myself in a conservatory of tropical plants and flowers. Around three sides of the patio were spacious piazzas in two tiers, and upon these piazzas opened the living-rooms of the club,—about twenty in number,—like the boxes or stalls in the galleries of a European theater. On the southern side

12

of the patio was a large dining-room, and beyond this, occupying the whole width of the building and overlooking the street from a projecting balcony, was the reading-room. This was a high, cool, spacious apartment comfortably furnished with easy-chairs, pictures, maps, hanging bookcases, a big library table covered with periodicals, and an American piano. The periodicals were not of very recent date, and the piano was somewhat out of tune, but I was so delighted with the shady, flower-bordered courtyard and the comfort and apparent cleanliness of the club as a whole that I felt no disposition to be hypercritical. To find such a haven of refuge at all in a city like Santiago was unexpected good fortune.

To one who is unfamiliar with the distinctive peculiarities of Spanish-American architecture, nothing, at first, is more surprising than the contrast between the gloomy and unpromising exterior of a Cuban residence and the luxury and architectural beauty which one often finds hidden behind its grated windows and thick stuccoed walls. It is more surprising and striking in Santiago, perhaps, than in most Spanish-American cities, on account of the narrowness and filthiness of the streets on which the houses even of the wealthiest citizens stand. In the course of the first week that I spent in the city I had occasion to enter a number of Spanish houses of the better class, and I never failed to experience a little shock of surprise when I went from what looked like a dirty and neglected back alley into what seemed to be a jail, and found myself suddenly in a beautiful Moorish court, paved with marble, shaded by graceful, feathery palms, cooled by a fountain set in an oasis of greenery and flowers, and surrounded by rows of slender stone columns, and piazzas twenty-five feet in width. The wealthy Spaniard or Cuban wastes no money in beautifying the outside of his house, because, standing as it does on a narrow, dirty street, it cannot be made attractive or imposing by any possible method of architectural treatment; but upon the ornamentation and embellishment of the patio, or interior court, he lavishes all his taste and skill.   The patio of the Anglo-American Club was not nearly as large and attractive as the courtyards of private residences on Heredia Street, to which I gained access later, but as it was the first house of the kind that I had seen in Cuba, it made a very pleasant impression upon me.

Upon presentation of my introduction from Mr. Elwell, the steward gave me one of the best rooms in the club, but said that it would be impossible to furnish me with food until he could get a cook and servants.   The club had been closed for weeks; all of its employees had fled from the city, and he had been left entirely alone.   I told him that I would try to forage for myself,—at least, for the present,—and that, if worst should come to worst, I could live two or three days on the hard bread and baked beans that I had brought with me from the ship.   Refreshing myself with a bath, a cracker of hard bread, and a drink of lukewarm tea from my canteen, I left my baggage in the steward's care and set out to explore the city.

The only part of Santiago which then presented anything like a clean and civilized appearance is that which adjoins the so-called "palace" of the Spanish governor, on the crest of the hill at the head of Marina Street.   There, around a small, dusty, bush-planted plaza, or park, stand the governor's residence, the old twin-belfried cathedral, the San Carlos or Cuban Club, the "Venus" restaurant, the post-office, and a few other public or semi-public buildings which make some pretensions to architectural dignity.   With the exception of the massive stone cathedral, however, they are all low, one-story or two-story brick houses covered with dirty white stucco, and would be regarded anywhere except in Santiago as cheap, ugly, and insignificant.

In the course of my walk from the club to the plaza I met

a few Cuban negroes in dirty white-cotton shirts and trousers, and half a dozen or more pale-faced Spanish soldiers, but the streets in that part of the city seemed to be almost wholly deserted.   Beyond the plaza, however, on Enramadas Street, I began to meet the stream of destitute refugees returning to the city from Caney, and a more dirty, hungry, sick, and dejected-looking horde of people I had never seen. When General Shafter gave notice to the Spanish military authorities that if Santiago were not surrendered it would be bombarded, fifteen thousand men, women, and children abandoned their homes and fled, most of them on foot, to various suburban villages north of the city.   Most of these fugitives went to Caney, where, for nearly two weeks, they camped out in the streets, suffering everything that human beings can suffer from hunger, sickness, and exposure.   Both General Shafter and the Red Cross made every possible effort to relieve them by sending provisions to them from Siboney; but the distance from that base of supplies was fifteen miles or more over a terrible road, the number of horses and mules available for transportation was hardly adequate to supply even our own army with ammunition and food, and the most that could be done for the refugees at Caney was to keep them from actually starving to death.   Hundreds of them perished, but they died from exposure, exhaustion, and sickness, rather than from starvation.   As soon as Santiago surrendered, these fugitives began to stream back into the city, and it was the advance-guard of them that I met on Enramadas Street on Tuesday morning.   They represented both sexes, all ages, all complexions, and all classes of the population, from poor Cuban or negro women carrying huge bundles on their heads and leading three or four half-naked children, to cultivated, delicately nurtured, English-speaking ladies, wading through the mud in bedraggled white gowns, carrying nothing, perhaps, except a kitten or a cage of pet birds.

Many of them were so ill and weak from dysentery or malarial fever that they could hardly limp along, even with the support of a cane, and all of them looked worn, exhausted, and emaciated to the last degree. Hundreds of these refugees died, after their return to Santiago, from diseases contracted in Caney, and if it had not been for the prompt relief given them by the Red Cross as soon as they reached the city, they would have perished by the thousand. With the aid and coöperation of Mr. Ramsden, son of the British consul, Mr. Michelson, a wealthy resident merchant, and two or three other foreign residents of Santiago, Miss Barton opened a soup-kitchen on shore, as soon as provisions enough had been landed from the *State of Texas* to make a beginning, and before Tuesday night the representatives of the Red Cross had given bread and hot soup to more than ten thousand sick and half-starved people, most of them returned refugees from Caney, who could not get a mouthful to eat elsewhere in the city, and who were literally perishing from hunger and exhaustion.

CHAPTER XVI

THE FEEDING OF THE HUNGRY

THE problem of supplying myself with food and drink in the half-starved city of Santiago, after the steamer had been quarantined against me, proved to be even more serious than I had anticipated. In my walk up Marina and Enramadas streets and out to the Caney road on Tuesday forenoon I passed two or three restaurants bearing such seductive and tantalizing names as "Venus," "Nectar," and "Delicias," etc., but they were all closed, and in a stroll of two miles through the heart of the city I failed to discover any food more "delicious" than a few half-ripe mangoes in the dirty basket of a Cuban fruit-peddler, or any "nectar" more drinkable than the water which ran into the gutter, here and there, from the broken or leaky pipes of the city water-works. Hot, tired, and dispirited, I returned about noon to the Anglo-American Club, took another drink of lukewarm tea from my canteen, nibbled a piece of hard bread, and opened a can of baked beans. The beans proved to be flavored with tomato sauce, which I dislike; the hard bread was stale and tasted of the haversack in which I had brought it ashore; and the tea was neither strong enough to inebriate nor yet cool enough to cheer. There did not seem to be any encouraging probability that I should be fed by Cuban ravens or nourished by manna from the blazing Cuban skies, and in the absence of some such miraculous interposition of Providence I should evidently have either to go with a tin cup to the Red Cross soup-kitchen and beg for a portion of soup on the ground that I was a destitute and starving reconcentrado, or else return to the pier where the *State of Texas* lay, hail somebody on deck, and ask to have food lowered to me over the ship's side. I could certainly drink a cup of coffee and eat a plate of corned-beef hash on the dock without serious danger of infecting the ship with yellow fever, typhus, cholera, or smallpox; and if the captain should object to my being fed in that way on the ground that the ship's dishes might be contaminated by my feverish touch, I was fully prepared to put my pride in my pocket and meekly receive my rations in an old tomato-can or a paper bag tied to the end of a string.

With all due respect for Red Cross soup, and the most implicit confidence in Red Cross soup-kitchens, I inclined to the belief that I should fare better if I got my nourishment from the *State of Texas*—even at the end of a string—than if I went to the Cuban soup-kitchen and claimed food as a reconcentrado, a refugee, or a repentant prodigal son. In the greasy, weather-stained suit of brown canvas and mud-bespattered pith helmet that I had worn at the front, I might play any one of these rôles with success, and my forlorn and disreputable appearance would doubtless secure for me at least two tincupfuls of soup; but what I longed for most was coffee, and that beverage was not to be had in the Cuban soup-kitchen. I resolved, therefore, to go to the pier, affirm with uplifted hand that I was not suffering from yellow fever, typhus fever, remittent fever, malarial fever, pernicious fever, cholera, or smallpox, and beg somebody to lower to me over the ship's side a cup of coffee in an old tomato-can and a mutton-chop at the end of a fishing-line. I was ready to promise that I would immediately fumigate the fishing-line and throw the empty tomato-can into the bay, so that the

State of Texas should not run the slightest risk of becoming infected with the diseases that I did not have.

About half-past one, when I thought Miss Barton and her staff would have finished their luncheon, I walked down Gallo Street to the pier where the steamer was discharging her cargo, hailed a sailor on deck, and asked him if he would please tell Mrs. Porter (wife of the Hon. J. Addison Porter, secretary to the President) that a Cuban refugee in distress would like to speak to her at the ship's side. In two or three minutes Mrs. Porter's surprised but sympathetic face appeared over the steamer's rail twenty-five or thirty feet above my head. Raising my voice so as to make it audible above the shouting of the stevedores, the snorting of the donkey-engine, and the rattle of the hoisting-tackle, I told her that I had not been able to find anything to eat in the city, and asked her if she would not please get my table-steward "Tommy" to lower to me over the ship's side a few slices of bread and butter and a cup of coffee. A half-shocked and half-indignant expression came into her face as she mentally grasped the situation, and she replied with emphasis: "Certainly! just wait a minute." She rushed back into the cabin to call Tommy, while I sat down on a bag of beans with the comforting assurance that if I did not get something to eat that afternoon there would be a fracas on the *State of Texas*. Mrs. Porter evidently regarded it as an extraordinary state of affairs which forced the vice-president of the Red Cross to go hungry in a starving city because a ship flying the Red Cross flag refused to allow him on board.

In five minutes more Tommy appeared in the starboard gangway of the main-deck, and lowered down to me on a tray a most appetizing lunch of bread and butter, cold meats, fried potatoes, preserved peaches, ice-water, and coffee. I resumed my seat on the bag of beans, holding the tray on my knees, and gave myself up to the enjoyment of the first meal I had had in Santiago, and the best one, it seemed to me, that ever gladdened the heart of a hungry human being in any city. The temperature in the fierce sunshine which beat down on my back was at least 130° F.; the cold meats were immediately warmed up, the butter turned to a yellowish fluid which could have been applied to bread only with a paint-brush, and perspiration ran off my nose into my coffee-cup as I drank; but the coffee and the fried potatoes kept hot without the aid of artificial appliances, and I emptied the glass of ice-water in two or three thirsty gulps before it had time to come to a boil. Mrs. Porter watched me with sympathetic interest, as if she were enjoying my lunch even more than she had enjoyed her own, and when I had finished she said: "It is absurd that you should have to take your meals on that hot, dirty pier; but if you 'll come down every day and call for me, I 'll see that you get enough to eat, even if they don't allow you on board."

All the rest of that week I slept in the Anglo-American Club and took my meals on the pier of the Juragua Iron Company, Mrs. Porter keeping me abundantly supplied with food, while I tried to make my society an equivalent for my board by furnishing her, three times a day, with the news of the city. Getting my meals in a basket or on a tray over the ship's side and eating them alone on the pier was rather humiliating at first, and made me feel, for a day or two, like a homeless tramp subsisting on charity; but when General Wood, the military governor of the city, and Dr. Van De Water, chaplain of the Seventy-first New York, came down to the *State of Texas* one afternoon to see Mrs. Porter and were not allowed to go on board, even for a drink of water, my self-respect was measurably restored. Dr. Van De Water had walked into the city from the camp of his regiment, a distance of two or three miles, in the fierce tropical sunshine, and was evidently suffering acutely from fatigue and thirst;

but the *State of Texas*, where, under the Red Cross flag, he naturally expected to find rest and refreshment, was barred against him, and he had to get his drink of water, as I got my daily bread, over the ship's side. The quarantine of the steamer against the shore would perhaps have been a little more consistent, as well as more effective, if the officers who superintended the unloading and storing of the cargo had not been permitted to visit every day the lowest and dirtiest part of the city and then return to the steamer to eat and sleep, and if the crew had not been allowed to roam about the streets in search of adventures at night; but I suppose it was found impracticable to enforce the quarantine against everybody, and the most serious and threatening source of infection was removed, of course, when General Wood, Dr. Van De Water, and the vice-president of the Red Cross were rigidly excluded from the ship.

While I was living at the Anglo-American Club and board-ing on the pier of the Juragua Iron Company the deserted and half-dead city of Santiago was slowly awakening to life and activity. The empty streets filled gradually with Ameri-can soldiers, paroled Spanish prisoners, and returning fugi-tives from Caney; shops that had long been shut and barred were thrown open under the assurance of protection given by the American flag; kerosene-lamps on brackets fastened to the walls of houses at the corners of the narrow streets were lighted at night so that pedestrians could get about without danger of tumbling into holes or falling over garbage-heaps; government transports suddenly made their appear-ance in the bay, and as many of them as could find accom-modation at the piers began to discharge cargo; six-mule army wagons rumbled and rattled over the rough cobblestone pavements as they came in from the camps after supplies; hundreds of hungry and destitute Cubans were set at work cleaning the filthy streets; and in less than a week Santiago had assumed something like the appearance that it must have presented before the siege and capture. The thing that it needed most in the first fortnight after the surrender was a hotel, and a hotel it did not have. Newspaper correspondents, officers who had come into the city from the camps, and passengers landed from the steamers had no place to go for food or shelter, and many of them were forced to bivouac in the streets. Captain William Astor Chanler, for example, tied his saddle-horse to his leg one night and lay down to sleep on the pavement of the plaza in front of the old cathedral.

The urgent need of a hotel finally compelled the steward of the Anglo-American Club to throw open its twenty or more rooms to army officers, cable-operators, and newspaper correspondents who had no other place to stay, and to make an attempt, at least, to supply them with food. A few cases of canned meat and beans and a barrel of hard bread were obtained from the storehouse of the Red Cross; a cook and three or four negro waiters were hired; and before the end of the first week after the capture of the city the club was furnishing two meals a day to as many guests as its rooms would accommodate, and had become the most interesting and attractive place of social and intellectual entertainment to be found on the island. One might meet there, almost any night, English war correspondents who had campaigned in India, Egypt, and the Sudan; Cuban sympathizers from the United States who had served in the armies of Gomez and Garcia; old Indian fighters and ranchmen from our Western plains and mountains; wealthy New York club-men in the brown-linen uniform of Roosevelt's Rough Riders; naval officers from the fleet of Admiral Sampson; and speculators, coffee-planters, and merchant adventurers from all parts of the western hemisphere. One could hardly ask a question with regard to any part of the

habitable globe or any event of modern times that somebody
in the club could not answer with all the fullness of personal
knowledge, and the conversation around the big library table
in the evening was more interesting and entertaining than
any talk that I had heard in months.   But the evenings were
not always given up wholly to conversation.   Sometimes Mr.
Cobleigh of the New York "World," who had a very good
tenor voice, would seat himself at the piano and sing "White
Wings," "Say au revoir, but not good-by," or "The Banks
of the Wabash," and then Mr. Cox, resident manager of the
Spanish-American iron-mines, would take Cobleigh's place at
the instrument and lead the whole assembled company in
"John Brown's Body," "My country, 't is of thee," and "The
Star-Spangled Banner," until the soldiers of the Ninth Infantry, quartered in the old theater across the way, would join in
the chorus, and a great wave of patriotic melody would roll
down Gallo Street to the bay, and out over the tranquil water
to the transports lying at anchor half a mile away.   Sitting
in that cheerful, comfortably furnished club-room under the
soft glow of incandescent electric lights, and listening to
the bright, animated conversation, the laughter, and the old
familiar music, I found it almost impossible to realize that I
was in the desperately defended and recently captured city
of Santiago, where the whole population was in a state of
semi-starvation, where thousands of sick or wounded were
languishing in crowded hospitals and barracks, and where,
within a few days, I had seen destitute and homeless Cubans
dying of fever in the streets.

Miss Barton began the work of relieving the wide-spread
distress and destitution in Santiago with characteristic
promptness and energy.   To feed twenty or thirty thousand
people at once, with the limited facilities and the small
working force at her command, and to do it systematically
and economically, without wastefulness and without confu-

sion, was a herculean task; but it was a task with which experience and training in many fields had made her familiar,
and she set about it intelligently and met the difficulties of
the situation with admirable tact and judgment. Her first
step was to ask the ablest, most influential, and most re-
spected citizens of Santiago to consult with her with regard
to ways and means and to give her the benefit of their local
knowledge and experience. The object of this was to secure
the coöperation and support of the best elements of the
population, and strengthen the working force of the Red
Cross by adding to it a local contingent of volunteer assistants who were thoroughly acquainted with the city and its
inhabitants and who would be able to detect and prevent
fraud or imposition. There was danger, of course, that
people who did not need food, or were not entitled to it,
would seek to obtain it on false pretenses, and that others,
who perhaps were really in distress, would try to get more
food than they actually required in order that they might
make a little money by selling the surplus. In anticipation
of this danger, Miss Barton decided to put the distribution
of food largely under local control. In the first place, a central committee of three was appointed to exercise general
supervision over the whole work. The members of this
committee were Mr. Ramsden, son of the British consul;
Mr. Michelson, a wealthy and philanthropic merchant engaged in business in Santiago; and a prominent Cuban
gentleman whose name I cannot now recall. This committee
divided the city into thirty districts, and notified the residents of each district that they would be expected to elect
or appoint a commissioner who should represent them in all
dealings with the Red Cross, who should make all applications
for relief in their behalf, and who should personally superintend the distribution of all food allotted to them on requisitions approved by the central committee. This scheme of

organization and distribution was intelligently and judiciously devised, and it worked to the satisfaction of all. Every commissioner was instructed to make a requisition for food in writing, according to a prescribed form, stating the number and the names of heads of families needing relief in his district, the number of persons in each family, and the amount of food required for the district as a whole and for each family or individual in detail. The commissioner then appended to the requisition a certificate to the effect that the petitioners named therein were known to him and that he believed they were really in need of the quantities of food for which they respectively made application. The requisition then went to the central committee, and when approved by it was filled at the Red Cross warehouse and retained there as a voucher.

I heard it asserted in Santiago more than once that food issued by the Red Cross to people who were supposed to be starving had afterward been sold openly on the street by hucksters, and had even been carried on pack-mules in comparatively large quantities to suburban villages and sold there; but I doubt very much the truth of this assertion. Miss Barton caused an investigation to be made of several such cases of alleged fraud, and found in every instance that the food said to have been obtained from the Red Cross had really come from some other source, chiefly from soldiers and government transports, whose provisions, of course, could not be distinguished from ours after they had been taken out of the original packages. Be this, however, as it may, the checks upon fraud and imposition in the Red Cross scheme of distribution were as efficient as the nature of the circumstances would allow, and I doubt whether the loss through fraudulent applications or through collusion between commissioners and applicants amounted to one tenth of one per cent. The Red Cross furnished food in bulk to thirty-two thousand half-starved people in the first five days after Santiago surrendered, and in addition thereto fed ten thousand people every day in the soup-kitchens managed by Mr. Michelson. I do not wish to make any unjust or invidious comparisons, but I cannot refrain from saying, nevertheless, that I did not happen to see any United States quartermaster in Cuba who, in the short space of five days, had unloaded and stored fourteen hundred tons of cargo, given hot soup daily to ten thousand soldiers, and supplied an army of thirty-two thousand men with ten days' rations. It is a record, I think, of which Miss Barton has every reason to be proud.

But her beneficent work was not confined to the mere feeding of the hungry in Santiago. She sent large quantities of cereals, canned goods, and hospital supplies to our own soldiers in the camps on the adjacent hills; she furnished medicines and food for sick and wounded to the Spanish prison camp as well as to the Spanish army hospital, the civil hospital, and the children's hospital in the city; she directed Dr. Soyoso of her medical staff to open a clinic and dispensary, where five surgeons and two nurses gave medical or surgical aid to more than three thousand sick or sickening people every day; she sent hundreds of tons of ice from the schooner *Morse* to the hospitals, the camps, and the transports going North with sick and wounded soldiers; she put up tents to shelter fever-stricken Spanish prisoners from the tropical sunshine while they were waiting to be taken on board the vessels that were to carry them back to Spain; and in every way possible, and with all the facilities that she had, she tried to alleviate the suffering caused by neglect, incompetence, famine, and war.

CHAPTER XVII

MORRO CASTLE

IN the course of the first week after I landed in Santiago, I made a number of interesting excursions to points in the vicinity of the harbor, for the purpose of ascertaining the real nature and strength of the Spanish fortifications and intrenchments. From the front of our army, after the battle of July 1–2, I had carefully examined, with a strong glass, the blockhouses and rifle-pits which defended the city on the land side; and from the bridge of the *State of Texas*, two weeks later, I had obtained a general idea of the appearance of Morro Castle and the batteries at the mouth of the harbor which protected the city from an attack by water; but I was not satisfied with this distant and superficial inspection. External appearances are often deceptive, and forts or earthworks that look very formidable and threatening from the front, and at a distance of half a mile, may prove to have little real strength when seen from the other side and at a distance of only a few yards. I wished, therefore, to get into these forts and batteries before any changes had been made in them, and before their guns had been removed or touched, so that I might see how strong they really were and how much damage had been done to them by the repeated bombardments to which they had been subjected.

The first excursion that I made was to Morro Castle and

the fortifications at the entrance to the harbor. It was my intention to start at 4 A. M., so as to reach the castle before it should get uncomfortably hot; but as I had no alarm-clock, and as no one in the club ever thought of getting up before six, I very naturally overslept myself, and by the time I had dressed, eaten a hasty breakfast of oatmeal, hard bread, and tea, and filled my canteen with boiled water, it was after seven. The air ought to have been fresh and cool even then; but on the southeastern coast of Cuba the change from the damp chilliness of night to the torrid heat of the tropical day is very rapid, and if there is no land-breeze, the rays of the unclouded sun, even as early as seven o'clock in the morning, have a fierce, scorching intensity that is hardly less trying than the heat of noon. The only really cool part of the day is from four to six o'clock in the morning.

I put a can of baked beans and a few crackers of hard bread into my haversack for lunch, threw the strap of my field-glass over my shoulder, took my canteen in my hand, and hurried down Gallo Street to the pier of the Juragua Iron Company, where I had engaged a colored Cuban fisherman to meet me with a sail-boat at 4 A. M. He had been waiting for me, patiently or impatiently, more than three hours; but he merely looked at me reproachfully, and pointed to the sun, as if to say, "You agreed to be here at daybreak, and now see where the sun is." I laid my head down sidewise on the palm of my hand, shut my eyes, snored vociferously, and explained to him in Russian that I had overslept myself. I was gratified to see that he understood my Russian perfectly. In communicating with Cubans and Spaniards I have always made it a practice to address them in Russian, for the obvious reason that, as they are foreigners, and Russian is a foreign tongue, they must necessarily understand that language a little better than they could possibly understand English. It may seem like an absurd idea, but I have

13

no hesitation in saying that a skilful and judicious combination of Russian with the sign-language is a good deal more intelligible to a Cuban fisherman than either Pidgin-English or Volapük. Voltaire once cynically remarked that "paternosters will shave if said over a good razor." So Russian will convey a perfectly clear idea to a Cuban fisherman if accompanied by a sufficiently pictorial pantomime. I tried it repeatedly on my boatman, and became convinced that if I only spoke Russian a little more grammatically, and gesticulated the sign-language a little more fluently, I could explain to him the outlines of cosmic philosophy and instruct him in the doctrines of esoteric Buddhism. I never should have got to Morro Castle and back with him if I had not been able to draw diagrams in the air with both hands and my head simultaneously, and then explain them to him in colloquial Russian.

The surface of the bay, as we pushed off from the pier, was almost as smooth and glassy as an expanse of oil; and although my negro boatman whistled persuasively for a breeze, after the manner of sailors, and even ejaculated something that sounded suspiciously like "Come up 'leven!" as he bent to his clumsy oars, he could not coax the Cuban Æolus to unloose the faintest zephyr from the cave of the winds in the high blue mountains north of the city. He finally suspended his whistling to save his breath, wiped his sweaty face on his shirt-sleeve, and made a few cursory remarks in Spanish to relieve his mind and express his unfavorable opinion of the weather. I shared his feelings, even if I could not adopt his language, and, pantomimically wringing the perspiration out of my front hair, I remarked in Russian that it was *zharko* (hot). Encouraged by what he took for sympathetic and responsive profanity on my side, he scowled fiercely and exclaimed, "Mucha sol—damn!" whereupon we smiled reciprocally and felt much cooler.

We crept slowly down the eastern side of the bay, past the conical hill crowned with a cubical blockhouse which marks the southern boundary of the city, around the end of the long iron trestle of the Juragua Iron Company, past the flat-topped mesa on which stands the harbor signal-station, and finally into the narrow neck of the Santiago water-bottle which Hobson vainly tried to cork with the collier *Merrimac*. From this point of view we could see, between the steep bluffs which form the entrance to the bay, a narrow strip of blue, sunlit ocean, and on its left the massive gray bastions of Morro Castle, projecting in a series of huge steps, like ledges or terraces of natural rock, from the crest of the eastern promontory.

All the maps of Santiago harbor that I have seen show another castle, called Socapa, nearly opposite Morro on the western side of the channel; but I have never been able to discover it. If it still exists, it must be in ruins and so overgrown with vegetation as to be completely hidden. The only fortification I could find on that side of the bay is the so-called "western battery," a recently constructed earthwork situated on the crest of the long, flat-topped hill which forms the outer coast-line. This earthwork could never have been known as a "castle"; it is at least three hundred yards west of the point indicated on the map as the site of Socapa, and it cannot be seen at all from the channel, or even from the highest parapet of Morro. Unless Socapa Castle, therefore, is so small and inconspicuous as to have escaped my notice, it must have fallen into ruins or been destroyed. There is no castle on the western side of the entrance now that can be seen from the water, from the Estrella battery, or from Morro.

After passing Cayo Smith, the sunken collier *Merrimac*, and the dismantled wreck of the *Reina Mercedes*, we turned abruptly to the left, opposite the Estrella battery, and entered

a deep, sheltered cove, directly behind the Morro promontory
and almost under the massive walls of the castle itself. Landing at a little wooden pier on the northern side of the minia-
ture bay, I walked up to the road leading to the Estrella
battery, and there stopped and looked about me. The cove
was completely shut in by high hills, and the only road or
path leading out of it, so far as I could see, was the one on
which I stood. This began, apparently, at the Estrella battery, ran around the head of the cove, and then, turning to
the right, climbed the almost precipitous side of the Morro
promontory, in a long, steep slant, to a height of one hundred
and fifty feet. There it made another turn which carried it
out of sight behind a buttress of rock under the northwestern
corner of the castle. Near the mouth of the cove, on my
right, rose the white, crenellated, half-ruined wall of the
Estrella battery—a dilapidated open stone fort of the eighteenth century, which contained no guns, and which, judging
from its appearance, had long been abandoned. It occupied,
however, a very strong position, and if the Spaniards had had
any energy or enterprise they would have put it in repair
and mounted in it a modern mortar which lay on a couple of
skids near the pier, and two or three small rapid-fire guns
which they might have obtained from one of Admiral Cervera's cruisers. Antiquated and obsolete as it was, it might
then have been of some use.

Near the head of the cove was an old ordnance storehouse,
or magazine, which proved upon examination to contain
nothing more interesting than a few ancient gun-carriages,
a lot of solid six-inch projectiles, an assortment of rammers
and spongers for muzzle-loading cannon, and a few wooden
boxes of brass-jacketed cartridges for Remington rifles.
Three long smooth-bore iron culverins lay on the ground
between this magazine and the pier, but they had not been
fired, apparently, in a century, and were so eaten and pitted

by rust that I could not find on them any trace of inscription or date. There was nothing really useful, effective, or modern, either in the Estrella battery or in the magazine, except the Remington rifle-cartridges and the unmounted mortar.

Finding nothing else of interest in the vicinity of the cove, I started up the road that led to the front or western face of Morro Castle. I call it a "road" by courtesy, because it did show some signs of labor and engineering skill; but it was broken every few yards into rude steps by transverse ledges of tough, intractable rock, and how any wheeled vehicle could ever have been drawn up it I cannot imagine. The fringe of plants, bushes, and low trees that bordered this road was bright with flowers, among which I noticed the white spider-lily (apparently a variety of *Cleome pungens*), the so-called "Cuban rose" (a flower that flaunts the scarlet and yellow of the Spanish flag and looks a little like *Potentilla la Vésuve*), and a beautiful climbing vine with large violet blossoms which resembled in shape and color the butterfly-pea (*Centrosema*).

In and out among these plants and bushes ran nimble lizards of at least half a dozen different kinds: lizards that carried their tails curled up over their backs like pug-dogs; lizards that amused themselves by pushing out a whitish, crescent-shaped protuberance from under their throats and then drawing it in again; lizards that changed color while I watched them; and big gray iguanas, two or three feet in length, which, although perfectly harmless, looked ugly and malevolent enough to be classed with Cuban land-crabs and tarantulas. I saw no animals except these lizards, and no birds except the soaring vultures, which are never absent from Cuban skies, and which hang in clouds over every battle-field, fort, city, and village on the island.

The road from the head of the Estrella cove to the crest

of the Morro promontory forks at a distance of seventy-five
or one hundred yards from the cable-house, one branch of it
turning to the left and climbing a steep grade to the summit
of the ridge east of the castle, where stand the lighthouse
and the barracks, while the other branch goes straight on in a
rising slant to a rocky buttress situated almost perpendicu-
larly over the point where the southern shore of the cove in-
tersects the eastern margin of the harbor channel.   Turning
to the left around this buttress, it runs horizontally southward
along a shelf-like cornice in the face of the precipice until
it reaches a spacious terrace, or esplanade, cut out of the
solid rock, at a height of one hundred and fifty feet above
the water. This terrace, which is on the western face of
the castle and directly under its lower bastions, seems to
have been intended originally for a gun-platform, but there
is nothing there now to indicate that guns were ever mounted
on it.   It has no parapet, or battlement, and is merely a wide,
empty shelf of rock, overhanging the narrow entrance to the
harbor, and overhung, in turn, by the walls of the fortress.
In the mountain-side back of it are four or five quadrangular
apertures, which look from a distance like square port-holes,
or embrasures, for heavy cannon, but which prove upon
closer examination to be doors leading to huge subterranean
chambers, designed, I presume, for the safekeeping of ammunition and explosives.   At the time when I went through
them they contained nothing more dangerous than condemned shovels and pickaxes, empty bottles, old tin cans,
metal lamps, dirty straw hats, discarded hammocks, and cast-
off shoes. I found nothing in the shape of ammunition except
two or three dozen spherical iron cannon-balls, which lay
scattered over the rocky floor of the esplanade, as if the
soldiers of the garrison had been accustomed to play croquet
with them there, just to pass away the time in the intervals
between Admiral Sampson's bombardments.

After looking about the esplanade and exploring the dim recesses of the gloomy ammunition-vaults, I climbed a crooked flight of disintegrating stone steps and entered, between two massive quadrangular bastions,[1] the lower story—if I may so call it—of the castle proper. As seen from the ocean outside of the harbor, this ancient fortress appears to consist of three huge cubes of gray masonry, superimposed one upon another in such a manner as to present in profile the outline of three rocky terraces; but whether this profile view gives anything like a correct idea of the real shape of the building I am unable to say. From the time when I entered the gateway at the head of the flight of stone steps that led up from the esplanade, I was lost in a jumbled aggregation of intercommunicating corridors, bastions, grated cells, stairways, small interior courtyards, and huge, gloomy chambers, which I could not mentally group or combine so as to reduce them to intelligible order or bring them into anything like architectural harmony. The almost complete absence of windows made it impossible to orient one's self by glancing occasionally at some object of known position outside; the frequent turns in the passages and changes of level in the floors were very confusing; the small courtyards which admitted light to the interior afforded no outlook, and I simply roamed from bastion to bastion and from corridor to corridor, without knowing where I was, or what relation the place in which I stood bore to the castle as a whole. Now and then I would ascend a flight of stone steps at the side of a courtyard and come out unexpectedly upon what seemed to be a flat roof, from which I could see the entrance to the harbor

---

[1] I use the word "bastion" in a very loose, untechnical way to designate projecting parts or semi-detached wings of the main building. I doubt whether the castle contains anything that would be called a bastion by a military engineer; but I cannot think of any other word to describe the cubical masses of masonry that are joined to the main work only on one side.

and the white walls of the Estrella battery hundreds of feet below; but as soon as I went back into the maze of passages, chambers, and bastions on that level, I lost all sense of direction, and five minutes later I could not tell whether I was on the northern side of the castle or the southern side, nor whether I was in the second of the three cubes of masonry or the third.

The most surprising thing about the castle, to me, was its lack of offensive power. Its massive stone walls gave it, of course, a certain capacity for endurance, and even for resistance of a passive kind; but it was almost as incapable of inflicting injury on an enemy as a Dutch dike or a hillock of the mound-builders would be. Until I reached what, for want of a better name, I shall have to call the roof of the uppermost cube, I did not find anywhere a single round of ammunition, nor a gun of any caliber, nor a casemate intended for a gun, nor an embrasure from which a gun could have been fired. So far as architectural adaptation to the conditions of modern warfare is concerned, it was as harmless as an old Norman keep, and might have been planned and built two centuries before guns were used or gunpowder invented. I have been unable to ascertain the date of its erection; but the city of Santiago was founded by Diego Velasquez in 1514, and all the evidence furnished by the castle itself would seem to indicate that it dates back to the sixteenth, or at latest to the seventeenth, century. There is certainly nothing in its plan or in its appearance to show that the engineers who designed it were acquainted even with the art of fortification as developed in the seventeenth century by Vauban. It is simply an old feudal castle, with moat, drawbridge, and portcullis, built after the model of medieval strongholds before heavy siege-ordnance came into general use. The idea that it could have done any serious damage to Admiral Sampson's fleet seems absolutely ludicrous when one has explored the interior of it and taken stock of its antiquated, not to say obsolete and useless, armament.

After wandering about for half an hour in the two lower stories, I climbed a crooked flight of stone steps, half blocked up with debris from a shattered parapet above, and came out on the flat roof of the highest and largest of the three cubes that together make up the fortress. It was a spacious battlemented floor, of rectangular but irregular outline, having an extreme length of perhaps one hundred and fifty feet, with an average width of seventy-five to one hundred.[1] On its eastern side it overlooked a deep, wide moat, intended to protect the wall from an assault made along the crest of the promontory, while on the other three sides one might look down hundreds of feet to the wide blue plain of the ocean, the narrow mouth of the harbor, and the deep sheltered cove of the Estrella battery. The city of Santiago was hidden behind the flat-topped hill on which the signal-station stands; but I could see a part of the beautiful bay, with the bare green mountains behind it, while eastward and westward I could follow the surf-whitened coast-line to the distant blue capes formed by the forest-clad slopes of Turquino on one side and the billowy foot-hills of the Gran Piedra on the other. The fleet of Admiral Sampson had disappeared; but its place had already been taken by a little fleet of fishing-smacks from Santiago, whose sun-illumined sails looked no larger, on the dark-blue expanse of the Caribbean, than the wings of white Cuban butterflies that had fallen into the sea.

For ten minutes after I reached the aërial platform of the bastion roof I had no eyes for anything except the magnificent natural cyclorama of blue water, rolling foot-hills, deep secluded valleys, and palm-fringed mountains that surrounded

[1] I neglected to ascertain the dimensions of this roof or gun-platform by pacing it, and the estimates given above are from memory.

me; but, withdrawing my gaze reluctantly at last from the enchanting scenery, I turned my attention again to the castle and its armament.   Scattered about here and there on the flat roof of the bastion were five short bronze mortars of various calibers and two muzzle-loading smooth-bore cannon, mounted, like field-pieces, on clumsy wooden carriages with long "trails" and big, heavy wheels.   It was evident at a glance that neither of the cannon would be likely to hit a battle-ship at a distance of five hundred yards without a special interposition of Providence; and as the mortars had no elevating, training, or sighting gear, and could be discharged only at a certain fixed angle, it is doubtful whether they could drop a shell upon a floating target a mile in diameter—and yet these five mortars and two eighteen-pounder muzzle-loading guns were all the armament that Morro Castle had.

After looking the pieces over superficially and forming from mere inspection a judgment as to their value, I proceeded to examine them closely for dates.   The larger of the two cannon, which was trained over the northern parapet as if to bombard the city of Santiago. bore the following inscription:

MARS

PLURIBUS NEC IMPAR [1]

12 Iun 1748

PAR IEAN MARITZ

ULTIMO RATIO REGUM [2]

LOUIS CHARLES DE BOURBON
COMPTE D'EU
DUC D'AUMALE

The other cannon, which was trained over the western

[1] "A fair match for numbers."

[2] "The last argument of kings."   Words engraved or cast on French cannon by order of Louis XIV.

parapet and aimed at the place where Socapa Castle ought to have been, was inscribed:

LE COMPTE DE PROVENCE

ULTIMO RATIO REGUM

LOUIS CHARLES DE BOURBON
COMPTE D'EU
DUC D'AUMALE
1755 ·

The mortars, which were embellished with Gorgons' heads and were fine specimens of bronze casting, bore inscriptions or dates as follows:

No. 1.   EL MANTICORA
                               1733

                    STRVXITDVCTOREXERC
                     IT^M REGISBEN꜀VE (*sic*)
                    _____

                    PHIL II HISPAN REX[1]
                    ELISA FAR HIS REGINA

No. 2.   VOĬE ABET FECIT
                           SEVILLE AÑO D
                               1724

No. 3.   EL COMETA
                               1737

No. 4.   1780

No. 5.   1781

From the above inscriptions and dates it appears that the most modern piece of ordnance in the Morro Castle battery was cast one hundred and seventeen years ago, and the oldest one hundred and seventy-four years ago. It would be interesting to know the history of the two French cannon which, in obedience to the order of Louis XIV, were marked

[1] Evidently an error; it should be Philip V

"ULTIMO RATIO REGUM." Iean Maritz, their founder, doubtless regarded them, a century ago, with as much pride as
Herr Krupp feels now when he turns out a fifteen-inch steel
breech-loader at Essen; but the *ultimo ratio regum* does
not carry as much weight on this side of the Atlantic in the
nineteenth century as it carried on the other side in the
eighteenth, and the recent discussions between Morro Castle
and Admiral Sampson's fleet proved conclusively that the
"last argument of kings" is much less cogent and convincing
than the first argument of battle-ships. It is doubtful,
however, whether these antiquated guns were ever fired at
Admiral Sampson's fleet. They were not pointed toward the
sea when the castle was evacuated; I could not find any
ammunition for them, either on the bastion roof where they
stood or in the vaults of the castle below; there were no
rammers or spongers on or about the gun-platforms, where
they would naturally have been left when the guns were
abandoned; and there was nothing whatever to show that
they had been fired in fifty years. But it could have made
little difference to the blockading fleet whether they were
fired or not. They were hardly more formidable than the
"crakys of war" used by Edward III against the French at
the battle of Crécy. As for the mortars, they were fit only
for a museum of antiquities, or a collection of obsolete im-
plements of war like that in the Tower of London. I hope
that Secretary Alger or Secretary Long will have "El Manticora" and "El Cometa" brought to the United States and
placed at the main entrance of the War Department or the
Navy Department as curiosities, as fine specimens of artistic
bronze casting, and as trophies of the Santiago campaign.

When I had finished copying the inscriptions on the cannon
and the mortars, I went down into the interior of the castle
to examine some pictures and inscriptions that I had noticed
on the walls of a chamber in the second story, which had

been used, apparently, as a guard-room or barrack. It was a large, rectangular, windowless apartment, with a wide door, a vaulted ceiling, and smooth stone walls which had been covered with plaster and whitewashed. Among the Spanish soldiers who had occupied this room there was evidently an amateur artist of no mean ability, who had amused himself in his hours of leisure by drawing pictures and caricatures on the whitewashed walls. On the left of the door, at a height of five or six feet, was a life-sized and very cleverly executed sketch of a Spaniard in a wide sombrero, reading a Havana newspaper. His eyes and mouth were wide open, as if he were amazed and shocked beyond measure by the news of some terrible calamity, and his attitude, as well as the horror-stricken expression of his elongated face, seemed to indicate that, at the very least, he had just found in the paper an announcement of the sudden and violent death of all his family. Below, in quotation-marks, were the words: "! ! ! Que BARBARIDAD. ! ! ! Han apresado UN VIVERO." ("What BARBARITY ! ! ! They have captured A FISHING-SMACK ! ! !")

This is evidently a humorous sneer at the trifling value of the prizes taken by the vessels of our blockading fleet off Havana in the early days of the war. But there is more in the Spanish words than can well be brought out in a translation, for the reason that *vivero* means a vessel in which fish are brought from the Yucatan banks *alive*, in large salt-water tanks. We had been accusing the Spaniards of cruelty and barbarity in their treatment of the insurgents. The artist "gets back at us," to use a slang phrase, by exclaiming, in pretended horror, "What barbarous cruelty! They have captured a boat-load of *living* fish!"

For a Spanish soldier, that is not bad; and the touch is as delicate in the sneer of the legend as in the technic of the cartoon.

A little farther along and higher up, on the same wall,
was a carefully executed and beautifully finished life-sized
portrait of a tonsured Roman Catholic monk—a sketch that
I should have been glad to frame and hang in my library, if
it had only been possible to get it off the wall without breaking the plaster upon which it had been drawn.   I thought of
trying to photograph it; but the light in the chamber was
not strong enough for a snap shot, and I had no tripod to
support my camera during a time-exposure.

There were several other sketches and caricatures on the
left-hand wall; but none of them was as good as were the
two that I have described, and, after examining them all carefully, I cast my eyes about the room to see what I could find
in the shape of "loot" that would be worth carrying away
as a memento of the place.   Apart from old shoes, a modern
kerosene-lamp of glass, a dirty blanket or two, and a cot-bed,
there seemed to be nothing worth confiscating except a couple
of Spanish newspapers hanging against the right-hand wall
on a nail.   One was "El Imparcial," a sheet as large as the
New York "Sun"; and the other, "La Saeta," an illustrated
comic paper about the size of "Punch."   They had no in-
trinsic value, of course, and as "relics" they were not particularly characteristic; but "newspapers from a bastion in
Morro Castle" would be interesting, I thought, to some of
my journalistic friends at home, so I decided to take them.
I put up my hand to lift them off the nail without tearing
them, and was amazed to discover that neither nail nor newspapers had any tangible existence.   They had been drawn
on the plaster, by that confounded soldier-artist, with a lead-
pencil!   I felt worse deceived and more chagrined than the
Greek pony that neighed at the painted horse of Apelles!
But I need not have felt so humiliated.   Those newspapers
would have deceived the elect; and I am not sure that the
keenest-sighted proof-reader of the "Imparcial" would not

have read and corrected a whole column before he discovered that the paper was plaster and that the letters had been made with a pencil. Major Greene of the United States Signal-Service, to whom I described these counterfeit newspapers, went to the castle a few days later, and, notwithstanding the fact that he had been forewarned, he tried to take "La Saeta" off the nail. He trusted me enough to believe that one of the papers was deceptive; but he felt sure that a real copy of "La Saeta" had been hung over a counterfeit "Imparcial" in order to make the latter look more natural. If the soldier who drew the caricatures, portraits, and newspapers in that guard-room escaped shot, shell, and calenture, and returned in safety to Spain, I hope that he may sometime find in a Spanish journal a translation of this chapter, and thus be made aware of the respectful admiration that I shall always entertain for him and his artistic talents.

In all the rooms of the castle that had been occupied by soldiers I found, scratched or penciled on the walls, checkerboard calendars on which the days had been successively crossed off; rude pictures and caricatures of persons or things; individual names; and brief reflections or remarks in doggerel rhyme or badly spelled prose, which had been suggested to the writers, apparently, by their unsatisfactory environment. One man, for example, has left on record this valuable piece of advice:

"Unless you have a good, strong 'pull' [*mucha influencia*], don't complain that your rations are bad. If you do, you may have to come and live in Morro Castle, where they will be much worse."

Another, addressing a girl named "Petenera," who seems to have gotten him into trouble, exclaims:

> Petenera, my life! Petenera, my heart!
> It is all your fault
> That I lie here in Morro

> Suffering pain and writing my name
> On the plastered wall.
>
> JOSÉ.

Probably "José" went to see "Petenera" without first obtaining leave of absence, and was shut up in one of the gloomy guard-rooms of Morro Castle as a punishment.

Another wall-writer, in a philosophic, reflective, and rather melancholy mood, says:

> Tu me sobreviviras.
> Que vale el ser del hombres
> Cuando un escrito vale mas!

You [my writing] will survive me.
What avails it to be a man, when a scrap of writing is worth more!

It is a fact which, perhaps, may not be wholly unworthy of notice that, among the sketches I saw and the mural inscriptions I copied in all parts of Morro Castle, there was not an indecent picture nor an improper word, sentence, or line. Spanish soldiers may be cruel, but they do not appear to be vicious or corrupt in the way that soldiers often are.

In wandering through the corridors and gloomy chambers of the castle, copying inscriptions on walls and cannon, and exploring out-of-the-way nooks and corners, I spent a large part of the day. I found that the masonry of the fortress had suffered even less from the guns of Admiral Sampson's fleet than I had supposed. The eastern and southeastern faces of the upper cube had been damaged a little; the parapet, or battlement, of the gun-floor had been shattered in one place, and the debris from it had fallen over and partly blocked up the steps leading to that floor from the second story; two or three of the corner turrets had been injured by small shells; and there was a deep scar, or circular pit, in the face of the eastern wall, over the moat, where the masonry had been struck squarely by a heavy projectile; but, with the exception of these comparatively trifling injuries, the old fortress remained intact. Newspaper men described it as "in ruins" or "almost destroyed" half a dozen times in the course of the summer; and the correspondent of a prominent metropolitan journal, who entered the harbor on his despatch-boat just behind the *State of Texas* the day that Santiago surrendered, did not hesitate to say: "The old fort is a mass of ruins. The stone foundation has been weakened by the shells from the fleet, causing a portion of the castle to settle from ten to twenty feet. Only the walls on the inner side remain. The terraces have been obliterated and the guns dismounted and buried in the debris. There are great crevices in the supporting walls, and the fort is in a general state of collapse."

How any intelligent man, with eyes and a field-glass, could get such an erroneous impression, or make such wild and reckless statements, I am utterly unable to imagine. As a matter of fact, the fleet never tried or intended to injure the castle, and all the damage done to it was probably accidental. I have no doubt that Admiral Sampson might have reduced the fortress to the condition that the correspondent so graphically describes,—I saw him destroy the stone fort of Aguadores in a few hours, with only three ships,—but he discovered, almost as soon as he reached Santiago, that the old castle was perfectly harmless, and, with the cool self-restraint of a thoughtful and level-headed naval officer, he determined to save it as a picturesque and interesting relic of the past. Most of the projectiles that struck it were aimed at the eastern battery, the lighthouse, or the barracks on the crest of the bluff behind it; and all the damage accidentally done to it by these shots might easily be repaired in two or three days. If Cuba ever becomes a part of the United States, the people of this country will owe a debt of

14

gratitude to Admiral Sampson for resisting the temptation
to show what his guns could do, and for preserving almost
intact one of the most interesting and striking old castles
in the world.

Leaving the fortress through the eastern gateway and
crossing the dry moat on a wooden trestle which had taken
the place of the drawbridge, I walked along the crest of the
bluff toward the eastern battery. It was evident, from the
appearance of the lighthouse and the one-story, tile-roofed
buildings on the crest of the hill, that if Morro Castle
escaped serious injury it was not because the gunners of
our fleet were unable to hit it.   Every other structure in its
vicinity had been shattered, riddled, or smashed. The lighthouse, which was a tapering cylinder of three-quarter-inch
iron twelve feet in diameter at the base and perhaps thirty
feet high, had been struck at least twenty or thirty times.
The western half of it, from top to bottom, had been carried
away bodily; there were eleven shot-holes in the other half;
the lantern had been completely demolished; and the ground
everywhere in the vicinity was strewn with fragments of
iron and glass.   The flagstaff of the signal-station had been
struck twice, slender and difficult to hit as it was, and the
walls and roofs of the barracks and ammunition storehouses
had been pierced and torn by shot and shell in a dozen different places. It is not likely, of course, that all this damage
was done at any one time or in any single bombardment.
The gunners of our fleet probably used these buildings as
targets, and fired at them, every time they got a chance,
just for amusement and practice. The white cylinder of
the lighthouse made a particularly good mark, and the eleven
shot-holes in the half of it that remained standing showed
that Admiral Sampson's gunners found no difficulty in hitting
a target ten feet by thirty at a distance of more than a mile.
The captain of the Spanish cruiser *Vizcaya* told Lieutenant

Van Duzer of the battle-ship *Iowa* that, at the height of the naval engagement off the mouth of the harbor on July 3, his vessel was struck by a shell, on an average, once a second. He spoke as if he had been greatly surprised by the extraordinary accuracy of our gunners' fire; but if he had taken one look at that Morro lighthouse before he ran out of the harbor he would have known what to expect.

After examining the shattered barracks and the half-demolished lighthouse, I walked on to the so-called "eastern battery," a strong earthwork on the crest of the ridge about one hundred and fifty yards from the castle. Here, in a wide trench behind a rampart of earth strengthened with barrels of cement, I found four muzzle-loading iron siege-guns of the last century, two modern mortars like the one that I had seen on the skids near the head of the Estrella cove, one smooth-bore cannon dated 1859, and two three-inch breech-loading rifles. The eighteenth-century guns were no more formidable than those on the roof of Morro, but the mortars and three-inch rifles were useful and effective. It was a shell from one of these mortars that killed or wounded eight sailors on the battle-ship *Texas*. One gun had been dismounted in this battery, but all other damage to it by the fleet had been repaired. Owing to the fact that its guns were in a wide trench, six or eight feet below the level of the hilltop, it was extremely difficult to hit them; and although Admiral Sampson repeatedly silenced this battery by shelling the gunners out of it, he was never able to destroy it.

The only other fortifications that I was able to find in the vicinity of Morro Castle were two earthworks known respectively as the "western battery" and the "Punta Gorda battery." The western battery, which was situated on the crest of the hill opposite Morro, on the other side of the harbor entrance, contained seven guns of various sizes and dates, but only two of them were modern. The Punta Gorda

battery, which occupied a strong position on a bluff inside
the harbor and behind the Estrella cove, had only two guns,
but both were modern and of high power.   In the three batteries—eastern, western, and Punta Gorda—there were only
eight pieces of artillery that would be regarded as effective
or formidable in modern warfare, and two of these were so
small that their projectiles would have made no impression
whatever upon a battle-ship, and could hardly have done
much damage even to a protected cruiser.   Six of these
guns were so situated that, although they commanded the
outside approach to the bay, they could not possibly hit an
enemy that had once passed Morro and entered the channel.
The neck of the bottle-shaped harbor, or, in other words,
the narrow strait between Morro Castle and the upper bay,
had absolutely no defensive intrenchment except the Punta
Gorda battery, consisting of two guns taken from the old
cruiser *Reina Mercedes*.

"Why," it may be asked, "did not Admiral Sampson fight
his way into the harbor, if its defenses were so weak?"

Simply because the channel was mined.   He might have
run past the batteries without serious risk; but in so narrow
a strip of water it was impossible to avoid or escape the
submarine mines, four of which were very powerful and
could be exploded by electricity.   He offered to force an
entrance if General Shafter would seize the mine-station
north of Morro; but the general could not do this without
changing his plan of campaign.   The coöperation of the
navy, therefore, was limited to the destruction of Cervera's
fleet and the bombardment of the city from the mouth of
Aguadores ravine.

CHAPTER XVIII

FEVER IN THE ARMY

THE most serious and threatening feature of the situation at Santiago after the capture of the city was the ill health of the army. In less than a month after it began its Cuban campaign the Fifth Army-Corps was virtually *hors de combat*. On Friday, July 22, I made a long march around the right wing from a point near the head of the bay to the Siboney road, and had an opportunity to see what the condition of the troops was in that part of our line. I do not think that more than fifty per cent. of them were fit for any kind of active duty, and if they had been ordered to march back to Siboney between sunrise and dark, or to move a distance of ten miles up into the hills, I doubt whether even forty per cent. of them would have reached their destination. There were more than a thousand sick in General Kent's division alone, and a surgeon from the First Division hospital—the only field-hospital of the Fifth Army-Corps—told me that a conservative estimate of the number of sick in the army as a whole would be about five thousand. Of course the greater part of these sick men were not in the hospitals. I saw hundreds of them dragging themselves about the camps with languid steps, or lying in their little dog-kennel tents on the ground; but all of them ought to have been in hospitals, and would have been had our hospital space and facilities been adequate. Inasmuch, however, as our hospital accommodations were everywhere deplorably inadequate, and inasmuch as our surgeons sent to the yellow-fever camps many patients who were suffering merely from malarial fever, a majority of our sick soldiers remained in their own tents, from necessity or from choice, and received only such care as their comrades could give them.

Yellow fever and calenture broke out among the troops in camp around Santiago about the same time that they appeared in Siboney. Calenture soon became epidemic, and in less than a fortnight there were thousands of cases, and nearly one half of the army was unfit for active service, if not completely disabled.

The questions naturally arise, Was this state of affairs inevitable, or might it have been foreseen as a possibility and averted? Is the climate of eastern Cuba in the rainy season so deadly that Northern troops cannot be subjected to it for a month without losing half their effective force from sickness, or was the sickness due to other and preventable causes? In trying to answer these questions I shall say not what I think, nor what I suppose, nor what I have reason to believe, but what I actually know, from personal observation and from the testimony of competent and trustworthy witnesses. I was three different times at the front, spent a week in the field-hospital of the Fifth Army-Corps, and saw for myself how our soldiers ate, drank, slept, worked, and suffered. I shall try not to exaggerate anything, but, on the other hand, I shall not suppress or conceal anything, or smooth anything over. Poultney Bigelow was accused of being unpatriotic, disloyal, and even seditious because he told what I am now convinced was the truth about the state of affairs at Tampa; but it seems to me that when the lives of American soldiers are at stake it is a good deal more patriotic and far more in accordance with the duty of a good citizen to tell a disagreeable and unwelcome truth that may lead to a reform than it is to conceal the truth and pretend that everything is all right when it is not all right.

The truth, briefly stated, is that, owing to bad management, lack of foresight, and the almost complete breakdown of the commissary and medical departments of the army, our soldiers in Cuba suffered greater hardships and privations, in certain ways, than were ever before endured by an American army in the field. They were not half equipped, nor half fed, nor half cared for when they were wounded or sick; they had to sleep in dog-kennel shelter-tents, which afforded little or no protection from tropical rains; they had to cook in coffee-cups and old tomato-cans because they had no camp-kettles; they never had a change of underclothing after they landed; they were forced to drink brook-water that was full of disease-germs because they had no suitable vessels in which to boil it or keep it after it had been boiled; they lived a large part of the time on hard bread and bacon, without beans, rice, or any of the other articles which go to make up the full army ration; and when wounded they had to wait hours for surgical aid, and then, half dead from pain and exhaustion, they lay all night on the water-soaked ground, without shelter, blanket, pillow, food, or attendance. To suppose that an army will keep well and maintain its efficiency under such conditions is as unreasonable and absurd as to suppose that a man will thrive and grow fat in the stockaded log pen of a Turkish quarantine. It cannot be fairly urged in explanation of the sickness in the army that it was due to the deadliness of the Cuban climate and was therefore what policies of marine insurance call an "act of God." The Cuban climate played its part, of course, but it was a subordinate part. The chief and primary cause of the soldiers' ill health was neglect, due, as I said before, to bad management, lack of foresight, and the almost complete breakdown of the

army's commissary and medical departments. If there be
any fact that should have been well known, and doubtless
was well known, to the higher administrative officers of the
Fifth Army-Corps, it is the fact that if soldiers sleep on the
ground in Cuba without proper shelter and drink unboiled
water from the brooks they are almost certain to contract
malarial fever; and yet twelve or fifteen thousand men were
sent into the woods and chaparral between Siboney and
Santiago without hammocks or wall-tents, and without any
vessel larger than a coffee-cup in which to boil water. I
can hardly hint at the impurities and the decaying organic
matter that I have seen washed down into the brooks by the
almost daily rains which fall in that part of Cuba in mid-
summer, and yet it was the unboiled water from these polluted brooks that the soldiers had to drink. One captain
whom I know took away the canteens from all the men in his
company, kept them under guard, and tried to force his
command to boil in their tin coffee-cups all the water that
they drank; but he was soon compelled to give up the plan as
utterly impracticable. In all the time that I spent at the
front I did not see a single camp-kettle in use among the
soldiers, and there were very few even among officers. Late
in July the men of the Thirty-fourth Michigan were bringing every day in their canteens, from a distance of two miles,
all the water required for regimental use. They had nothing
else to carry it in, nothing else to keep it in after they got
it to camp, and nothing bigger than a tin cup in which to
boil it or make coffee.

In the matter of tents and clothing the equipment of the
soldiers was equally deficient. Dog-kennel shelter-tents will
not keep out a tropical rain, and when the men got wet they
had to stay wet for lack of a spare suit of underclothes.
The officers fared little better than the men. A young lieutenant whom I met in Santiago after the surrender told me

that he had not had a change of underclothing in twenty-seven days. The baggage of all the officers was left on board of the transports when the army disembarked, and little, if any, of it was ever carried to the front.

Nothing, perhaps, is more important, so far as its influence upon health is concerned, than food, and the rations of General Shafter's army were deficient in quantity and unsatisfactory in quality from the very first. With a few exceptions, the soldiers had nothing but hard bread and bacon after they left the transports at Siboney, and short rations at that. A general of brigade who has had wide and varied experience in many parts of the United States, and whose name is well and favorably known in New York, said to me in the latter part of July: "The whole army is suffering from malnutrition. The soldiers don't get enough to eat, and what they do get is not sufficiently varied and is not adapted to this climate. A soldier can live on hardtack and bacon for a while, even in the tropics, but he finally sickens of them and craves oatmeal, rice, hominy, fresh vegetables, and dried fruits. He gets none of these things; he has come to loathe hard bread and bacon three times a day, and he consequently eats very little and is n't adequately nourished. Nothing would do more to promote the health of the men than a change of diet."

A sufficient proof that the soldiers were often hungry is furnished by the fact that men detailed from the companies frequently marched from the front to Siboney and back (from eighteen to twenty-five miles, over a bad road), in order to get such additional supplies, particularly in the shape of canned vegetables, as they could carry in their hands and haversacks or transport on a rude, improvised stretcher. Officers and men from Colonel Roosevelt's Rough Riders repeatedly came into Siboney in this way on foot, and once or twice with a mule or a horse, and begged food from the

Red Cross for their sick and sickening comrades in their camp at the front.

It is not hard to understand why soldiers contracted malarial fever in a country like Cuba, when they were imperfectly sheltered, inadequately equipped, insufficiently fed and clothed, forced to sleep on the ground, and compelled to drink unboiled water from contaminated brooks. But there was another reason for the epidemic character and wide prevalence of the calenture from which the army suffered, and that was exposure to exhalations from the malarious, freshly turned earth of the rifle-pits and trenches. All pioneers who have broken virgin soil with a plow in a warm, damp, wooded country will remember that for a considerable time thereafter they suffered from various forms of remittent and intermittent fever. Our soldiers around Santiago had a similar experience. The unexpected strength and fighting capacity shown by the Spaniards in the first day's battle, and their counter-attack upon our lines on the night of the following day, led our troops to intrench themselves by digging rifle-pits and constructing rude bomb-proofs as places of refuge from shrapnel. During the armistice these intrenchments were greatly extended and strengthened, and before Santiago surrendered they stretched along our whole front for a distance of several miles. In or near these rifle-pits and trenches our men worked, stood guard, or slept, for a period of more than two weeks, and the exhalations from the freshly turned earth, acting upon organisms already weakened by hardships and privations, brought about an epidemic of calenture upon the most extensive scale.

By August 3 the condition of the army had become so alarming that its general officers drew up and sent to General Shafter the following letter:

We, the undersigned officers, commanding the various brigades, divisions, etc., of the army of occupation in Cuba, are of the unanimous opinion that this army should be at once taken out of the island of Cuba and sent to some point on the northern sea-coast of the United States; that it can be done without danger to the people of the United States; that yellow fever in the army at present is not epidemic; that there are only a few sporadic cases, but that the army is disabled by malarial fever, to the extent that its efficiency is destroyed, and that it is in a condition to be practically entirely destroyed by an epidemic of yellow fever, which is sure to come in the near future.

We know from the reports of competent officers and from personal observation that the army is unable to move into the interior, and that there are no facilities for such a move if attempted, and that it could not be attempted until too late. Moreover, the best medical authorities of the island say that with our present equipment we could not live in the interior during the rainy season without losses from malarial fever, which is almost as deadly as yellow fever.

This army must be moved at once or perish. As the army can be safely moved now, the persons responsible for preventing such a move will be responsible for the unnecessary loss of many thousands of lives.

Our opinions are the result of careful personal observation, and they are also based on the unanimous opinion of our medical officers with the army, and who understand the situation absolutely.

This letter was signed by Generals Kent, Bates, Chaffee, Sumner, Ludlow, Ames, and Wood, and Colonel Roosevelt.

In view of such a state of affairs as that disclosed by this letter there was, of course, only one thing to be done. The War Department decided to remove the Fifth Army-Corps at once from Cuba, and before the middle of August a large part of General Shafter's command was on its way to Montauk Point.

As a result, I presume, of sleeping without shelter from the heavy dew in the field-hospital at the front, and over-exerting myself by walking around the lines of the army in the blazing sunshine of midday, I was finally prostrated with illness myself. At three o'clock on the night of Tuesday, July 26, I awoke in a chill, and before morning I had all the symptoms of calenture, with a temperature of 104.

Calenture, or Cuban malarial fever, comes on rather suddenly with a chill of greater or less severity and a violent headache. The temperature frequently rises to 105, and the fever, instead of being intermittent, runs continuously with little, if any, diurnal variation. If the attack is not a very severe one the headache gradually subsides; the temperature falls to 102 or 103, and in the course of three or four days the disease begins to yield to treatment. In some cases the fever is interrupted by a second chill, followed by another rise of temperature; but, as a rule, there is only one chill, and the fever, after running from four days to a week, gradually abates. The treatment most favored in Santiago consists of the administration of a large dose of sulphate of magnesia at the outset, followed up with quinine and calomel, or perhaps quinine and sulphur. The patient is not allowed to take any nourishment while the fever lasts, and if he keeps quiet, avoids sudden changes of temperature, and does not fret, he generally recovers in a week or ten days. He suffers from languor and prostration, however, for a fortnight or more, and if he overeats, moves about in the sunshine, or exposes himself to the night air, he is liable to have another chill, with a relapse, in which the fever is higher and more obstinate, perhaps, than at first. Under ordinary circumstances the fever is not dangerous, and the worst thing about it is the wretched, half-dead, half-alive condition in which it leaves one. My attack was not a very severe one, and in the course of ten days I was able to walk about again; but the first time I went out into the sunshine I had a relapse, which reduced me to such a state of weakness and helplessness that I could no longer care for myself, and had either to leave the country or go into one of the crowded

Santiago hospitals and run the risk of being sent as a "suspect" to the yellow-fever camp near Siboney.   Upon the advice of Dr. Egan, I decided to take the first steamer for New York, and sailed from Santiago on August 12, after a Cuban campaign of only seven weeks.

CHAPTER XIX

THE SANTIAGO CAMPAIGN

IT is my purpose, in the concluding chapters of this volume, to review as fully and dispassionately as I can the series of military operations known collectively as "the Santiago campaign," including, first, the organization and equipment of the expedition of General Shafter at Tampa; second, the disembarkation of troops and the landing of supplies at Daiquiri and Siboney; third, the strategic plan of the campaign and its execution; and, fourth, the wrecking of the army by disease after the decisive battle of July 1–2. The point of view from which I shall regard this campaign is not that of a trained military expert or critic, but merely that of an attentive and fair-minded civilian observer. I do not pretend to speak *ex cathedra*, nor do I claim for my judgments any other value than that given to them by such inherent reasonableness and fairness as they may seem to have. I went to Cuba without any prejudice for or against any particular plan of operations; I had very little acquaintance with or knowledge of the officers of the Fifth Army-Corps; and the opinions and conclusions that I shall here set forth are based on personal observations made in the field without conscious bias or prepossession of any kind.

In reviewing a military campaign, an arctic expedition, a voyage of discovery, or any other enterprise involving the employment of a certain force for the accomplishment of a certain purpose, the first question to be considered is the question of responsibility. Who is to be held accountable for the management and the results of this enterprise—the leader who directed and had charge of it, or the superior power which gave him his orders, furnished him with his equipment, and sent him into the field? When General Shafter was ordered to "go and capture the garrison at Santiago and assist in capturing the harbor and the fleet," did he become personally responsible for the management and the results of the campaign, or did he share that responsibility with the War Department? Unless there is some evidence to the contrary, the presumption in such a case is that the general in command of the army is told in due time where he is to go and what he is expected to do, and is then allowed to make his own plan of campaign, and to call upon the War Department for such supplies and means of transportation as, in the exercise of his individual judgment, he may think necessary for the successful execution of that plan. If he is given time enough to acquaint himself thoroughly with the field in which he is to operate, if his plan of campaign, in its general outlines, is approved, and if all his requisitions for vessels, horses, mules, wagons, ambulances, tents, guns, ammunition, and miscellaneous supplies are duly honored, there is no reason that I can see why he should not be held to a strict personal accountability for results, both generally and in detail. He has made his own plan; he has had everything that he asked for; and if the campaign does not go as it should, he, and not the War Department, is to blame. If, however, the department, after selecting him and approving his plan, does *not* furnish him with the transportation and the stores that he needs and has called for, he ought to protect himself and his own reputation by referring respectfully to that fact in his report of the campaign, so that, if any of his bricks are imperfect for lack of straw, the people may know that he was not supplied with straw and had no means whatever of getting it in the field to which he was sent. The importance of this point will become apparent when an attempt is made to ascertain the causes and fix the responsibility for the wrecking of the Fifth Army-Corps by disease in the short space of one calendar month.

There is nothing in the official documents thus far published to indicate that General Shafter was unreasonably hurried, or that he failed to get from the War Department anything for which he made timely requisition. The invasion of eastern Cuba was planned as early as the first week in May—possibly much earlier than that, and, at any rate, long before Admiral Cervera's fleet took refuge in Santiago harbor. Colonel Babcock, Shafter's adjutant-general, told me on May 7 that the government had decided to send the army of invasion to the eastern end of the island, and to leave Havana and the western provinces unmolested until later in the season. Before General Shafter sailed from Tampa, therefore, he had nearly or quite six weeks in which to acquaint himself with the Santiago field and mature a plan of operations. The question whether or not he was furnished with all the means of transportation and all the supplies for which he made requisition is in more doubt; but, inasmuch as he seems to have made no complaint or protest, and does not refer in his official reports to deficiencies of any kind, it may be assumed, for the purposes of this review, that he had been furnished by the War Department with everything for which he asked. Upon this assumption he was unquestionably responsible for the whole Santiago campaign, and must not only be given credit for the success that crowned it, but be held accountable for the blunders and oversights by which it was marred. He can relieve himself from such accountability only by showing that his equipment was inadequate and that the inadequacy was the result of causes beyond his control.

We are now prepared to consider:

I. The organization and equipment of the Santiago expedition.

When a general is appointed to lead and direct an expedition in a foreign country, the first questions, I think, that he must ask himself are: (1) What is the nature of the field in which I am to operate, and what are the difficulties —especially the unusual and unfamiliar difficulties—with which I shall have to contend? (2) Can I disembark my army in a harbor, or shall I have to land it on an open, unprotected coast, and perhaps through surf? (3) Are there any roads leading back into the interior, and, if so, what is their nature, and what is likely to be their condition at this season of the year? (4) Is the climate of the country to which I am going an unhealthful one, and, if so, how can I best protect my men from the diseases likely to attack them?

It is not always practicable to obtain satisfactory answers to such questions as these; but that answers should be had, if possible, and that the equipment of the force and the plan of campaign should be made to accord with the information obtained by means of them, is unquestionable. In the particular case now under consideration there was no difficulty whatever in getting full and satisfactory replies, not only to all of the above questions, but to scores of others of a similar nature that might have been and ought to have been asked. For nearly a month before General Shafter sailed from Tampa the vessels of Admiral Sampson's fleet had been patrolling the southeastern coast of Cuba from Santiago harbor to Guantanamo Bay, and their officers were in a position to furnish all the information that might be desired with regard to the nature of the coast, the facilities for

landing an army, the strength and direction of the prevailing winds, the danger to be apprehended from heavy surf,
and a dozen other matters of vital importance to an invading army.   At Daiquiri, Siboney, and Santiago there were
stations of an American iron-mining company, and its officers
and employees, who might easily have been found, were in
a position to furnish any amount of accurate and trustworthy
information with regard to climate, topography, roads, rains,
surf, and local conditions generally, in the very field that
General Shafter's army was to occupy.

The sources of information above indicated were not the
only sources accessible at the time when the Santiago campaign was decided upon; but they were the most important
ones, and it is fair to presume that General Shafter made use
of them to the fullest possible extent.   If so, he was able to
answer the questions above suggested in some such way as
this:

1. The field to which I am going is a tropical field, and the
unusual and unfamiliar difficulties with which I shall have to
contend are probably those dependent upon climatic conditions.

2. There are no sheltered harbors on the southeastern coast
of Cuba between Cape Cruz and Cape Maysi except the harbor of Santiago and the Bay of Guantanamo.   The former
is in possession of the enemy, and cannot, therefore, be used,
while the latter is too far away from the city of Santiago,
which I am ordered to capture.   It is probable, therefore,
that I shall have to land my army on an unsheltered part of
the coast.   The prevailing winds in the summer are from the
east and southeast, and the swell that rolls in from the
Caribbean Sea often breaks on the exposed coast-line in heavy
and dangerous surf.

3. The roads leading back into the interior in the direction of Santiago are generally narrow and bad; they traverse

almost impenetrable jungles; and they are liable, at this season of the year, to be rendered impassable for wheeled vehicles by heavy and frequent rains.

4. The climate is unhealthful, and unless men from the North are well fed, suitably clothed, securely sheltered, and furnished with boiled water for drinking purposes, they are almost certain to suffer from calenture, the characteristic fever of the region, as well as from yellow fever and dysentery.

This, in the briefest possible summary, is the information that General Shafter had, or might have had, before he sailed from Tampa. What preparation did he make to meet the difficulties suggested by this knowledge, and how far is the influence of it to be traced in the organization and equipment of his command?

Take, first, the problem of disembarking an army of sixteen thousand men, with the supplies necessary for its maintenance, on an unsheltered coast.

In 1847, when General Scott had in contemplation the landing of an army of twelve thousand men on the open beach at Vera Cruz, he caused sixty-seven surf-boats to be built for that particular service, each of them capable of holding from seventy to eighty men. Every detail of the disembarkation had been carefully considered and planned; every contingency that could be foreseen had been provided for; and the landing was successfully made in the course of two or three hours, without a single error or accident.

When General Shafter sailed from Tampa, on June 14, with an army considerably larger than that of General Scott, his equipment for disembarkation on an exposed, surf-beaten coast consisted, according to his own report, of only two scows! One of these went adrift at sea, and the loss of it, the general says, "proved to be very serious and was greatly felt." I don't wonder! Two scows, for an army of sixteen thousand men and ten or fifteen ship-loads of supplies, was a sufficiently economical allowance; and when that number was reduced by half, and a whole army-corps became dependent upon one scow, I am not surprised to learn that "the disembarkation was delayed and embarrassed." There is a reference in the report to certain "lighters sent by the quartermaster's department," and intended, apparently, for use on the Cuban coast; but when and by what route they were "sent" does not appear, and inasmuch as they were lost at sea before they came into General Shafter's control, they can hardly be regarded as a part of his equipment.   All that he had with him was this flotilla of two scows.   I heard vague reports of a pontoon-train stowed away under hundreds of tons of other stuff in the hold of one of the transports; but whether it was intended to supplement the flotilla of scows, or to be employed in the bridging of rivers, I am unable to say.   I do not think it was ever unloaded in Cuba, and I am quite sure that it never was used.

The almost complete absence of landing equipment, in the shape of surf-boats, lighters, and launches, eventually proved, as I shall hereafter show, to be disastrous in the extreme; and if the navy had not come to the rescue, at Daiquiri and Siboney, it is not at all certain that General Shafter could have landed his army.   In a telegram to the War Department dated "Playa del Este, June 25," he frankly admits this, and says: "Without them [the navy] I could not have landed in ten days, and perhaps not at all."

Now, it seems to me that the responsibility for this lack of boats, which came near ruining the expedition at the outset and which hampered and embarrassed it for three weeks afterward, can be definitely fixed.   The difficulty to be overcome was one that might have been foreseen and provided for.   If General Shafter did not foresee and provide for it, as General Scott did at Vera Cruz, he, manifestly, is the person to blame; while, on the other hand, if he did fore-see it, but failed to get from the War Department the neces-sary boats, the department is to blame.   The committee of investigation which is holding its sessions at the time this book goes to press ought to have no trouble in putting the responsibility for this deficiency where it belongs.

Boats, however, were not the only things that were lack-ing in the equipment of General Shafter's army.   Next in importance to landing facilities come facilities for moving supplies of all kinds from the sea-coast to the front, or, in other words, means of land transportation.   In his official report of the campaign General Shafter says: "There was no lack of transportation, for at no time, up to the surrender, could all the wagons I had be used."   If I were disposed to be captious, I should say that the reason why the general could not use the wagons he had was that a large number of them lay untouched in the holds of the transports.   He might have said, with equal cogency, that there was no lack of food, be-cause at no time could all the hard bread and bacon in his ships be eaten.   The usefulness of food and wagons is de-pendent to some extent upon their location.   A superfluity of wagons on board a steamer, five miles at sea, is not neces-sarily a proof that there are more than enough wagons on shore.

When the army began its march in the direction of Santi-ago, without suitable tents, without hospital supplies, with-out camp-kettles, without hammocks, without extra clothing or spare blankets, and with only a limited supply of food and ammunition, there were one hundred and eighteen army wagons still on board the transport *Cherokee*.   When they were unloaded, if ever, I do not know, but they were not available in the first week of the campaign, when the army began its advance and when the roads were comparatively dry and in fairly good condition.   It must be observed, moreover, that transportation is not wholly a matter of wagons. Vehicles of any kind are useless without animals to draw them; and General Shafter does not anywhere say that he had a superfluity of mules, or that he could not use all the horses he had. It was in draft-animals that the weakness of the quartermaster's department became most apparent as the campaign progressed. There were never half enough mules to equip an adequate supply-train for an army of sixteen thousand men, even if that army never went more than ten or twelve miles from its base. If it had been forced to go fifty miles from its base, the campaign would have collapsed at the outset.

General Shafter seems disposed to attribute the difficulty that he experienced in supplying his army with food to the condition of the roads rather than to the lack of mules, packers, teamsters, and wagons. In an interview with a correspondent of the Boston "Herald" at Santiago on August 25 he is reported as saying: "There has been some question concerning the transportation facilities of the army. The facilities were all there, and the transportation equipment provided was all that it should have been; but our difficulties were enormous. There was only one road; to build another would have taken two years. The nature of the country, the weather, all these things helped to disorganize this department. The use of wagons was almost impossible. The pack-train, as a matter of fact, did the real service. I had not, at first, thought the pack-train would be of service; but if it had not been there, I do not know what the army would have done for food. The roads were practically impassable. With the bridges down, the wagons could not be worked. I had a great deal of concern when we were only able to get up one day's rations at a time, but as soon as we were able to get a few days' rations ahead, we knew we were prepared for anything."

It is hardly accurate to say, without qualification and without limitation as to time, that the "roads were practically impassable." They were unquestionably very bad, and perhaps impassable, at the last; but before they became so there was ample time to take over them, with a suitable supply-train, all the tents, cooking-utensils, clothing, medical supplies, and provisions that the army so urgently needed but did not have. The road from Daiquiri and Siboney to the front did not become impassable for loaded wagons until the end of the second week in July. For ten days after the army landed it was comparatively dry and good; and for ten days or two weeks more it was at least passable, and was constantly traversed, not only by pack-trains, but by wagons with loads.

Captain Henry L. Marcotte, a retired officer of the Seventeenth Infantry, who went with General Shafter's army as correspondent for the "Army and Navy Journal," describes the condition of the road as follows:

"The road from Daiquiri to Siboney, about seven miles, leads over the foot-hill slopes of the mountain-ranges and crosses a winding stream several times during that distance. The road-bed, being mostly of rock, and well shaded by tropical growths, with good water every few hundred yards, made the journey for the Gatling battery a picnic without obstacles. From Siboney to [a point] near El Pozo the road was as good as [from Daiquiri] to Siboney, with the exception of one part. This, with five minutes' work, was made passable for the battery and for the three army wagons which the quartermaster's department had ventured to send out. In fact, the road, all the way to Santiago, proved equal to most country roads, and there was not the slightest excuse for not using the hundred or more wagons stowed in the hold of the *Cherokee* to transport tentage, medical and other supplies close upon the heels of the slow-moving Fifth

Corps. . . . There is a mystery about the 'condition of the road' that may remain so unless it is fixed upon as the scape-goat for the lack of transportation. . . . The condition of the road at no time would have prevented a farmer from taking a load of hay to market. . . . There was no point from Daiquiri to the trenches which could not have been as easily reached by wagons as by pack-mules between June 22 and July 18."

Captain Marcotte, as a retired officer of the regular army, is better qualified than I am to express an opinion with regard to the availability of a road for military purposes, and he does not hesitate to say that the road from Daiquiri and Siboney to the front was practicable for loaded wagons up to July 18, or for a period of nearly a month subsequent to the landing of the army. During a part of that time, he says, its condition was not such as to prevent a farmer from taking a load of hay over it.

I myself went over this road from Siboney to the front four times between June 26 and July 9,—twice on foot, once in an ambulance, and once in an army wagon,—and my own judgment is that for ten days after the disembarkation of the army the road was comparatively dry and good. After that it became muddy and bad, but was by no means im-passable, even for heavily loaded wagons, when I traversed it for the last time, five days before the surrender of Santi-ago. With the fall of that city the army's base of supplies was transferred from Siboney to Santiago harbor, and the condition of the Siboney road ceased to be a factor in the transportation problem. When a dozen steamers, loaded with supplies of all kinds, anchored off the Santiago piers, on July 15, the bulk of the army was within two miles of them, and there ought to have been no difficulty in getting to the troops everything that they needed.

If the road from Siboney to the front was practicable for

both pack-mules and wagons from the time when the army landed to the time when its base of supplies was transferred to Santiago, and if, as General Shafter asserts, "the facilities were all there, and the transportation equipment provided was all that it should have been," why was the army left for almost a month without suitable tents, without adequate hospital supplies, without camp-kettles, without cooking-utensils other than tin plates, coffee-cups, and old tomato-cans, without hammocks, without extra clothing or spare blankets, and with only a limited supply of food? That this was the state of the army is beyond question.

Lieutenant John H. Parker of the Gatling-gun battery reported to Adjutant-General Corbin, under date of July 23, that he and his men had been entirely without tents for a period of twenty-eight days.

John Henry of the Twenty-first Infantry wrote to his cousin in Lowell, Massachusetts, that his regiment had been on the firing line seventeen days. For two days they had nothing at all to eat, and no shelter, and lay on the ground in puddles of water.

Ex-Representative F. H. Krebs of the Second Massachusetts Regiment says that for twenty-six consecutive days he had only hard bread, bacon, and coffee, and that for three days he lived on one hardtack a day. The soldiers of his regiment did all their cooking in tin plates and coffee-cups, and slept for two months on the wet ground, under what are called "shelter"-tents, for the reason, I suppose,—*lucus a non lucendo,*—that they do not shelter.

Dr. James S. Kennedy, first assistant surgeon of the Second Division hospital, wrote from the hospital camp near Santiago: "There is an utter lack of suitable medicines with which to combat disease. There has been so much diarrhea, dysentery, and fever, and no medicine at all to combat them, that men have actually died for want of it. Four days after my reporting here there was not a single medicine in the entire hospital for the first two diseases, and nothing but quinine for the fever."

Dr. Edward L. Munson reported to Surgeon-General Sternberg, under date of July 29, that "at the time of the battle of Las Guasimas there were absolutely no dressings, hospital tentage, or supplies of any kind on shore, within reach of the surgeons already landed. The medical department was compelled to rely upon its own energies and improvise its own transportation. I feel justified in saying that at the time of my departure [from Siboney] large quantities of medical supplies, urgently needed on shore, still remained on the transports, a number of which were under orders to return to the United States. Had the medical department carried along double the amount of supplies, it is difficult to see how, with the totally inadequate land and water transportation provided by the quartermaster's department, the lamentable conditions on shore could have been in any way improved. The regimental medical officers had no means of transportation even for their field-chests."

Lieutenant-Colonel Senn, chief of the surgical operating staff, in a letter to the "Medical Record," dated "Siboney, August 3," disclaimed responsibility for the want of medical and surgical supplies in the field-hospitals, and said: "The lack of proper transportation from the landing to the front cannot be charged to the medical department."

Finally, General Shafter himself, in a telegram to President McKinley, dated "Santiago, August 8," reported as follows: "At least seventy-five per cent. of the command have been down with malarial fever, from which they recover very slowly. . . . What put my command in its present condition was the twenty days of the campaign when they had nothing but meat, bread, and coffee, without change of clothes, and without any shelter whatever."

In view of the above statements, made, not by irresponsible "newspaper correspondents and camp-followers," but by the officers and men of the Fifth Army-Corps, and in view of the confirmation given to them by the commanding general himself in a telegram to the President, it is proper, I think, to press once more the question, Why was the army left for almost a month without suitable tents, without adequate hospital supplies, without camp-kettles, without cooking-utensils, without hammocks, without extra clothing or spare blankets, and with only a limited supply of food? The answer to the question, it seems to me, is obvious. The army had not half transportation enough to supply its wants. General Miles discovered this fact when he reached Siboney on July 11, and he immediately cabled the War Department for more draft-animals; but it was then too late to make good the deficiency. The troops were already breaking down, as General Shafter admitted in his telegram to the President, from "twenty days of meat, bread, and coffee, without change of clothes, and without any shelter whatever." I do not know how many draft-animals General Shafter had; but in four journeys over the road between Siboney and the front I happened to see only two pack-trains, one of them going forward with ammunition, and the other returning without load. But whatever may have been the strength of the pack-train equipment, it was certainly inadequate, and the common practice of detailing soldiers to march into Siboney after food and bring it back to the front on their shoulders or on improvised hand-litters showed the urgency of the need. Many such details or deputations came on board the *State of Texas*, obtained small quantities of hospital supplies or delicacies for the sick, and carried them back to the camps in their hands.

This inadequacy of transportation facilities was apparent to every one who had any knowledge of the condition of the army, and it was a subject of common talk in Siboney, in Daiquiri, on board the fleet, and in every one of our hospitals and camps. I shall try, in another chapter, to show how it affected the health and fighting efficiency of the troops, and how near it came to wrecking not only the Fifth Army-Corps, but the whole Cuban expedition. Suffice it to say, for the present, that General Shafter sailed from Tampa without a sufficient number of mules, teamsters, and packers to supply, equip, and maintain his army in the field. The responsibility for this deficiency, as well as the responsibility for the lack of boats, must rest either upon the War Department or upon the general in command. If the latter did not ask for adequate means of land and water transportation before he left Tampa, he is the person to be held accountable. If he asked and failed to obtain, the War Department must stand in the gap.

CHAPTER XX

THE SANTIAGO CAMPAIGN (*Continued*)

WHEN, on June 14, General Shafter's army sailed for the southeastern coast of Cuba, without adequate facilities for disembarkation, and without a sufficient number of mules, packers, teamsters, and army wagons to insure its proper equipment, subsistence, and maintenance in the field, it was, *ipso facto*, predestined to serious embarrassment and difficulty, if not to great suffering and peril. No amount of zeal, energy, and ability on the part of quartermasters and commissaries, after the army had reached its destination, could possibly make up for deficiencies that should have had attention before the army sailed. Boats, mules, and wagons were not to be had at Siboney, and when the urgent need of them became apparent it was too late to procure them from the United States. General Shafter cabled the War Department for lighters and steam-tugs almost as soon as he reached the Cuban coast, and General Miles telegraphed for more draft-animals before he had been in Siboney twenty-four hours; but neither the boats nor the mules came in time to be of any avail. Cuban fever waits for no man, and before the boats that should have landed more supplies and the mules that should have carried them to the front reached Siboney, seventy-five per cent. of General Shafter's command had been prostrated by disease, due, as he himself admits, to insufficient food, "without change of clothes, and without any shelter whatever." [1]

But the lack of adequate land and water transportation was not the only deficiency in the equipment of the Fifth Army-Corps when it sailed from Tampa. It was also ill provided with medical stores and the facilities and appliances needed in caring for sick and wounded soldiers. Dr. Nicholas Senn, chief of the operating staff of the army, says that "ambulances in great number had been sent to Tampa, but they were not unloaded and sent to the front." I myself passed a whole train-load of ambulances near Tampa in May, but I never saw more than three in use at the front, and, according to the official report of Dr. Guy C. Godfrey, commanding officer of the hospital-corps company of the First Division, Fifth Army-Corps, "the number of ambulances for the entire army was limited to three, and it was impossible to expect them to convey the total number of wounded from the collecting-stations to the First Division hospital." [2]

Lieutenant-Colonel Jacobs of the quartermaster's department, who was assistant to General Humphreys in Cuba, testified before the Investigating Commission on November 16 that he had fifty ambulances at Tampa, and that he was about to load them on one of the transports when General Shafter appeared and ordered them left behind.

The surgeon-general declared, in a letter to the "Medical Record," dated August 6, that "General Shafter's army at Tampa was thoroughly well supplied with the necessary medicines, dressings, etc., for field-service; but, owing to insufficient transportation, he left behind at Tampa his reserve medical supplies and ambulance corps."

General Shafter himself admits that he had not enough

---

[1] Telegram of General Shafter to the President, August 8.
[2] Report to the surgeon-general from Santiago, July 28.

medical supplies, but seems to assert, by implication, that he was not to blame for the deficiency. In a telegram to Adjutant-General Corbin, dated "Santiago, August 3," he said: "From the day this expedition left Tampa until to-day there has never been sufficient medical attendance or medicines for the daily wants of the command, and three times within that time the command has been almost totally out of medicines. I say this on the word of the medical directors, who have in each instance reported the matter to me, the last time yesterday, when the proposition was made to me to take medicines away from the Spanish hospital. . . . The surgeons have worked as well as any men that ever lived, and their complaint has been universal of lack of means and facilities. I do not complain of this, for no one could have foreseen all that would be required; but I will not quietly submit to having the onus laid on me for the lack of these hospital facilities."

The state of affairs disclosed by these official reports and telegrams seems to me as melancholy and humiliating as anything of the kind ever recorded in the history of American wars. Three ambulances for a whole corps of sixteen thousand men; an army "almost totally out of medicines" three times in seven weeks; and a proposition to make up our own deficiencies by seizing and confiscating the medical supplies of a Spanish hospital! I do not wonder that General Shafter wishes to escape responsibility for such a manifestation of negligence or incompetence; but I do not see how he can be allowed to do so. It is just as much the business of a commanding general to know that he has medicines and ambulances enough as it is to know that he has food and ammunition enough. He is the man who plans the campaign, and, to a certain extent, predetermines the number of sick and wounded; he is the man who makes requisition upon the War Department for transports, mules,

and wagons enough to carry the army and its equipment
to the field where it is to operate; and he is the man who
should consider all contingencies and emergencies likely to
arise as a result of climatic or other local conditions, and
who should see that ample provision is made for them. General Shafter says that "no one could have foreseen all that
would be required." That is probably true; but any one, it
seems to me, could have foreseen that an army of sixteen
thousand men, which was expected to attack intrenched
positions, would need more than three ambulances for the
transportation of the wounded, to say nothing of the sick.
The same remark applies to medicines and medical supplies.
Every one knew that our army was going to a very unhealthful region, and it was not difficult to foresee that it would
require perhaps two or three times the quantity of medical
supplies that would be needed in a temperate climate and a
more healthful environment. The very reason assigned for
General Shafter's hurried advance toward Santiago is that he
knew his army would soon be disabled by disease, and wished
to strike a decisive blow while his men were still able to
fight. If he anticipated the wrecking of his army by sickness that could not be averted nor long delayed, why did he
not make sure, before he left Tampa, that he had medical
supplies and hospital facilities enough to meet the inevitable emergency? His telegram to Adjutant-General Corbin
seems to indicate that he was not only unprepared for an
emergency, but unprepared to meet even the ordinary demands of an army in the field, inasmuch as he declares,
without limitation or qualification, that from June 14 to
August 3 he never had medicines enough for the daily
wants of his command.

It may be thought that the view here taken of the responsibility of the commanding general for everything that
pertains to the well-being and the fighting efficiency of his

command is too extreme and exacting, and that he ought not to be held personally accountable for the mistakes or the incompetence of his staff-officers. Waiving a discussion of this question on its merits, it need only be said that, inasmuch as General Shafter has officially recommended all of his staff-officers for promotion on account of "faithful and meritorious services throughout the campaign," he is estopped from saying now that they did not do their duty, or that they made errors of judgment so serious as to imperil the lives of men, if not the success of the expedition. The responsibility for the lack of medical supplies and hospital facilities, therefore, as well as the responsibility for the lack of boats, mules, and wagons, must rest either upon the War Department or upon the general in command. If the latter made timely requisition for them, and for transports enough to carry them to the Cuban coast, and failed to obtain either or both, the War Department must be held accountable; while, on the other hand, if General Shafter did not ask for medical supplies enough to meet the probable wants of his army in a tropical climate and an unhealthful environment, he must shoulder the responsibility for his own negligence or want of foresight.

I shall now try to show how this lack of boats, mules, wagons, and medical supplies affected General Shafter's command in the field.

II. The landing at Daiquiri and Siboney.

The points selected for the disembarkation of the army and the landing of supplies were the best, perhaps, that could be found between Santiago harbor and Guantanamo Bay; but they were little more, nevertheless, than shallow notches in the coast-line, which afforded neither anchorage nor shelter from the prevailing wind. There was one small pier erected by the Spanish-American Iron Company at Daiquiri, but at Siboney there were no landing facilities whatever, and the

16

strip of beach at the bottom of the wedge-shaped notch in the precipitous wall of the coast was hardly more than one hundred yards in length. The water deepened so suddenly and abruptly at a distance of fifty yards from the shore that there was practically no anchorage, and General Shafter's fleet of more than thirty transports had to lie in what was virtually an open roadstead and drift back and forth with the currents and tides. The prevailing winds were from the east and southeast, and the long swell which rolled in from the Caribbean Sea broke in heavy and at times dangerous surf upon the narrow strip of unsheltered beach where the army had to land. All of these local conditions were known, or might have been known, to General Shafter before he left Tampa; but when he arrived off the coast they seemed to take him wholly by surprise. He had brought with him neither surf-boats, nor steam-launches, nor suitable lighters, nor materials with which to construct a pier. How he ever would have disembarked his command without the assistance of the navy, I do not know. I doubt whether a landing could have been effected at all. Fortunately, the navy was at hand, and its small boats and steam-launches, manned by officers and sailors from the fleet, landed the whole army through the surf with the loss of only two men. The navy then retired from the scene of action, and General Shafter was left to his own devices—and deplorably weak and ineffective they proved to be.

The engineer corps found near the railroad at Siboney a few sticks of heavy timber belonging to the Iron Company, out of which they improvised a small, narrow pier; but it was soon undermined and knocked to pieces by the surf. The chief quartermaster discovered on or near the beach three or four old lighters, also belonging to the Iron Company, which he used to supplement the service rendered by the single scow attached to the expedition; but as he put them in charge of soldiers, who had had no experience in handling boats in broken water, they were soon stove against the corners of the pier, or swamped in the heavy surf that swept the beach. All that could be done then was to land supplies as fast as possible in the small rowboats of the transports. If General Shafter had had competent and experienced officers to put in command of these boats, and steam-launches to tow them back and forth in strings or lines of half a dozen each, and if he had made provision for communication with the captains of the steamers by means of wigwag flag-signals, so as to be able to give them orders and control their movements, he might have landed supplies in this way with some success. But none of the difficulties of the situation had been fore-seen, and no arrangements had been made to cope with them. The captains of the transports put their vessels wherever they chose, and when a steamer that lay four or five miles at sea was wanted closer inshore, there was no means of send-ing orders to her except by rowboat. The captains, as a rule, did not put officers in charge of their boats, and the sailors who manned them, having no competent direction, acted upon their own judgment. Finally, boats which could have made a round trip between the transports and the shore in half an hour if towed by a steam-launch often used up the greater part of two hours in toiling back and forth through a heavy sea under oars.

It is not a matter for surprise that, with such facilities and under such conditions, General Shafter found it almost im-possible to land even food and ammunition enough to keep his army properly supplied. In his official report of the cam-paign he says: "It was not until nearly two weeks after the army landed that it was possible to place on shore three days' supplies in excess of those required for daily consump-tion."

In addition to all the unnecessary difficulties and embarrassments above described, there was another, almost, if not quite, as serious, arising from the manner in which the transports had been loaded at Tampa. Stores were put into the steamers apparently without any reference to the circumstances under which they would be taken out, and without any regard to the order in which they would be needed at the point of destination. Medical supplies, for example, instead of being put all together in a single transport, were scattered among twenty or more vessels, so that in order to get all of them it was necessary either to bring twenty steamers close to shore, one after another, and take a little out of each, or send rowboats around to them all where they lay at distances ranging from one mile to five.[1] Articles of equipment that would be required as soon as the army landed were often buried in the holds of the vessels under hundreds of tons of stuff that would not be needed in a week, and the army went forward without them, simply because they could not be quickly got at. Finally, I am inclined to believe, from what I saw and heard of the landing of supplies at Siboney, that there was not such a thing as a bill of lading, manifest, or cargo list in existence, and that the chief quartermaster had no other guide to the location of a particular article than that furnished by his own memory or the memory of some first mate. I do not assert this as a fact; I merely infer it from the difficulty that there seemed to be in finding and getting ashore quickly a particular kind of stores for which there happened to be an immediate and urgent demand. After the fight of the Rough Riders at Guasimas, for example, General Wood found himself short of ammunition for his Hotchkiss rapid-fire guns. He sent Lieutenant Kilbourne back to General Shafter at Siboney with a request that a fresh supply be forwarded at the earliest possible moment. General Shafter said that he had no idea where

[1] Report of Dr. Edward L. Munson to the surgeon-general, dated July 29.

that particular kind of ammunition was to be found, and referred the applicant to Quartermaster Jacobs at Daiquiri. Lieutenant Kilbourne walked seven miles to Daiquiri, only to find that the quartermaster had no more idea where that ammunition was than the commanding general had. He thereupon returned to Guasimas, after a march of more than twenty miles, and reported to General Wood that ammunition for the rapid-fire guns could not be had, because nobody knew where it was. If the commanding general and the quartermaster could not put their hands on ammunition when it was needed, they could hardly be expected to find, and forward promptly, articles of less vital importance, such as camp-kettles, hospital tents, clothing, and spare blankets.

It would be easy to fill pages with illustrations and proofs of the statements above made, but I must limit myself to a typical case or two relating to medical supplies, which seem to have been most neglected.

In a report to Surgeon-General Sternberg dated July 29, Dr. Edward L. Munson, commander of the reserve ambulance company, says that for two days after his arrival at Siboney he was unable to get any transportation whatever for medical supplies from the ships to the shore. On the third day he was furnished with one rowboat, but even this was taken away from him, when it had made one trip, by direct order of General Shafter, who wished to assign it to other duty. Some days later, with the boats of the *Olivette, Cherokee,* and *Breakwater,* he succeeded in landing medical supplies from perhaps one third of the transports composing the fleet. " I appealed on several occasions," he says, "for the use of a lighter or small steamer to collect and land medical supplies, but I was informed by the quartermaster's department that they could render no assistance in that way. . . . At the time of my departure large quantities of medical supplies, urgently needed on shore, still remained on the transports, a number of which were under orders to return to the United States." "In conclusion," he adds, "it is desired to emphasize the fact that the lamentable conditions prevailing in the army before Santiago were due (1) to the military necessity which threw troops on shore and away from the possibility of supply, without medicines, instruments, or hospital stores of any kind; and (2) to the lack of foresight on the part of the quartermaster's department in sending out such an expedition without fully anticipating its needs as regards temporary wharfage, lighters, tugs, and despatch-boats."

Dr. Frank Donaldson, assistant surgeon attached to Colonel Roosevelt's Rough Riders, states in a letter to the Philadelphia "Medical Journal," dated July 12, that "a desperate effort" was made to secure a few cots for the sick and wounded in the field-hospitals at the front. There were hundreds of these cots, he says, on one of the transports off Siboney, but it proved to be utterly impossible to get any of them landed. Whether they were all carried back to the United States or not I do not know; but large quantities of supplies, intended for General Shafter's army, *were* carried back on the transports *Alamo, Breakwater, Vigilancia,* and *La Grande Duchesse.*

I do not mean to throw any undeserved blame upon the quartermasters and commissaries at Siboney. Many of them worked day and night with indefatigable energy to get supplies on shore and forward them to the army; but they were hampered by conditions over which they had no control, and for which, perhaps, they were not in any way responsible; they were often unable to obtain the assistance of steamer captains and other officers upon whose coöperation the success of their own efforts depended, and they probably did all that could be done by individuals acting as separate units rather than as correlated parts of an organized and intelligently directed whole. The trouble at Siboney was the same trouble that became apparent at Tampa.   There was at the head of affairs no controlling, directing, and energizing brain, capable of grasping all the details of a complex situation and making all the parts of a complicated mechanism work harmoniously together for the accomplishment of a definite purpose.

III. The strategic plan of campaign and its execution.

As this branch of the subject will be discussed—if it has not already been discussed—by better-equipped critics than I can pretend to be, I shall limit myself to a brief review of the campaign in its strategic aspect as it appears from the standpoint of a civilian.

I understand, from officers who were in a position to know the facts, that the original plan of attack on the city of Santiago provided for close and effective coöperation of the army with the navy, and for a joint assault by way of Aguadores and Morro Castle.   General Shafter was to move along the line of the railroad from Siboney to Aguadores, keeping close to the coast under cover of the guns of the fleet, and, with the assistance of the latter, was to capture the old Aguadores fort and such other intrenchments as should be found at the mouth of the Aguadores ravine.   This, it was thought, might be accomplished with very little loss, because the fleet could shell the Spaniards out of their fortifications, and thus make it possible for the army to occupy them without much fighting.   Having taken Aguadores, General Shafter was to continue his march westward along the coast, still under the protection of Admiral Sampson's guns, until he reached Morro.   Then, without attempting to storm or reduce the castle, he was to go down through the ravine that leads to the head of the Estrella cove, and seize the submarine-mine station at the mouth of Santiago harbor.   When electrical connection between the station and the mines had been destroyed, and the mines had thus been rendered harmless, Admiral Sampson was to force an entrance, fighting his way in past the batteries, and the army and fleet were then to advance northward toward the city along the eastern side of the bay.

This plan had many obvious advantages, the most important of which was the aid and protection that would be given to the army, at every stage of its progress, by the guns of perhaps thirty or forty ships of war. In the opinion of naval officers, Admiral Sampson's cruisers and battle-ships could sweep the country ahead of our advance with such a storm of shot and shell that the Spaniards would not be able to hold any position within a mile of the coast. All that the army would have to do, therefore, would be to occupy the country as fast as it was cleared by the fire of the fleet, and then open the harbor to the latter by cutting communication with the submarine mines which were the only effective defense that the city had on the water side. General Shafter's army, moreover, would be all the time on high, sea-breeze-swept land, and therefore comparatively safe from malarial fever, and it would not only have a railroad behind it for the transportation of its supplies, but be constantly within easy reach of its base by water.

Why this plan was eventually given up I do not know. In abandoning it General Shafter voluntarily deprived himself of the aid that might have been rendered by three or four hundred high-powered and rapid-fire guns, backed by a trained fighting force of six or eight thousand men. I do not know the exact strength of Sampson's and Schley's combined fleets, but this seems to me to be a conservative estimate. A prominent officer of the battle-ship *Iowa* told me in Santiago, after the surrender, that the fighting ships under Admiral Sampson's command, including the auxiliary cruisers and mosquito fleet, could concentrate on any given field a fire of about one hundred shells a second. This included, of course, small projectiles from the rapid-fire and one-pound machine guns. He did not think it possible for Spanish infantry to live, much less fight, in the field swept by such a fire, and this was his reason for believing that the fleet could have cleared the way for the army if the latter had advanced along the coast instead of going back into the interior. The plan of attack by way of Aguadores and Morro was regarded by the foreign residents of Santiago as the one most likely to succeed; and a gentleman who lived eight years at Daiquiri, as manager of the Spanish-American Iron Company, and who is familiar with the topography of the whole region, writes me: "I have always thought that the great mistake of the Santiago campaign was that they assaulted the city at its most impregnable point, instead of taking possession of the heights at Aguadores, which would have been tantamount to the fall of Morro, the possession of the harbor entrance and of the harbor itself. The forces of the Spaniards were not sufficient to maintain any considerable number of men there, and it seems to me that, with the help of the fleet shelling the heights, they could have been reached very easily along the Juragua Railroad. If General Duffield had pressed on when he was there, it is probable that he would have met with only a thin skirmish-line, or, if the fleet had done its work, with no resistance at all."

The reason assigned for General Shafter's advance through the valleys and over the foot-hills of the interior, instead of along the high land of the coast, is that he had been ordered to "capture the garrison at Santiago and assist in capturing the harbor and the fleet." He did not believe, it is said, that he could "capture the garrison" without completely investing the city on the east and north. If he attacked it from the southern or Morro side, he might take the city, but the garrison would escape by the Cobre or the San Luis road. This seems like a valid and reasonable objection to the original plan of campaign; but I doubt very much whether the Spanish army would have tried to escape in any event, for the reason that the surrounding country was almost wholly destitute of food, and General Linares, in the hurry and confusion of defeat, would hardly have been able to organize a provision-train for an army of eight or ten thousand men, even if he had had provisions to carry. The only place where he could hope to find food in any quantity was Manzanillo, and to reach that port he would have had to make a forced march of from twelve to fifteen days. But the question whether the interior line of advance or the coast-line was the better must be left to strategists, and I express no opinion with regard to it.

The operations and manœuvers of our army in front of Santiago have already been described and commented upon by a number of expert observers, and the only additional criticisms that I have to make relate to General Shafter's neglect of reconnaissances, as a means of ascertaining the enemy's strength and position; his apparent loss of grip after the battle of July 1–2; and his failure not only to prevent, but to take any adequate steps to prevent, the reinforcement of the Santiago garrison by a column of five thousand regulars from Manzanillo under command of Colonel Escarrio. If I am correctly informed, the only reconnaissances made from the front of our army, after it came within striking distance of the enemy's intrenched line, were made by General Chaffee and a few other commanding officers upon their own responsibility and for their own information. General Shafter knew little more about the topography of the country in front of his advance picket-line than could be ascertained by mere inspection from the top of a hill. He received information to the effect that General Pando, with a strong column of Spanish regulars, was approaching Santiago from the direction of Manzanillo; but he never took any adequate steps to ascertain where General Pando was, when and by what road he might be expected to arrive, or how many men he was bringing with him.   In the course of a single day— July 3—General Shafter sent three telegrams to the War Department with regard to the whereabouts of Pando, in each of which he located that officer in a different place.   In the first he says: "Pando has arrived at Palma" (a village about twenty-five miles northwest of Santiago on the Cobre road).   In the second he declares that Pando is "six miles north of Santiago," "near a break in the [San Luis] railroad," and that he thinks "he will be stopped."   In the third he says: "Pando, I find to-night, is some distance away and will not get into Santiago."

We know now—and General Shafter should have known then—that the column of reinforcements from Manzanillo was not led by General Pando, but by Colonel Escarrio, and that at the very time when Shafter, in successive telegrams, was placing it "at Palma," "six miles north," "near a break in the railroad," and "some distance away," it was actually in the Santiago intrenchments, ready for business.

I take this case as an illustration on account of its extreme importance.   A column of five thousand Spanish regulars is not to be despised; and when it is within a few days', or perhaps a few hours', march, knowledge of its exact location may be a matter of life and death to a thousand men.   Was there any reason why General Shafter should not have informed himself accurately with regard to the strength and the position of this column of reinforcements?   I think not. When Admiral Sampson arrived off the entrance to Santiago harbor, it was of vital importance that he should know with certainty the location of Cervera's fleet.   He did not hastily telegraph the War Department that it was reported at Cienfuegos; that it was said to be in the Windward Passage; that it was five miles north of Morro, or that it was near a reef in the Este Channel and would be stopped.   He sent Lieutenant Victor Blue ashore to make a thorough and careful reconnaissance.   Lieutenant Blue made a difficult and dangerous journey of seventy miles, on foot, around the city of Santiago, saw personally every vessel in the harbor, and then returned to the flagship, and reported that Cervera's fleet was all there.   I do not know whether this was good strategy on the part of Admiral Sampson or not, but it was certainly good common sense.   Suppose that General Shafter had asked General Wood to pick out from the Rough Riders half a dozen experienced scouts and Indian fighters to make a reconnaissance, with Cuban guides, in the direction of Manzanillo, and ascertain exactly where that column of reinforcements was, and when it might be expected to arrive.   Would not the men have been forthcoming, and would not the desired information have been obtained?   I have confidence enough in the Rough Riders to answer this question emphatically in the affirmative.   The capable men are not all in the navy, and if General Shafter did not have full information with regard to Colonel Escarrio's movements, it was simply because he did not ask any of his officers or men to get it for him—and it was information well worth having.   If that column of five thousand Spanish regulars had reached Santiago two days earlier—the evening before instead of the morning after the battle of July 1-2—I doubt very much whether we should have taken either Caney or San Juan Hill, and General Shafter might have had better reason than he did have to "consider the advisability of falling back to a position five miles in the rear." [1]

If General Shafter believed that these Spanish reinforcements were "some distance away" and that they would "not get into Santiago," it is difficult to understand why he should have so far lost his grip, after the capture of Caney and San

[1] Statement furnished to the press by General Miles, September 8, 1898.

Juan Hill, as to telegraph the War Department that he was "seriously considering the advisability of falling back to a position five miles in the rear." His troops had not been defeated, nor even repulsed; they had been victorious at every point; and the Spaniards, as we afterward learned in Santiago, were momentarily expecting them to move another mile to the front, rather than five miles to the rear. It is the belief of many foreign residents of Santiago, including the English cable-operators, who had the best possible means of knowing the views of the Spanish commanders, that if our army had continued the attack after capturing Caney and San Juan Hill it might have entered the city before dark. This may or may not be so; but the chance—if chance there was—vanished when Colonel Escarrio, on the morning after the battle, marched around the head of the bay and into the city with a reinforcing column of five thousand regulars. General Shafter says, in his official report, that "the arrival of General Escarrio was not anticipated" because "it was not believed that his troops could arrive so soon." The time when a reinforcing column of five thousand men will reach the enemy ought not to be a matter of vague belief—it should be a matter of accurate foreknowledge; and if General Shafter had sent a couple of officers with a few Rough Riders out on the roads leading into Santiago from Manzanillo, he might have had information that would have made the arrival of Colonel Escarrio less unexpected. But he seems to have taken no steps either to ascertain the movements of the latter or to prevent his junction with Linares.

General O. O. Howard, in an interview published in the New York "Tribune" of September 14, 1898, explains the apparent indifference of General Shafter to the approach of these reinforcements as follows: "In regard to the Cubans allowing the Spanish reinforcements to enter Santiago from Manzanillo, I would say that I met General Shafter on board the *Vixen*, and from my conversation with him I infer that he intended to allow the Spaniards to enter the city, so as to have them where he could punish them more."

It is to be hoped that General Howard misunderstood General Shafter, because such strategy as that indicated would suggest the tactics of the pugnacious John Phœnix, who, in a fight in the editorial room, put his nose into the mouth of his adversary in order to hold the latter more securely.

The explanation of the entrance of the Spanish reinforcements given by General Shafter in his official report of the campaign is as follows: "General Garcia, with between four and five thousand Cubans, was intrusted with the duty of watching for and intercepting the reinforcements expected. This, however, he failed to do, and Escarrio passed into the city along my extreme right and near the bay."

General Garcia himself, however, in his report to his own government, states that he was directed by General Shafter to occupy and hold a certain position on the right wing of the army, and that, without disobeying orders and leaving that position, he could not possibly intercept the Manzanillo troops.

As it happened, Escarrio's column did not become a controlling or decisive factor in the campaign, and the question why he was allowed to reinforce the Santiago garrison has therefore only a speculative interest. If, however, these reinforcements had happened to arrive two days earlier—in time to take part in the battle of July 1-2—the whole course of events might have been changed. The Spanish garrison of the city, according to the English cable-operators and the foreign residents, consisted of three thousand regulars, one thousand volunteers, and about one thousand sailors and marines from Cervera's fleet—a force, all together, of not more than five thousand men. This comparatively small army, fighting in intrenchments and in almost impregnable

positions, came so near repulsing our attack on July 1 that
General Shafter "seriously considered the advisability of
falling back to a position five miles in the rear." If the five
thousand men in the Spanish blockhouses and rifle-pits had
been reinforced July 1 instead of July 3 by the five thousand
regulars from Manzanillo, the Santiago campaign might
have ended in a great disaster. Fortunately for General
Shafter, and unfortunately for General Toral, "Socorro de
España ó tarde ó nunca" ("Spanish reinforcements arrive
late or never").

CHAPTER XXI

THE SANTIAGO CAMPAIGN (*Concluded*)

IV. The wrecking of the army by disease after the decisive battle of July 1–2.

The army under command of General Shafter left Tampa on the fourteenth day of June, and arrived off the Cuban coast near Santiago on the 20th of the same month. Disembarkation began at Daiquiri on the 22d, and ended at Siboney on the 24th. On the morning of June 25 the whole army was ashore, and was then in a state of almost perfect health and efficiency. One week later the soldiers at the front began to sicken with malarial and other fevers, and two weeks later, according to General Shafter's report, "sickness was increasing very rapidly, and the weakness of the troops was becoming so apparent that I was anxious to bring the siege to an end." On July 21, less than four weeks after the army landed, Colonel Roosevelt told me that not more than one quarter of his men were fit for duty, and that when they moved five miles up into the hills, a few days before, fifty per cent. of the entire command fell out of the ranks from exhaustion. On July 22 a prominent surgeon attached to the field-hospital of the First Division stated to me that at least five thousand men in the Fifth Army-Corps were then ill with fever, and that there were more than one thousand sick in General Kent's division alone.

On August 3 eight general officers in Shafter's command signed a round-robin in which they declared that the army had been so disabled by malarial fevers that it had lost its efficiency; that it was too weak to move back into the hills; that the epidemic of yellow fever which was sure to occur would probably destroy it, and that if it were not moved North at once it "must perish." At that time, according to General Shafter's telegram of August 8 to the War Department, "seventy-five per cent. of the command had been ill with a very weakening malarial fever, which leaves every man too much broken down to be of any use." In the short space of forty days, therefore, an army of sixteen thousand men had lost three fourths of its efficiency, and had been reduced to a condition so low that, in the opinion of eight general officers, it must inevitably "perish" unless immediately sent back to the United States. Early in August, after a stay in Cuba of only six weeks, the Fifth Army-Corps began to move northward, and before September 1 the whole command was in camp at Montauk Point, Long Island. Of the eighteen thousand men who composed it, five thousand were very ill, or soon became very ill, and were sent to the general hospital; while five thousand more, who were less seriously sick, were treated in their tents.[1] Eight thousand men out of eighteen thousand were nominally well, but had been so enfeebled by the hardships and privations of the campaign that they were no longer fit for active Cuban service, and, in the opinion of General Miles, hardly one of them was in sound health.[2] I think it is not an exaggeration to describe this state of affairs as "the wrecking of the army by disease." It is my purpose in the present chapter to inquire whether such wrecking of the army was inevitable, and if not, why it was allowed to happen.

[1] Statement of General Wheeler, New York "Sun," September 3.
[2] New York "Sun," September 21.
17

A review of the history of campaigns in tropical countries
seems to show that Northern armies in such regions have
always suffered more from disease than from battle; but it
does not by any means show that the virtual destruction of
a Northern army by disease in a tropical country is inevitable
now. When the British army under the Earl of Albemarle
landed on the Cuban coast and attacked Havana in 1762,
it lost nearly one half its efficiency, as a result of sickness, in
about four weeks; but at that time the fact that nine tenths
of all tropical diseases are caused by microscopic germs, and
are therefore preventable, was not known. The progress
made in sanitary science in the present century renders unnecessary and inexcusable in 1898 a rate of sickness and
mortality that was perhaps inevitable in 1762. Northern
soldiers, if properly equipped and cared for, can live and
maintain their health now under conditions which would have
been absolutely and inevitably fatal to them a century ago.

In April last there was an interesting and instructive discussion of this subject, or of a subject very closely connected
with this, at a meeting held in the rooms of the Royal Geographical Society, London, and attended by many of the best-
known authorities on tropical pathology in Great Britain.
Most of the gentlemen who took part in the debate were of
opinion that there is no reason whatever why the white man
should not be able to adapt himself to the new conditions of
life in the tropics, and protect himself against the diseases
that prevail in those regions. The popular belief that the
white man cannot successfully colonize the tropics is dis-
proved by the fact that he has done so. It is undoubtedly
true that many Northerners who go to equatorial regions
contract disease there and die; but in the majority of such
cases the man is the victim of his obstinate unwillingness
to change his habits in respect to eating, drinking, and clothing, and to conform his life to the new conditions.

The chief diseases, both acute and chronic, of tropical

countries—those which formerly caused such ravages among the white settlers, and gave rise to the prevalent theory that Europeans can live only in the temperate zone—are all microbic in origin, and consequently in great measure preventable. We cannot expect, of course, to see them absolutely wiped out of existence; but their sting may be extracted by means of an improved public and private hygiene and other prophylactic measures. A comparison of the healthfulness of the West India Islands under enlightened British rule with that of the two under Spanish misrule shows what can be done by sanitation to convert a pest-hole into a paradise. Indeed, as Dr. L. Sambon, in opening the discussion, well said, sanitation within the last few decades has wrought wonderful changes in all tropical countries as regards health conditions, and the changes in some places have been so great that regions once considered most deadly are now even recommended as health resorts.

Dr. Patrick Manson, than whom there is no greater authority on the pathology of equatorial regions, began his remarks with the confession that in former years, under the influence of early training, he shared in the pessimistic opinions then current about tropical colonization by the white races. In recent years, however, his views on this subject had undergone a complete revolution—a revolution that began with the establishment of the germ theory of disease. He now firmly believed in the possibility of tropical colonization by the white races. Heat and moisture, he contended, are not, in themselves, the direct cause of any important tropical disease. The direct causes of ninety-nine per cent. of these diseases are germs, and to kill the germs is simply a matter of knowledge and the application of that knowledge —that is to say, sanitary science and sanitation.[1]

The fact that ninety-nine per cent. or more of the diseases

[1] "British Medical Journal" of April 30, 1898, quoted in the "Journal of the Military Service Institution."

that prevail in the tropics are caused by germs was known, of course, to the surgeon-general of our army, and ought to have been known to General Shafter and the Secretary of War. It was, therefore, their duty, collectively and individually, to protect our soldiers in Cuba, not only by informing them of the best means of escaping the dangers threatened by these micro-organisms, but also by furnishing them with every safeguard that science and experience could suggest in the shape of proper food, dress, equipment, and medical supplies. The rules and precautions which it is necessary to observe in order to escape the attacks of micro-organisms and maintain health in the tropics were well known at the time when the invasion of Cuba was planned, and had been published, long before the army left Tampa, in hundreds of periodicals throughout the country. Cuban physicians and surgeons, Americans who had campaigned with Gomez and Garcia, and travelers who, like Hornaday, had spent many years in tropical forests and jungles, all agreed that if our soldiers were to keep well in Cuba they should drink boiled water, they should avoid sleeping on the ground, they should have adequate protection from rain and dew at night, and they should be able to change their clothing, or at least their underwear, when wet.[1] By observing these very simple precautions Dr. Hornaday maintained his health throughout five years of almost constant travel and exploration in the woods and jungles of Cuba, South America, India, the Malay Archipelago, and Borneo. If our soldiers went to Cuba, or marched from Siboney to Santiago, without the equipment required for the observance of these precautions, it was not the result of necessary ignorance on the part of their superiors. As the Philadelphia "Medical Journal" said, ten days before the army sailed: "The climate and sani-

[1] "Health Hints for Cuba," by William T. Hornaday, director of the New York Zoölogical Society; New York "Sun," May 22, 1898.

tary—or rather unsanitary—conditions of Cuba have been much discussed, and it is well known what our troops will have to contend against in that island." The "Army and Navy Journal," about the same time, pointed out the grave danger to be apprehended from contaminated drinking-water, and said: "The government should provide itself with heating and distilling apparatus on an adequate scale. Sterilized water is cheaper than hospitals and an army of nurses, to say nothing of the crippling of the service that sickness brings." In an article entitled "Special Sanitary Instructions for the Guidance of Troops Serving in Tropical Countries," published in the "Journal of the American Medical Association" for May, Dr. R. S. Woodson described fully the adverse sanitary conditions peculiar to Cuba, and called especial attention to the danger of drinking impure water and sleeping on the ground. Finally, the highest medical officers of our army, including the surgeon-general, the chief surgeon of the Fifth Army-Corps, and Dr. John Guiteras, published instructions and suggestions for the maintenance of the health of our soldiers in the field, in which attention was again called to the danger of drinking unboiled water and sleeping in wet clothing on the ground.[1]

In spite of all these orders, instructions, and suggestions, and in defiance of the advice and warnings of all competent authorities, General Shafter's army sailed from Tampa without its reserve medical supplies and ambulance corps, and, having landed on the Cuban coast, marched into the interior without wall-tents, without hammocks, without a change of clothing, and without a single utensil larger than a coffee-cup in which to boil water.

[1] Circular of the surgeon-general, dated April 25, 1898; Memorandum of Instructions to Soldiers, by Lieutenant-Colonel B. F. Pope, chief surgeon of the Fifth Army-Corps; and General Order No. 8, Fifth Army-Corps, Tampa, June 2, 1898.

The question naturally arises, Why? If everybody, without exception, who knows the climate of Cuba warns you that your soldiers must not sleep on the ground, in wet clothing, why not provide them with hammocks, rain-sheets, and extra underwear? If your own surgeon-general and the chief surgeon of your own corps advise you officially that the drinking of unboiled water will almost certainly cause disease, why not supply your men with camp-kettles? I can think of only three possible answers to these questions. Either (1) the War Department did not furnish General Shafter with these articles, or with adequate transportation for them; or (2) General Shafter did not believe in microbes and the germ theory of disease, and regarded the suggestions of medical and other experts as foolish and nonsensical; or (3) the commanding general expected to capture Santiago before his troops should be put *hors de combat* by disease, and did not care particularly what happened to them afterward. If there be any other explanation of the officially admitted facts, it does not at this moment occur to me.

Some of the defenders of the War Department and of General Shafter seek to convey the idea, by implication at least, that the wrecking of our army was inevitable—that it was a sort of divine visitation, which could not have been averted, and for which no one, except the Creator of microbes and the Cuban climate, was responsible. But this theory accords neither with the facts nor with General Shafter's explanation of them. In his telegram of August 8 to President McKinley, he does not say, "What put my command in its present condition was a visitation of God"; he says: "What put my command in its present condition was the twenty days of the campaign when they had nothing but meat [fat bacon], bread, and coffee, without change of clothes, and without any shelter whatever." From this admission of the commanding general it is clear that the wrecking of the army was not due primarily to uncontrollable climatic conditions, but rather to lack of foresight, mismanagement, and inefficiency.   This conclusion is supported and greatly strengthened by the record of another body of men, in a different branch of the service, which spent more time in Cuba than the Fifth Army-Corps spent there, which was subjected to nearly all the local and climatic influences that are said to have wrecked the latter, but which, nevertheless, escaped disease and came back to the United States in perfect health. I refer to the battalion of marines under command of Colonel Huntington.   This small naval contingent landed on the western shore of Guantanamo Bay on June 10—two weeks before the Fifth Army-Corps finished disembarkation àt Daiquiri and Siboney.   It was almost immediately attacked by a superior force of Spanish regulars, and was so harassed, night and day, by the fire of the latter that some of its officers slept only two hours out of one hundred and fifteen. As soon as it had obtained a foothold it went into camp on a slight elevation in the midst of an almost impenetrable jungle, surrounded itself with defensive trenches, and there lived, for a period of ten weeks, exposed to the same sun, rain, and malaria that played havoc with the troops of General Shafter.   On the sixth day of August, after eight weeks on Cuban soil and in a tropical climate, its condition, as reported by Admiral Sampson, was as follows: "The marine battalion is in excellent health.   Sick-list two and one half per cent.   The fleet surgeon reports that they are in better condition for service in this climate than they were when they arrived South in June.   I do not think it necessary to send them North."[1]   Almost exactly at the same time when this report was made, General Shafter was telegraphing the War Department that seventy-five per cent. of his command had been disabled by fever, and eight general

[1] Telegram to Secretary Long, dated "Playa, Cuba, August 6, 1898."

officers of the Fifth Army-Corps were signing a round-robin in which they declared that if the army were not immediately moved North it "must perish."

Late in August it was decided that the marines should return to the United States, notwithstanding their satisfactory state of health, and on the 26th of that month they reached Portsmouth, New Hampshire, with only two men sick. They had been gone a little more than eleven weeks, ten of which they had spent in Cuba, and in that time had not lost a single man from disease, and had never had a higher sick-rate than two and one half per cent.

In view of this record, as compared with that of any regiment in General Shafter's command, we are forced to inquire: What is the reason for the difference? Why should a battalion of marines be able to live ten weeks in Cuba, without the loss of a single man from disease, and with a sick-rate of only two and one half per cent., while so hardy and tough a body of men as the Rough Riders, under substantially the same climatic conditions, had become so reduced in four weeks that seventy-five per cent. of them were unfit for duty, and fifty per cent. of them fell out of the ranks from exhaustion in a march of five miles?

The only answer I can find to these questions is that the marines had suitable equipment and intelligent care, while the soldiers of General Shafter's command had neither. When the marines landed in Guantanamo Bay, every tent and building that the Spaniards had occupied was immediately destroyed by fire, to remove any possible danger of infection with yellow fever. When General Shafter landed at Siboney, he not only disregarded the recommendation of his chief surgeon to burn the buildings there, but allowed them to be occupied as offices and hospitals, without even so much as attempting to clean or disinfect them. Yellow fever made its appearance in less than two weeks. The marines at Guantanamo were supplied promptly with light canvas uniforms suitable for a tropical climate, while the soldiers of General Shafter's army sweltered through the campaign in the heavy clothing that they had worn in Idaho or Montana, and then, just before they started North, were furnished with thin suits to keep them cool at Montauk Point in the fall. The marines drank only water that had been boiled or sterilized, while the men of General Shafter's command drank out of brooks into which the heavy afternoon showers were constantly washing fecal and other decaying organic matter from the banks. The marines were well protected from rain and dew, while the regulars of the Fifth Army-Corps were drenched to the skin almost every day, and slept at night on the water-soaked ground. The marines received the full navy ration, while the soldiers had only hardtack and fat bacon, and not always enough of that. Finally, the marines had surgeons enough to take proper care of the sick, and medicines enough to give them, while General Shafter, after leaving his reserve medical supplies and ambulance corps at Tampa, telegraphs the adjutant-general on August 3 that "there has never been sufficient medical attendance or medicines for the daily wants of the command." In short, the marines observed the laws of health, and lived in Cuba according to the dictates of modern sanitary science, while the soldiers, through no fault of their own, were forced to violate almost every known law of health, and to live as if there were no such thing as sanitary science in existence.

Governor Tanner, General Grosvenor, and Secretary Alger may declare that the wrecking of the army by disease was inevitable, that Northern soldiers cannot maintain their health in the tropics, and that "when troops come home sick and worn, it is a part of war"; but, in view of the record made at Guantanamo Bay, we may say to them, seriously and respectfully, rather than flippantly: "Tell that to the marines!"

The record of the marine battalion, taken in connection with General Shafter's admission that his command was disabled by "twenty days of bread, meat, and coffee, without change of clothes, and without any shelter whatever," seems to show conclusively that the epidemic of disease which wrecked the army was the direct result of improper and insufficient food, inadequate equipment, and utter neglect of all the rules prescribed by sanitary science for the maintenance of health in tropical regions. The questions then recur, Why did not the army have such food, clothes, and equipment as would have made obedience to the laws of health possible? Why should they have been directed by their chief surgeon to boil all drinking-water, to avoid sleeping on the ground, and to change their clothing when wet, if it was not the intention to give them camp-kettles in which to boil the water, hammocks in which to sleep, and clothing enough for a change? The American people, certainly, are both able and willing to pay for the proper support and equipment of their army. If it had cost five million dollars, or ten million dollars, to supply every company in General Shafter's command with hammocks, waterproof rain-sheets, extra clothing, and camp-kettles, the money would have been appropriated and paid without a grumble or a murmur. We are not a stingy people, nor even an economical people, when the question is one of caring for the men that we send into the field to fight for us. If, then, the financial resources of the War Department were unlimited, and if it had supreme power, why could it not properly equip and feed a comparatively small invading force of only sixteen or eighteen thousand men? Were the difficulties insuperable? Certainly not! It is safe, I think, to say that there were a thousand business firms in the United States which, for a suitable consideration, would have undertaken to keep General Shafter's army supplied, at every step of its progress from Siboney to Santiago, with hammocks, waterproof tents, extra clothing, camp-kettles, and full rations of food. The trouble was not lack of money or lack of facilities at home; it was lack of foresight, of system, and of administrative ability in the field.

Lieutenant Parker of the Thirteenth Infantry has pointed out the fact that the army was not properly equipped and fed "even after the surrender [of Santiago] had placed unlimited wharfage at our disposal within two and a half miles of the camps over excellent roads."[1] A week or ten days after the surrender, officers were coming into Santiago on horseback and carrying out to the camps over the pommels of their saddles heavy hospital tents for which they could get no other transportation and of which their men were in urgent need. As late as August 13—nearly a month after the surrender—the soldiers of the Ninth Massachusetts were still sleeping on the ground in dog-kennel tents, toasting their bacon on the ends of sticks, and making coffee in old tomato-cans, although at that very time there were hundreds of large wall-tents piled up in front of the army storehouse on the Santiago water-front and hundreds of tons of supplies, of all sorts, in the storehouses and on the piers.

The state of affairs in the hospitals was not much better than it had been a month before. In a signed letter dated "Santiago, August 12," Dr. James S. Kennedy, first assistant surgeon of the Second Division hospital, declared that there was "an utter lack of suitable medicines with which to combat disease. There has been so much diarrhea, dysentery, and fever, and no medicine at all to combat them, that men have actually died for want of it. Four days after my reporting here there was not a single medicine in the entire hospi-

1 "Some Lessons of the War from an Officer's Standpoint," by Lieutenant John H. Parker; "Review of Reviews," October, 1898.

tal for the first two diseases, and nothing but quinine for the fever. Yesterday, August 11, a certain regiment left its encampment to go on board ship for the North, and ten hours afterward a private who had been left behind started back to his former encampment to sleep, no private soldiers being allowed in Santiago after dark. On reaching his camp he found ten men abandoned—no medicines, no food, no nurses or physicians—simply abandoned to starvation or suicide."

If these statements are not true, Dr. Kennedy should be brought to trial by court martial for conduct prejudicial to good order and discipline, if not conduct unbecoming an officer and a gentleman, in publicly making injurious charges that have no foundation in fact. If they are true, they furnish another proof that the lack of medical supplies and medical attention in the army was due to official negligence and inefficiency. In June and July it might have been urged with some show of plausibility that a sudden and unexpected emergency, in the shape of a wide-spread epidemic of fever, had taken the army by surprise and found it unprepared; but with the coast of the United States only four or five days distant, with uninterrupted telegraphic communication, and with good landing facilities in a safe and sheltered harbor, there was no excuse for a lack of medicines and hospital supplies on August 12—seven weeks after the army landed and four weeks after it entered the city of Santiago.

Defenders of General Shafter and the War Department try to excuse the wrecking of the army by saying that "the invasion of Cuba was not a pleasure excursion," that "war is not strictly a hygienic business," that "the outcry about sickness and neglect is largely sensational and for the manufacture of political effect," and that the general criticism of the management of the campaign is "a concerted effort to hide the glories of our magnificent triumph under alleged faults and shortcomings in its conduct"; but these excuses and counter-charges do not break the force of the essential and officially admitted fact that our army landed on the Cuban coast on June 24 in a high state of health and efficiency, and in less than six weeks had not only lost seventy-five per cent. of its effective strength, but had been reduced by disease to a condition so low that, in the opinion of eight of its general officers, it "must perish" unless immediately sent back to the United States. Secretary Alger declares that management which produces these results "is war"; but I should rather describe it as incapacity for war. If we do not learn a lesson from the Santiago campaign—if we continue to equip, feed, and manage our armies in the field as we equipped, fed, and managed the Fifth Army-Corps in Cuba —our newly acquired tropical possessions will cost us more in pensions than they will ever produce in revenue.